*With respect and thanks to the late
Paul Banks, Peter Waters, and Christopher Clarkson.
We miss you.*

Flood in Florence, 1966: A Fifty-Year Retrospective

Proceedings of Symposium

November 3 and 4, 2016
University of Michigan
Ann Arbor, Michigan

Edited by Paul Conway and
Martha O'Hara Conway

Ann Arbor
Maize Books
2018

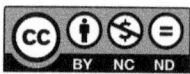
Published in the United States of America by
Michigan Publishing

DOI: http://dx.doi.org/10.3998/mpub.9310956

ISBN 978-1-60785-456-2 (paper)
ISBN 978-1-60785-457-9 (e-book)

An imprint of Michigan Publishing, Maize Books serves the publishing needs of the University of Michigan community by making high-quality scholarship widely available in print and online. It represents a new model for authors seeking to share their work within and beyond the academy, offering streamlined selection, production, and distribution processes. Maize Books is intended as a complement to more formal modes of publication in a wide range of disciplinary areas.

http://www.maizebooks.org

Contents

THEME PANEL: CONSERVATION
EDUCATION AND TRAINING

CLOSING KEYNOTE

Welcome

James L. Hilton

It's wonderful and perhaps just a little bit odd to gather together to commemorate a natural disaster. But in truth we are here today to recognize and honor the work that conservators have done over the past fifty years to make useable and available the world's cultural artifacts for teaching and research. The net result of the skilled work of conservators is to instill in all of us a joyous appreciation of the tangible knowledge found in centuries of books, manuscripts, and works of art.

The focus of this symposium is on lessons learned from five decades of salvage and recovery from the 1966 Florence Flood and how those lessons have influenced the way we think about preservation and conservation, from the physical to the digital. It is fitting that this symposium is happening at this time and in this place. Preservation has always been mission critical for research universities. For much longer than the past fifty years, higher education has been a growth economy. The common goals of universities have always been to provide educational opportunities that are as broad and deep as possible and to foster a good society, one young mind at a time. But we may be entering a new period of real differentiation among universities in terms of the social and economic value each one adds to society and to those students who we reach directly. Research universities and their libraries have the unique obligation and mission to preserve knowledge recorded in published and unpublished forms for current and future generations of scholars all over the world. The preservation and conservation work that happens on our campuses is vital to the long-term viability of our educational enterprise and to the distinctiveness of our campus community.

In welcoming you to the University of Michigan Library, I would like to recognize that participants in this symposium include several people who were in Florence for the initial salvage and restoration work in the aftermath of the flood. Also participating in the theme talks and panel discussions are those who learned from the expertise and experience of the Florence veterans and who are now passing their own knowledge to today's and tomorrow's preservation and conservation professionals, many of whom are also here today. In fact, this symposium is an extraordinary case study of cross generational knowledge transfer accomplished through the combination of apprenticeships, formal education, and the publication of the outcomes of both practice and research. I fully expect that the proceedings will document the rich ideas exchanged at this symposium and serve as a record of extraordinary progress in conservation since that flood five decades ago.

Flood in Florence, 1966: A Fifty-Year Retrospective

Edited by Paul Conway and
Martha O'Hara Conway

Introduction to the Symposium Proceedings

Paul Conway and Martha O'Hara Conway

This volume consists of the expanded and edited proceedings of a symposium on the occasion of the fiftieth anniversary of the Florence Flood of 1966. The symposium took place on Thursday and Friday, November 3 and 4, 2016, on the University of Michigan campus in Ann Arbor, Michigan. To the best of our knowledge, the symposium was the only academically oriented anniversary event in the world that has explored some of the implications of this distinctive natural disaster on the practices and perspectives of the preservation and conservation communities, as well as on education and training for several generations of preservation and conservation professionals. These proceedings are a selective lens on the five decades of progress made and the work to be done in these fields.

What happened to warrant such a commemoration? On Friday, November 4, 1966, the good citizens of Florence, Italy, awoke to find that their beloved Arno River had once again flooded its banks. The storm that produced the flood was caused by a cyclone that formed in the western Mediterranean and moved eastward toward Italy. Widespread damage occurred in Tuscany, at the northern Adriatic coast, and in the northeastern Italian Alps. One hundred and eighteen people in the area lost their lives; thirty-three died in Florence. Twenty thousand families lost their homes, fifteen thousand cars were destroyed, and six thousand shops went out of business, at least temporarily. According to several scientific studies on the aftermath, the storm's most peculiar characteristic was the wind, which picked up a large amount of warm, moist air and resulted in the highest storm surge ever recorded along the Venetian coast.[1]

The 1966 flood was by no means the first time the Arno had caused very significant damage to the city of Florence. Two of the dozens of disastrous floods recorded, those of 1333 and 1844, happened on the very same day of the year, the day of the 1966 flood: November 4. The second version of the famous Ponte Vecchio was damaged by floods in 1171 and 1269 and then finally destroyed by the flood of 1333. The present bridge withstood a major flood in 1557 and then took a serious beating in 1966. It still stands today.[2]

What places the 1966 flood in a special category, apart from the tragic deaths and the awesome scale of the flooding, is the impact on the material cultural heritage stored, largely uncataloged and unknown, in museums, libraries, and private residences throughout the city. The Arno flood of 1966 buried centuries of books, manuscripts, and works of art in muck and muddy, oily water. This symposium is about how some of the lessons learned during the long recovery have been passed on through generations of preservation and conservation professionals.

Loss Is the Norm

As we celebrate progress in building and nurturing a profession, we should be mindful of the broader context of our work. The fields of preservation and conservation may be the only professions that have in their purview the entire scope of recorded history, ranging from ancient papyrus to today's equally fragmentary resources in digital form. At the heart of what conservators and preservation specialists do is understand risk in material terms over time and then undertake the complex choreography of balancing the cost of investing in preventative or restorative actions with the value of the cultural heritage artifacts under their care. The sheer scale of the Flood in Florence challenged every then-existing notion of systematic action. The immediate consequence of early recovery efforts was the creation of a community of veterans committed not only to sustaining the recovery effort in Florence but also to nurturing the growth of the preservation field itself.

The preservation field has a history that predates the Flood in Florence and roots that are grounded in the development of the modern research library, the foundational principles of the archival profession, and the core mission of today's museums. In 1946, two full decades before the Florence Flood we are considering here, Pelham Barr had already coined the term *responsible custody* to describe the centrality of conservation to the library: "It is the only . . . function which should be continuously at work twenty-four hours a day. It is the only function which should be concerned with every piece of material in the library from the moment the selector becomes aware of its existence to the day it is discarded."[3] Indeed, preservation and conservation are two of the most important functions that unite all cultural heritage organizations.

Although the Flood in Florence of 1966 is a dramatic story of community action, it is also a cautionary tale about professional hubris. Social and community memory is understood from the fragments of what has survived the destruction of war, willful ignorance, and the ravages of Mother Nature. Over the course of recorded history, impulses to save and protect have always competed directly with motives to discard and struggles with the natural environment. It is surely ironic that we could not understand the classical world as well as we do without the dumps, wells, and latrines that held the first fragments of paper for millennia. Until the modern university vested libraries and archives with the responsibility to preserve sources for scholarship—merely two centuries ago—the rich, the powerful, and the religious chose what to keep and what to save. The human sciences would be an impossibility without the princes and priests who appreciated the beauty, rarity, or communicative power of books and works of art. In the symposium, we took a distinctively retrospective view of preservation over decades that many of us have experienced directly. Those of us committed to the societal value of conscious and systematic preservation and conservation must accept the tenuousness of our professional claims of virtue.

In the proceedings of the symposium, we offer few predictions on the future of our profession; but we are mindful of the shifting sands of resource allocation and the perceived decline in the essentialness of cultural artifacts.

Writing about the Florence Flood

Over the past fifty years, much has been written about the Florence Flood, particularly in the decade or so immediately following the disaster. Giorgio Batini provides a contemporary account of the damage to Florence's cultural property.[4] Sheila Waters draws extensively on the letters she exchanged with her husband, Peter Waters, as he led the British team's recovery and conservation efforts.[5] Peter Waters's own account of book and binding restoration is practically a primary source document for understanding the scale of the challenge in the immediate aftermath of the flood.[6] Katherine Taylor kept a diary in the period surrounding the flood and drew upon it for her remembrance on living through it.[7] Robert Clark provides a firsthand and accessible account of the Florence Flood and its impact on art without delving too deeply into the specifics of book and paper recovery and conservation.[8] Swietlan Kraczyna's photographic essay on the flood is a compelling documentary record of the Arno River's devastation, recorded on the day of and those following the flood.[9]

Not all the interesting writing on the Florence Flood are nonfictional accounts. Robert Hellenga's novel imagines the experience of one of the Mud Angels who volunteered to salvage, clean, and treat the thousands of damaged books pulled from libraries.[10] David Hewson's murder mystery, set in Florence, uses the 1966 flood as an anchor and a recurring theme.[11]

Perhaps most endearing is a collection of art created by children in the immediate aftermath of the Flood in Florence.[12] University of Florence professor Giuliana Pinto provides an afterthought to the proceedings on the therapeutic value of the art produced by children in Florence in the year after the flood. The Italian government adapted one of the drawings for a postage stamp commemorating the fiftieth anniversary of the flood[13] and released it (coincidentally) on the second day of the symposium in Ann Arbor.[14] A website developed by the Università degli Studi di Firenze assembled a host of commemorative projects, news items, and background information for events that took place in Florence around the time of the fiftieth anniversary.[15]

Sherelyn Ogden, who we were honored to welcome to the symposium, reviewed the library conservation literature written before and after the flood with an eye toward assessing impact on the field. She found that most of the changes that have occurred in professional practice since the flood had begun prior to it: "The flood brought conservation to public attention at a time when funds were available to exploit that attention, with the result that progress was accelerated rather than a new direction being taken."[16] In his comprehensive review of news coverage of the flood, David Alexander found a new, if temporary, status granted to the academic and technical expertise of the conservator.[17] In a more recent review, Luciana Lazzeretti and Francesco Capone credit the cross-fertilization between scientific and humanistic

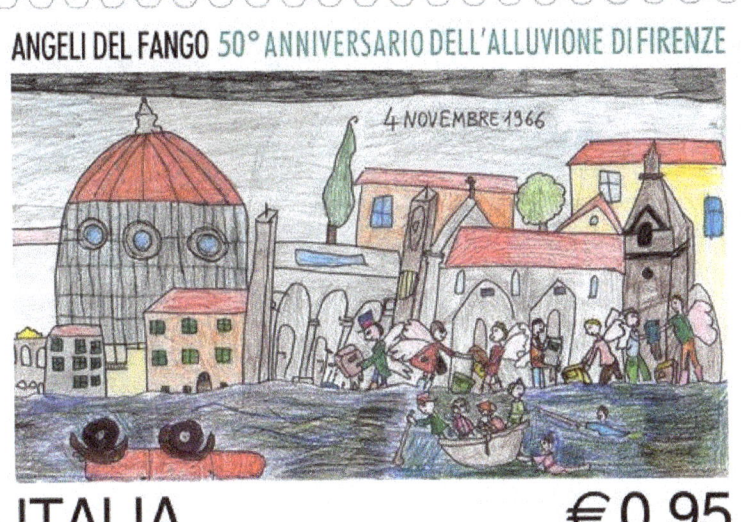

knowledge gathered in Florence for spurring significant new advances in chemistry within the conservation sciences.[18] On an even grander scale, Dennis Rodwell credits the Flood in Florence as the trigger event that led to the establishment of the UNESCO World Heritage program, which now has more than one thousand sites.[19]

In 2006, ten years ago, the Villa La Pietra in Florence and the New York University Conservation Center collaborated to host an international symposium on the occasion of the fortieth anniversary of the Flood in Florence. Major support from the Andrew W. Mellon Foundation fostered a reunion of dozens of experts who had rushed to Florence and spent weeks, months, or even years in salvage and recovery activities. British conservator Christopher Clarkson noted at the symposium that, in training people to do the work of recovery, "we started to deliberatively apply the word 'conservation' to our activities" in an attempt to "show a distinct philosophical break with [the] hand-binding and tradecraft conventions" that had preceded them.[20] In the intervening years, the concept of conservation has come to be universally recognized as the suite of perspectives, techniques, and ethical standards that motivate actions to stabilize and restore the usability of cultural heritage artifacts across all media.

The proceedings of the 2006 symposium constitute a rearview mirror portrait of the immediate aftermath of the flood. The emphasis of that conference, driven in part by the priorities of the organizers, was on artistic artifacts, including paintings and sculpture. The proceedings convey the vibrancy of the international collaborative effort and transmit four decades forward some of the energy and creativity marshaled in the several years immediately following the flood. The proceedings of the fortieth anniversary symposium summarize the most important lessons learned about physical treatment of water-damaged cultural resources of all forms across several millennia, lessons learned by experts, lessons learned from making mistakes under pressure and duress, and lessons learned through spontaneous innovation. For the fiftieth anniversary symposium, we elected not to revisit in detail the innovative recovery work done in Florence but instead to focus on the longer-term impacts of that innovation on subsequent conservation and preservation practices.

There remains some debate in the literature as to whether the work of recovery is finished. Scott Devine argues for completeness by pointing out that all materials damaged in the 1966 flood have been stabilized and adequate bibliographic control has been established for all materials that survived.[21] Others lament the lingering backlog of items needing conservation treatment. African conservation specialist Joe Nkrumah returned to Florence for the fortieth anniversary and found that "the job we started has never progressed and is far from its conclusion."[22] Antonio Paolucci highlights the impact of the restoration laboratory in Florence and its continuing commitment to treatment in spite of inadequate resources for the job at hand.[23] For the fiftieth anniversary symposium, we chose to avoid debate over progress in recovery from the Flood in Florence and instead cast a wider net on the idea of impact and the implications of the flood for the preservation and conservation professions.

The Symposium Program

To explore the impact of the 1966 Flood in Florence at the fiftieth anniversary mark, the organizing committee filled the better part of two days with two stage-setting presentations, four theme talks clustered around three panel discussions, and a closing keynote address. In the midst of the papers and panel discussion, a "movie night" at the University of Michigan Museum of Art screened two rare films made in the immediate aftermath of the flood. Following the symposium, participants inaugurated an exhibition in the Stephen S. Clark Library curated by Cathleen Baker on book and binding repair in Florence in the years immediately following the flood.

The symposium began with a photographic essay by University of Minnesota professor John Comazzi. He drew on a selection of images of the flood from the contemporary work of architectural photographer Balthazar Korab, who was present in Florence at the time of the flood.

The visual record communicates the damage of the flood more power-fully than even the words of witnesses recorded at the time.

Following the visual portrait was a personal memoir by Sheila Waters, the wife of distinguished conservator Peter Waters, who led the British team in establishing a systematic approach to the recovery and conservation of thousands of books in the Biblioteca Nazionale Centrale di Firenze. Waters's reflections on the innovative treatment strategies developed in Florence under great pressure established a bridge across the fifty years separating us from the aftermath of November 4, 1966. In association with the symposium, Sheila Waters unveiled her memoir of her life with Peter Waters in Florence.[24]

The first theme panel started with remarks by the distinguished conservator Don Etherington, who is one of the few living veterans of the rescue and salvage operation in Florence. Three conservators formed a panel to extend Etherington's insights as they have played out across multiple generations of professionals. Conservator Beth Doyle outlined the transmission of new conservation knowledge in print and through education and training programs, foreshadowing a full panel discussion on education at the end of the symposium. Conservator Sherelyn Ogden, who conducted the seminal analysis of the published literature on the Florence Flood, reflected on the impact of the recovery effort on the ethics of the conservation profession. Conservator Julia Miller turned a critical eye on how advances in conservation techniques and best practices are and are not communicated in the professional literature.

University of Michigan art historian Megan Holmes presented her scholarship on the consequences of the Flood in Florence on conserva-tion and connoisseurship of works of art. Her essay serves as an impor-tant link to the fortieth anniversary symposium proceedings and also serves as a reminder of the devastating (and lingering) impact of the flood on Florence's painting and sculpture collections.

As we know all too well, the larger destructive forces of natural and human-made disasters do not single out libraries, archives, and museums for special abuse. In the second of three theme panels, Jeanne Drewes, who is responsible for binding and collections care at the Library of Congress, introduced some of the most important top-ics that surround disaster preparation and mitigation of library col-lections. Being prepared and capable of rapid response in a natural or human-made disaster is a professional competency that can be traced directly to the lessons learned in Florence during recovery. Leading the panel discussion, preservation librarian Nancy Kraft demonstrated with stories from her own career how important it is to plan and train for water-based calamities. Preservation administrator Doris Hamburg provided a deeper dive into the development of disaster planning strat-egies and revealed the national and international networks of best prac-tices for responding to natural and human-made disasters. Conservator and preservation administrator Shannon Zachary brought the story of disaster mitigation into the digital age with a summary of how key ideas in traditional settings are being mapped to collections of digital information.

The third theme panel, on education and training, featured a thor-ough essay by Ellen Cunningham-Kruppa, who is a distinguished and accomplished educator of conservation and preservation profession-als. Cunningham-Kruppa reviewed the history of graduate education programs, beginning with the first formal degree program at Columbia University and ending with speculation on the road ahead for gradu-ate training. In her panel commentary, conservator Morgan Adams reported on her experience of cotraining in library and archives con-servation in an art conservation graduate program. Conservator and publisher Cathleen Baker recounted the path of conservation train-ing since the early 1980s and focused attention on the potential of an emergent graduate education program. The third panelist, conserva-tor John Dean, broadened the perspective on conservation educa-tion to encompass international training programs in Southeast Asia and beyond.

The closing keynote was presented by Michael Suarez, SJ, who directs the Rare Book School at the University of Virginia and is on the faculty of the Department of English. At the symposium, he had the unenviable task of focusing the attention of participants on the lessons of the Flood in Florence for dealing with a flood of a different sort that is sweeping across the land—a veritable deluge of digital data from two streams: the digitization of cultural heritage resources at scale and the ubiquitous presence of born-digital documents. Lessons learned from a half century of conservation treatment efforts may shed important light on the enduring values of the material world of books and works of art and help inform strategies for preservation in a digital environment.

Participants in the symposium were treated to the rare experience of viewing two important and rare films on the Flood in Florence that have never been screened together. For these proceedings, special collections conservator Bryan Draper introduced *Florence: Days of Destruction*, shot in the immediate aftermath of the flood by the Florentine film director Franco Zeffirelli, who was editing his *Taming of the Shrew* in Rome when the flood struck. The English version of the film that was screened in Ann Arbor is narrated by Richard Burton. Cathleen Baker introduced the second film, *The Restoration of Books, Florence, 1968* by Roger Hill, instructor of filmmaking at the Royal College of Art, London. The film documented the conservation and restoration efforts at the Biblioteca Nazionale Centrale di Firenze, where hundreds of thousands of books were damaged during the flood. The film has scenes of the conservation of mud-covered, battered books as well as hands-on demonstrations of a limp vellum binding by Christopher Clarkson and a full-leather binding completed by Peter Waters.

Preparing the Proceedings

The proceedings are an edited compendium of the remembrances, facts, and ideas presented at the fiftieth anniversary symposium. The leaders of each of the three theme sessions (book and paper conservation, disaster preparedness, education and training) prepared a draft paper in advance of the symposium and circulated it to the panelists, who then prepared their own draft remarks cognizant of the major points made in the theme papers. Following the symposium, which was recorded in full, participants received a transcript of their remarks and were invited to revise and extend their contributions for the published proceedings. The organizing committee reviewed all the submissions, and the editors of the symposium proceedings made editorial changes to improve readability and consistency of presentation, seeking input from authors as appropriate.

The symposium proceedings are published simultaneously in print and digital formats by Michigan Publishing Services of the University of Michigan. The imprint represents a new model of publishing that makes high-quality scholarship widely available in print and online through streamlined selection, production, and distribution processes. The imprint is optimized for scholarship produced under the auspices of the University and operates on a cost-recovery model to minimize production overhead.

Some Salient Insights

The symposium organizers clustered the presentations into themes that we thought would resonate with the participants. As revised and extended papers, however, the proceedings volume lends itself to finding crosscutting ideas. Here are five for the consideration of readers. There are surely more to be found.

Almost every speaker mentioned the challenges of funding conservation treatment work and the ongoing education of conservators. A consistent point in the education and training panel is the vital and ongoing role that the Andrew W. Mellon Foundation has played in the emergence of conservation education as a graduate degree specialization. The Mellon Foundation supported the fortieth anniversary symposium and continues to foster the endowment of professional conservator positions in research libraries across the country. Credit is also due to the Mellon Foundation for helping reenvision conservation education in the future. Often in parallel over the years, the National Endowment for the Humanities has supported initial graduate education initiatives at Columbia University and then at the University of Texas. Other federal granting agencies, particularly the Institute for Museum and Library Services, have encouraged innovation in practice-based internships and continuing professional education initiatives.

At least half of the symposium papers stress the high level of technical skill and manual dexterity that is required for effective and efficient conservation treatment. The speakers differ markedly, however, in the role that materials science, organic chemistry, and other hard sciences play in the education and training of conservators and in bench practice. Several papers come close to claiming conservation as a science unto itself, while other papers suggest that the requirement for core science skills limits diversity of student pools and lends a false sense of rigor to physical treatments, which may be as much art as science.

The requirement in Florence to work at scale—hundreds of thousands of bound volumes and hundreds of works of art needed prompt attention—has profoundly influenced the ethics, the practice, and the training of conservation. Indeed, Christopher Clarkson (through the fortieth anniversary proceedings) and Don Etherington (at the symposium) emphasize that the very nature of conservation works at scale and in phases, seeking to maximize impact and efficiency while minimizing treatment work beyond what is necessary to make bindings and texts usable into the future. The focus on scale also plays out in triage activities that become necessary in the wake of water or fire disasters. In spite of an ethical focus on scale and impact, conservation treatment in the end takes place one item at a time and remains costly and time consuming.

In assembling the symposium program, the organizers were acutely aware that the passage of fifty years from the Florence Flood of 1966 means that knowledge lives and grows only through cross-generational transfer. The symposium participants demonstrate through their presence and distinctive perspectives on conservation and preservation that the field is alive and thriving, if challenged in a number of important ways. Two scholars (Comazzi and Holmes) provided intellectual depth and context to the events in Florence in 1966. Two of the papers (Etherington and Waters) represent the views of the first generation of conservators and educators who learned directly from the Florence Flood recovery efforts. We were graced by their presence in Ann Arbor. Another group of three papers (Baker, Dean, and Ogden) demonstrate the impact of learning directly from those who were present.

This "second generation" translated these associations into a passion to combine treatment with the education and training of the next generation. The symposium featured seven presentations by professionals (Cunningham-Kruppa, Drewes, Hamburg, Kraft, Miller, and Zachary) across a range of archive and library specialties who might collectively be called the "third post-Florence generation." One common denominator of this group of "mature" professionals is their experience with and commitment to preservation administration that encompasses both leadership in conservation treatment as well as a full suite of preventive preservation activities, especially disaster preparedness and building environment management. The symposium also produced two papers from a cohort of "fourth-generation" preservation and conservation professionals (Adams and Doyle). Formally trained, technically sophisticated, and savvy with social media and communications, this generation carries on the tradition of professional commitments that emerged from the waters of Florence.

A final crosscutting theme of the symposium papers is the continuing social, cultural, economic, and research value of the original artifact. We most certainly are living in a digital world that is rapidly transforming access to and use of cultural heritage resources. But the special aura of the rare book, unique manuscript, or original work of art telegraphs human creativity across time and space in ways that flat and dissembled digital data cannot accomplish. The artifacts collected, protected, and served in the nation's libraries, archives, and museums embed honest truths about the human condition and, through their conservation and preservation, stand as testimony to our resilience.

Notes

1. De Zolt, S., Lionello, P., Nehu, A., and Tomasin, A. "The Disastrous Storm of 4 November 1966 on Italy." *Natural Hazards and Earth Systems Science* (Copernicus Publications on behalf of the European Geosciences Union) 6, no. 5 (2006): 861–79.
2. Panattoni, Lorenzo, and James R. Wallis. "The Arno River Flood Study (1971–1976)." *EOS: Transactions of the American Geophysical Union* 60, no. 1: 1–5.

3. Barr, Pelham. "Book Conservation and University Library Administration." *College & Research Libraries* 7 (July 1946): 214–19.

4. Batini, Giorgio. *4 November 1966: The River Arno in the Museums of Florence: Galleries, Monuments, Churches, Libraries, Archives and Masterpieces Damaged by the Flood.* Translated from Italian by T. Paterson. Florence: Bonech, 1967.

5. Waters, Sheila. *Waters Rising: Letters from Florence.* Ann Arbor, MI: Legacy Press, 2016.

6. Waters, Peter. "Book Restoration after the Florence Floods." *Penrose Annual* 62 (1969): 83–93.

7. Taylor, Kathrine Kressmann. *Diary of Florence in Flood.* New York: Simon and Schuster, 1967.

8. Clark, Robert. *Dark Water: Art, Disaster, and Redemption in Florence.* New York: Anchor Books, 2009.

9. Kraczyna, Swietlan Nicholas. *The Great Flood of Florence, 1966: A Photographic Essay.* Syracuse, NY: Syracuse University Press, 2007.

10. Hellenga, Robert. *The Sixteen Pleasures.* New York: Soho Press, 2009.

11. Hewson, David. *The Flood: A Mystery Set in Florence, Italy.* Sutton, UK: Severn House, 2015.

12. Pescioli, Idana. *Com'era L'acqua: I bambini de Firenze raccontano.* 1967; Pontedera (Pi): Tagate Edizioni, 2016.

13. Loria, Danilo. "50° anniversario dell'alluvione di Firenze: Un francobollo celebrerà gli 'angeli del fango' Per approfondire." Strettoweb, November 3, 2016. http://www.strettoweb.com/2016/11/50-anniversario-dellalluvione -di-firenze-un-francobollo-celebrera-gli-angeli-del-fango/477717/. Accessed March 18, 2018. See our translation from Italian:

> On November 4, the Ministry of Economic Development will issue a commemorative stamp of the "Angels of the mud," on the 50th anniversary of the Florence flood. The stamp, worth €0.95, is printed by the Istituto Poligrafico e Zecca dello Stato S.p.A., in rotogravure, on white paper, patinated neutral, self-adhesive, non-fluorescent; in five colors and a circulation of eight hundred thousand copies. The image depicts the 1966 Florence flood "interpreted," through a drawing, by the children of a school group. The sketch was edited by the "2016 Progetto Firenze" Committee, with the optimization of the Philatelic Center of the Directorate for Card Production and Traditional Productions Office of the Poligrafico Institute and Mint of the State S.p.A. The stamp "ANGELI DEL FANGO" and "50th ANNIVERSARY OF THE FLOODING OF FLORENCE," the inscription "ITALY" and the value "€0.95" complete the stamp.

14. PosteItalieane. "Angeli del fango." https://www.poste.it/angeli-del-fango -filatelia.html. Accessed March 18, 2018.

15. Firenze 2016: 50th Anniversary of the Florence Flood. http://toscana
.firenze2016.it/en/the-project/. Accessed October 13, 2017.

16. Ogden, Sherelyn. "The Impact of the Florence Flood on Library Conservation in the United States of America: A Study of the Literature Published
1956–1976." *Restaurator* 3 (January 1979): 1–36.

17. Alexander, David. "The Florence Flood: What the Papers Said." *Environmental Management* 4, no. 1 (1980): 27–34.

18. Lazzeretti, Luciana, and Francesco Capone. "Innovation and Innovators in
a Resilient City: The Case of Chemical Innovations after the 1966 Flood
in Florence." *City, Culture and Society* 6, no. 3: 83–91.

19. Rodwell, Dennis. "The UNESCO World Heritage Convention, 1972–2012:
Reflections and Directions." *Historic Environment: Policy & Practice* 3, no. 1:
64–85.

20. Spande, Helen (ed.). *Conservation Legacies of the Florence Flood of 1966:
Proceedings of the Symposium Commemorating the 40th Anniversary*. London:
Archetype, 2009.

21. Devine, Scott W. "The Florence Flood of 1966: A Report on the Current
State of Preservation and the Libraries and Archives of Florence." *The Paper
Conservator* 29, no. 1: 15–24.

22. Spande. *Conservation Legacies*, 85.

23. Paolucci, Antonio. *Il laboratorio del restauro a Firenze [The restoration laboratory in Florence]*. Turin, Italy: Istituto Bancario San Paolo di Torino, 1986.

24. Waters. *Waters Rising*.

Acknowledgments

A symposium planning committee was responsible for putting the program together and taking care of all the logistical details required for a successful event. The committee consisted of the following:

- Cathleen A Baker, conservation librarian emerita, University of Michigan Library
- Martha O'Hara Conway, director, Special Collections Research Center, University of Michigan Library
- Paul Conway, associate professor, University of Michigan School of Information
- Shannon Zachary, head of preservation and conservation, University of Michigan Library

The symposium and these proceedings could not have been possible without generous financial support from three University of Michigan departments and two external sponsors.

The University of Michigan Library and the University of Michigan School of Information shared equally in the costs of bringing the speakers and panelists to Ann Arbor. The Carnegie Fund of the School of Information subsidized the preparation and publication of the proceedings.

The University of Michigan Museum of Art hosted the symposium's "movie night" on November 3.

The Northeast Document Conservation Center in Andover, Massachusetts, and Preservation Technologies, LP, in Cranberry Township, Pennsylvania, supported hosting costs and offset the expense of preparing the program booklet. Thank you to Bill Veillette, executive director of NEDCC, and Robert Strauss, vice president of Preservation Technologies, for their long-standing commitment to preservation and their generosity toward our symposium.

The editors of these proceedings thank Christian and Monica Korab for their generosity in contributing a selection of photographs from Balthazar Korab's extraordinary work in Florence in the immediate aftermath of the flood. The striking photograph on the cover is described by John Comazzi on page 9.

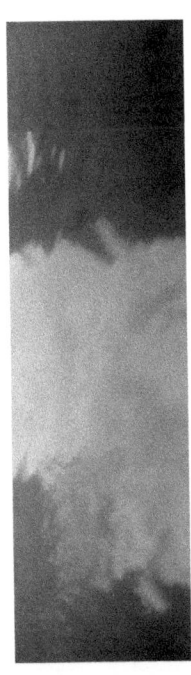

SETTING
THE SCENE

THE FLORENCE FLOOD AND ITS AFTERMATH: THE PHOTOGRAPHY OF BALTHAZAR KORAB

John Comazzi

It was daybreak on November 4, 1966, when the Arno River began to reveal its true destructive potential to the waking inhabitants of Florence. The rising depth and increased velocity of the river were to be expected given the extraordinary amount of rainfall that had soaked northern and central Italy throughout the month of October. However, it was the makeup of contents swirling in the river that signaled the severity of destruction inflicted upon towns upstream and foreshadowed the devastation about to be unleashed on the Florentines and their city. At first, the debris was seemingly innocuous, a typical mix of detritus one would expect to see floating in a swelling river: tree branches, leaves, litter, and the grimy froth that surfaces in a rapid flow. But it was not long before the river began to deliver a more ominous mix of wreckage: household items, furniture, fuel tanks, and the occasional bovine carcass.[1]

Up in the hills of Settignano, a small town northeast of Florence, news of the raging Arno brought a different kind of urgency to a Hungarian

American photographer who was still settling into his apartment after arriving in Italy with his wife and two young children only ten days prior. His working knowledge of Italian was good enough to decipher the periodic radio broadcasts delivering updates on the intense situation unfolding in the city center. And while he had arrived in Italy without any commissioned projects planned for his year-long "sabbatical," that morning, he knew where he needed to be. So he quickly packed his medium format Hasselblad camera, a 35 mm Leica, and whatever film he had—five rolls of 120 format film (twelve exposures each) and a handful of 35 mm Kodachrome rolls—and convinced his wife to drive him down to the city center, or as near as they could get in their Fiat Cinquecento.

Approaching from the east, they made a circuitous path to the northwest corner of the city, where he disembarked the car in the vicinity of the Fortezza da Basso and the Santa Maria Novella train station. Leaving him behind, his wife was forced to plot a different path back to Settignano—one that entailed numerous harrowing turns including a heartrending drive along the raised bed of a rail line in order to avoid the rising waters. She would later admit that she was not certain she would ever see her husband again.[2]

From Budapest to Florence by Way of the United States: A Brief Introduction to Balthazar Korab

Balthazar Korab was born in Budapest, Hungary, in 1926 and spent his early childhood in a stable upper-middle-class household, benefitting from his daily interactions within a culturally rich capital city.[3] By the time he reached his adolescence, he was well aware of his own advanced artistic skills and declared his desire to pursue a career as a painter. His parents, however, encouraged him to parlay his talents into a more "respectable" career in architecture, as his uncle had done before him. However, his plans to pursue a degree in architecture were interrupted during the German occupation of Hungary in March 1944. By October, the Russian army was advancing west, with the occupying German forces determined to defend Budapest at all costs. So the Korab family packed their essential belongings in two horse-drawn wagons and fled the city. Among his most essential personal items, Korab packed a sketchbook and a Russian-made 35 mm Leica camera that his father purchased from a soldier retreating from the eastern front.

It is important to emphasize that Korab's artistic sensibilities were maturing at a time of great turmoil in his home city and country, and he used his skills in visual representation to grapple with the disruptive events in his life. It was also during this time that he began to experiment with photography. The majority of his earliest photographs are somewhat casual snapshots of his family and fellow refugees. However, several of his photographs from this period seem to originate from a different kind of perceptual sensitivity—one that deepened Korab's emotional response to his extraordinary circumstances. This use of visual representation as a coping mechanism to make sense of the dramatic experiences in his life helped shape Korab's overall "habits of depiction" that would prove instrumental for his future practices as a photographer of architecture.[4]

Korab began his architecture education at the Budapest Polytechnic in 1945, shortly after the end of the Second World War. His time in the university coincided with the Soviet occupation of Hungary and major political upheavals that led to the unjust imprisonment of his father in 1948. Shortly after his father's release, Korab fled the country in January 1949 with his younger brother (Antoni) and a friend from architecture school (László Kollár). He eventually traveled to Paris, where he was accepted into the architecture program at the École des Beaux-Arts and completed his architecture training (1950–54). He obtained his diploma of architecture in 1954 and then moved to the United States with his first wife, Sally Dow, an American pianist whose family lived outside Detroit.

Soon after his arrival in the United States, Korab sought and was offered a job as a designer in the architecture office of Eero Saarinen and Associates. However, it was his skill with a camera that quickly caught the attention of Saarinen and the senior associates, and before long, he was responsible for integrating photography into the firm's design-development and documentation processes. Due largely to positive reception of his published photography from his time in the Saarinen office, Korab began to receive numerous professional commissions from other architects throughout the United States and eventually opened an independent photography studio in 1958.

By the early 1960s, Korab's reputation continued to grow as he became one of the most sought-after professional photographers of architecture, and in 1964, he was awarded first prize in the national competition for the American Institute of Architects' (AIA) Gold Medal for Excellence in Photography. It was during this time of intense professional development that Korab and his second wife, Monica (née Kane), decided to take a self-imposed one-year sabbatical to Italy, beginning in the fall of 1966, with their children, Christian (b. 1960) and Alexandra (b. 1964). While Korab went to Italy with no grand plan, the opportunity proved to have an enormous influence on his career and personal development as a photographer, as he produced a series of portfolios and publications that contain some of the most historically significant images in his archive.

L'Aqua Alta

Korab's trek through the flooding city began as he moved cautiously through the dense network of streets in the Santa Maria Novella neighborhood leading to Via de' Tornabuoni and the Piazza Santa Trinita. From there, he ventured across the Ponte Santa Trinita to the Lungarno Guicciardini along the south bank of the Arno to gain a sweeping view back of the city center at a time when the Arno had reached its most violent levels of intensity and force.

Realizing that he was moving dangerously close to the lower ground in the Santo Spirito and Borgo San Jacopo neighborhoods of "Oltrarno" (beyond the Arno), he headed back across the river in the direction of Santa Maria Novella and continued to venture north into the San Marco neighborhood.

As the high waters continued to flood the city streets farther to the north from the Arno, Korab found himself navigating the

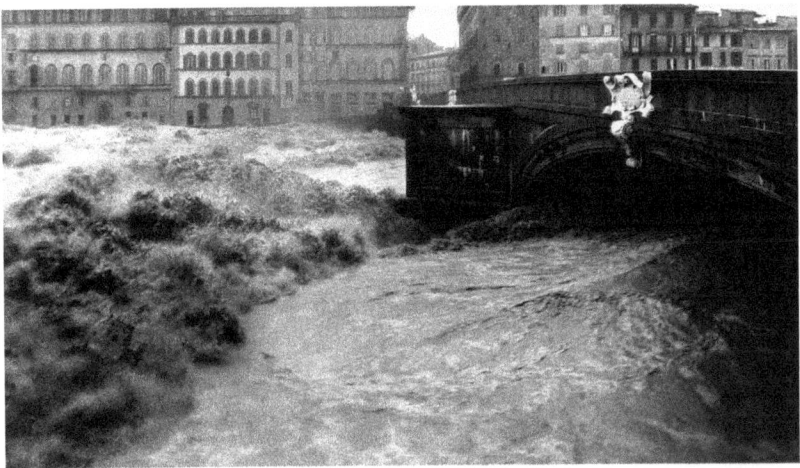

Florence Flood, November 4, 1966. View from the south bank of the Arno River, Florence, Italy. The river rages just beneath the stone arches of the Ponte Santa Trinita. Photo by Balthazar Korab.

historic center of the city by first heading east toward Piazza Santissima Annunziata. Blocked by chest-high waters, he backtracked and moved south down Via Ricasoli in the direction of the Piazza del Duomo, ultimately arriving at the heart of the city's religious center: between the steps of the Cattedrale di Santa Maria del Fiore (the Duomo) and the Battistero di San Giovanni (the Baptistery of Saint John).

At times submerged up to his chest, Korab moved through the frigid waters to capture some of the most extraordinary images of the flood and its immediate aftermath. The next morning, he drove to Rome to process the film and prepare the images for distribution through organizations such as the Associated Press news service and *Life* magazine, which purchased the rights for several images for a feature article on the flood that was published two weeks later.[5]

During the days and weeks immediately following the flood, Korab spent much of his time in the city documenting the damage to the city's architecture, monuments, and works of art, as well as the numerous professionals, students, and volunteers from around the world who traveled to Florence to aid in the conservation efforts focused on the

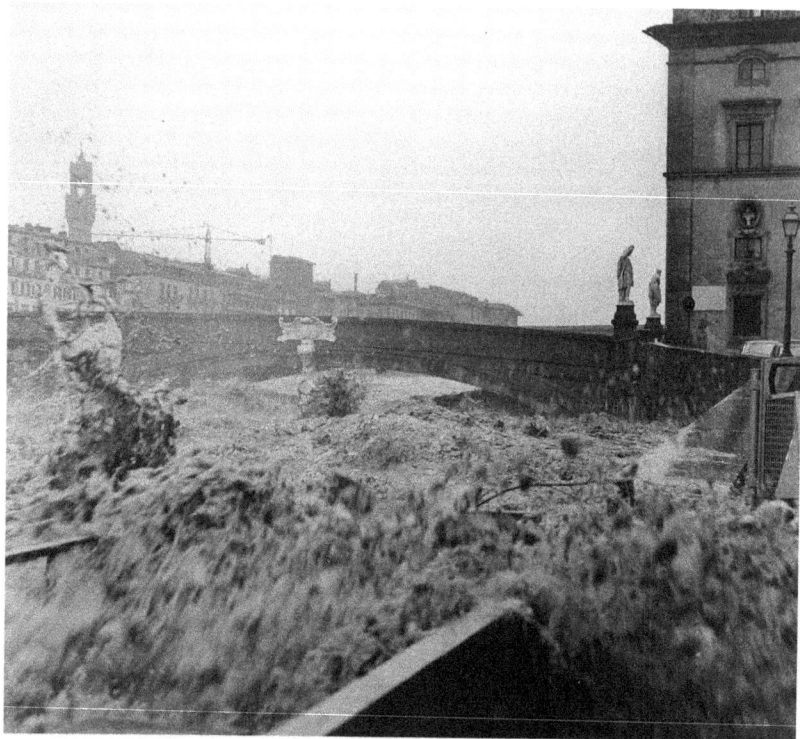

Florence Flood, November 4, 1966. View from the south bank of the Arno
River, Florence, Italy. Raging water floods over the south embankment of Lungarno
Guicciardini and the Ponte Santa Trinita. Photo by Balthazar Korab.

most precious archival materials from the Galleria degli Uffizi, the Istituto e Museo di Storia della Scienza (Institute and Museum of the History of Science; now the Museo Galileo), and the Biblioteca Nazionale
Centrale di Firenze (Florence National Central Library).

Due largely to the publication of images made during and in the
aftermath of the flood, Korab received a plum commission by *National
Geographic* to record the restoration and conservation efforts to repair
damaged art and rare books from churches, galleries, libraries, and
other archives throughout the city.[6]

This commission from *National Geographic* helped establish numerous connections between Korab and leaders of the city's major cultural
institutions, including the Uffizi and the National Central Library, who

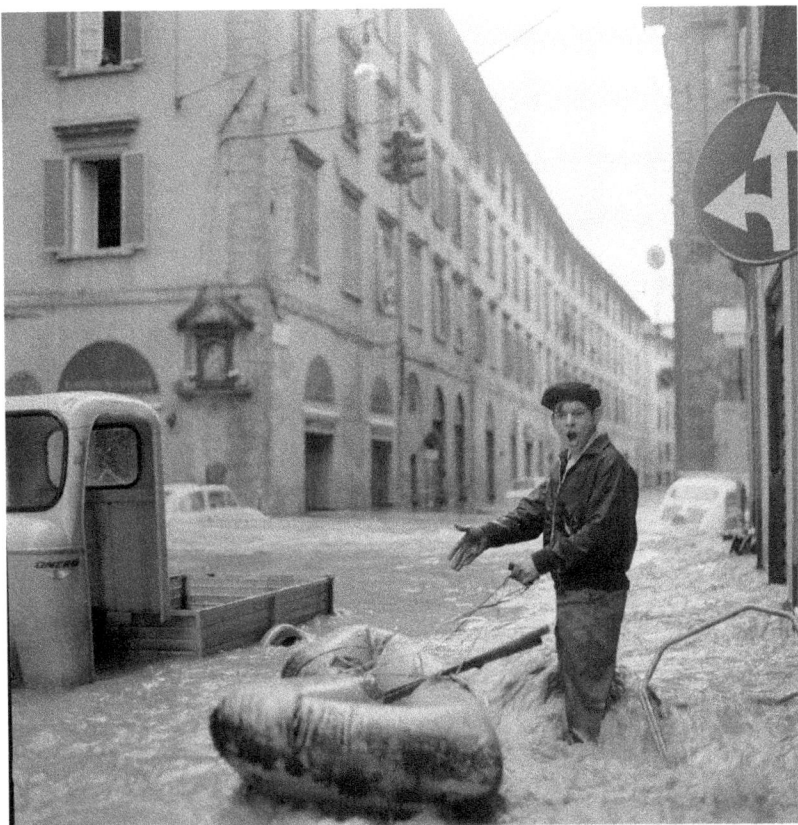

Florence Flood, November 4, 1966. View looking to the southwest down Via Nazionale at Via Guelfa toward the Stazione Santa Maria Novella. This photo captured the raw intensity of the events as they developed throughout the morning. Taken around 11:00 a.m., this image depicts a young boy (age fifteen at the time) named Stefano Londi who was attempting to secure a small inflatable raft that he had been using throughout the morning to navigate the rising floodwaters. Mr. Londi, now age sixty-five, was recently identified through a social media campaign and was present to recall his story during the opening of an exhibition of Korab photographs commemorating the fiftieth anniversary of the Florence Flood held at the Tethys Gallery in Florence, Italy, on October 27, 2016. Photo by Balthazar Korab.

enlisted Korab to aid in the process of cleaning, restoring, and organizing the many thousands of photographic plates and archival transparencies held in their respective collections. The Korabs had moved from their small apartment in Settignano to a flat on the Villa I Tatti estate, which gave them rare access to the gardens and the *limonaia*. With the

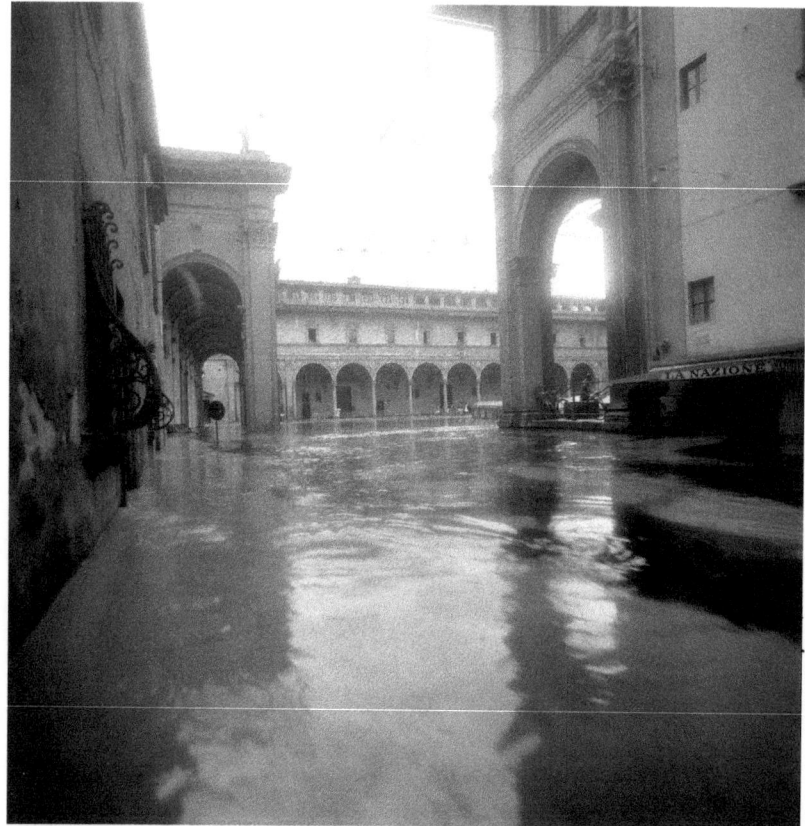

Florence Flood, November 4, 1966. View southeast down Via Cesare Battisti toward Piazza della Santissmia Annunziata and the Ospedale degli Innocenti. In an interview with the author in 2008, Korab recalled that he could feel the immense pressure of the frigid water on his torso as he moved through the chest-high waters of the Piazza. Photo by Balthazar Korab.

help of his family, Korab fashioned a series of drying racks made of bamboo harvested from the gardens to assist in the cleaning and drying of the rare archival photographic plates.

Luisa Becherucci, director of the Uffizi; Professor Ugo Procacci, superintendent of fine art for the Florence region; and Umberto Baldini, director of restorations at the Uffizi all met with Korab frequently throughout his documentation of the restorations being undertaken by their respective institutions.[7]

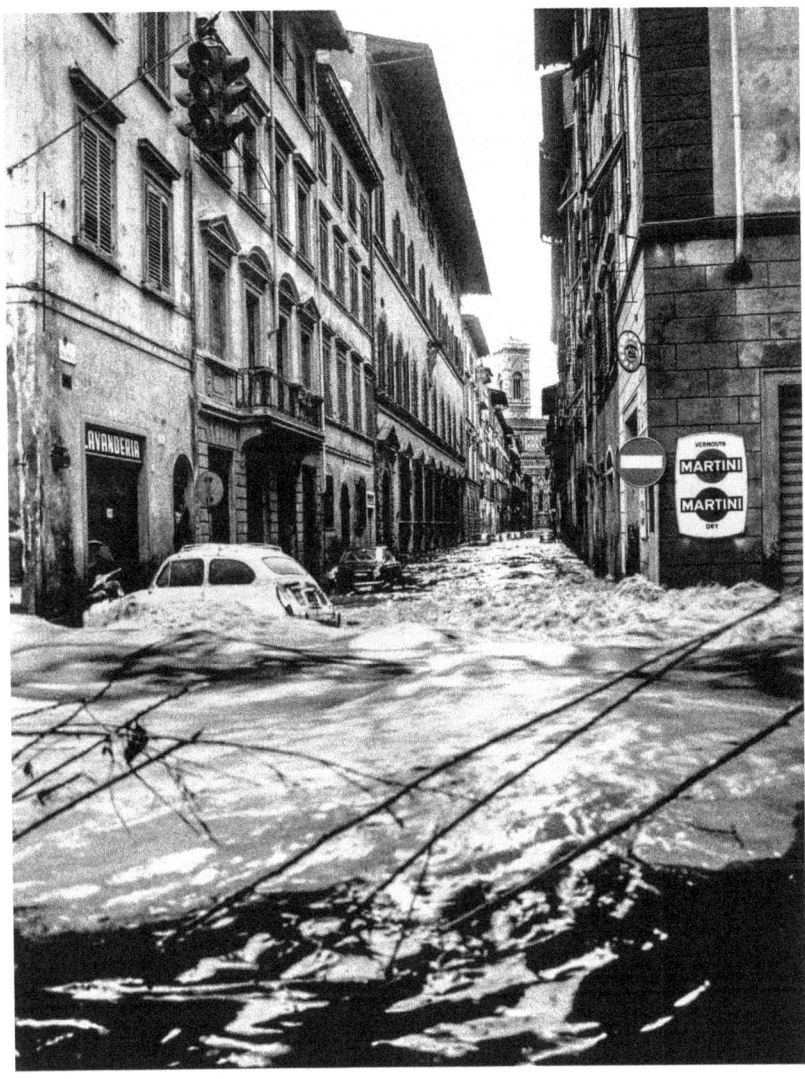

Florence Flood, November 4, 1966. View southwest down Via Ricasoli at Via degli Alfani toward the Duomo (Basilica of Santa Maria del Fiore). The campanile di Giotto (or Giotto's bell tower) is visible rising above the basilica at the end of Via Ricasoli as the floodwaters consume a Fiat 500 in the foreground. Photo by Balthazar Korab.

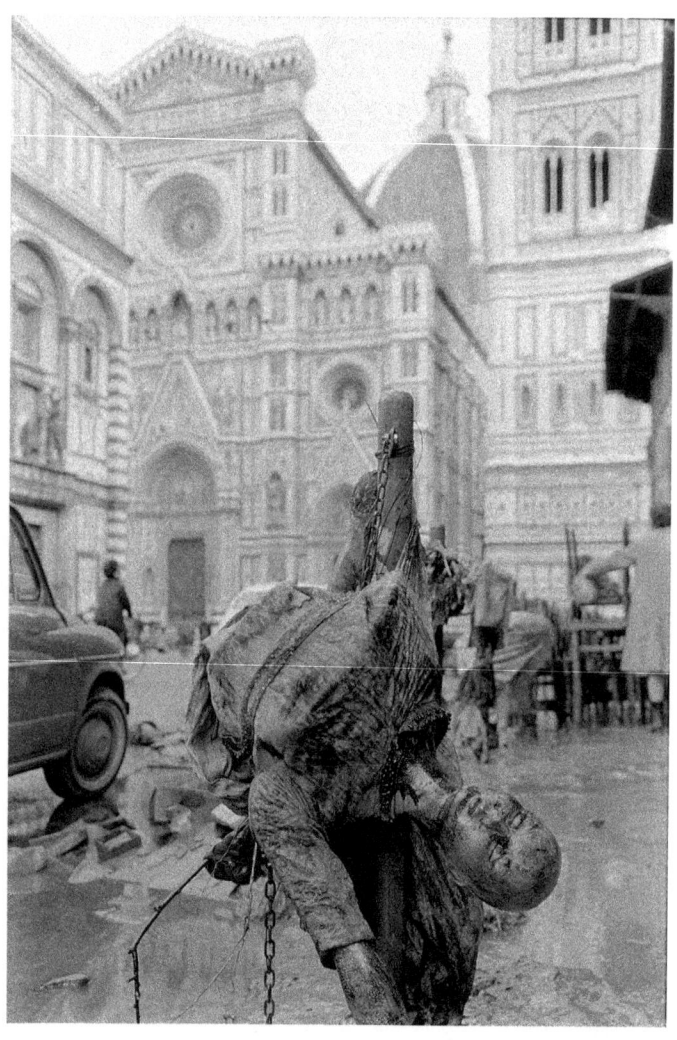

Florence Flood, November 4, 1966. A mannequin and miscellaneous debris from shops and restaurants were left strewn about the Piazza del Duomo with a view of the façade of Duomo (Basilica of Santa Maria del Fiore), the Battistero di San Giovanni (Baptistry of St. John), and the campanile di Giotto (or Giotto's bell tower) beyond. Photo by Balthazar Korab.

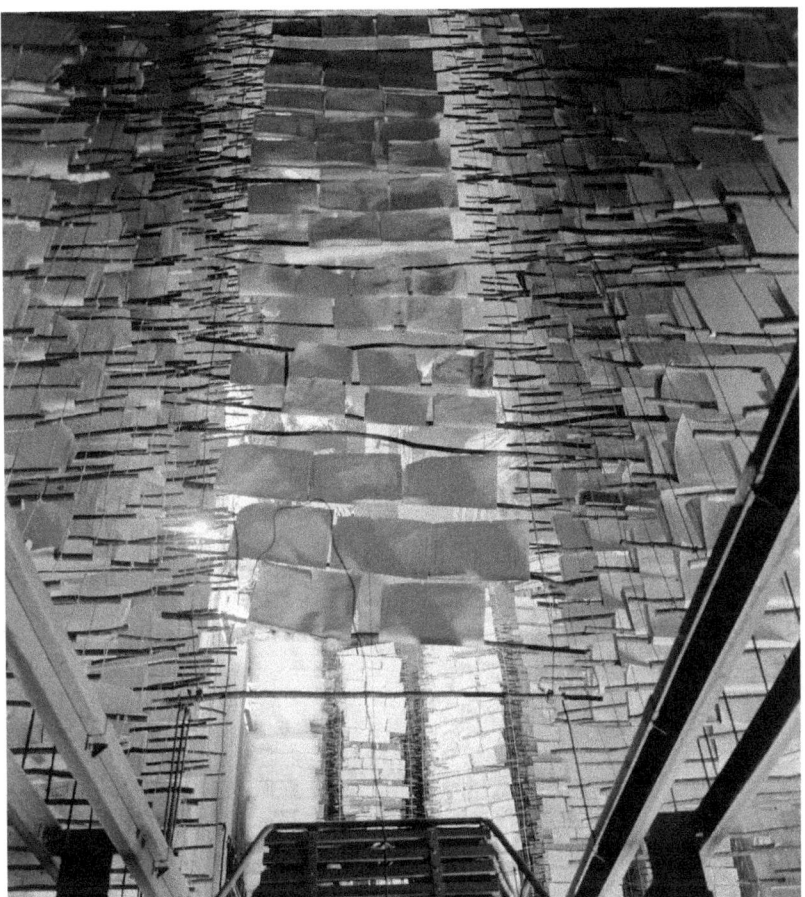

Rare books, manuscripts, and other documents hanging to dry in the heating plant of the Santa Maria Novella rail terminal. Pages were first cleaned, then pressed to remove moisture, and finally hung to dry for several hours in the heating plant. Photo by Balthazar Korab.

In addition to providing Korab with the rare opportunity to document the historically significant restoration practices developed following the floods, these commissions secured from international publications also created an unanticipated source of income, allowing the Korabs to extend their sabbatical in Italy for an additional year.[8] During the remainder of their stay, Korab produced several other significant portfolios, including one of the gardens at the Villa Gamberaia, another of the working landscapes and hill towns of Tuscany and Umbria, and a unique collaboration

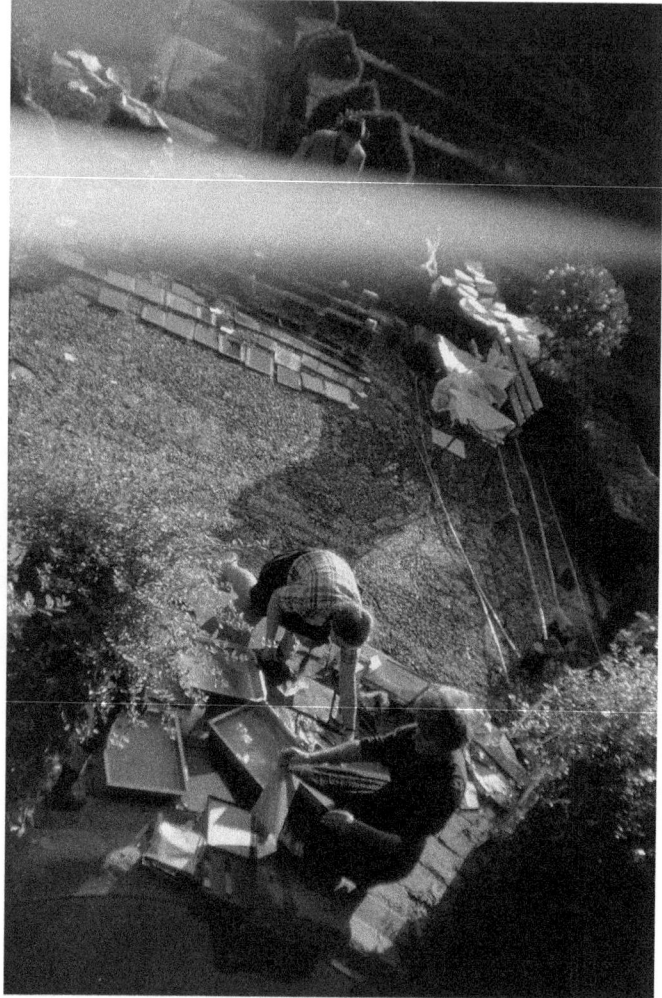

The Korab family was enlisted by the leadership of the Uffizi and the Biblioteca Nazionale to help clean glass negatives and transparencies in the gardens of Villa I Tatti, where they were renting a flat at the time. Photo by Balthazar Korab, c. 1967.

with Astra Zarina, an acquaintance from Michigan, documenting the roofscapes of Rome.[9] In what proved to be an extraordinarily expansive survey, Korab produced an estimated 3,200 images, 226 of which were later selected for publication in a book, *I tetti di Roma: Le terrazze—le altane—i belvedere* (*The rooftops of Rome: Terraces—high loggias—overlooks*).[10]

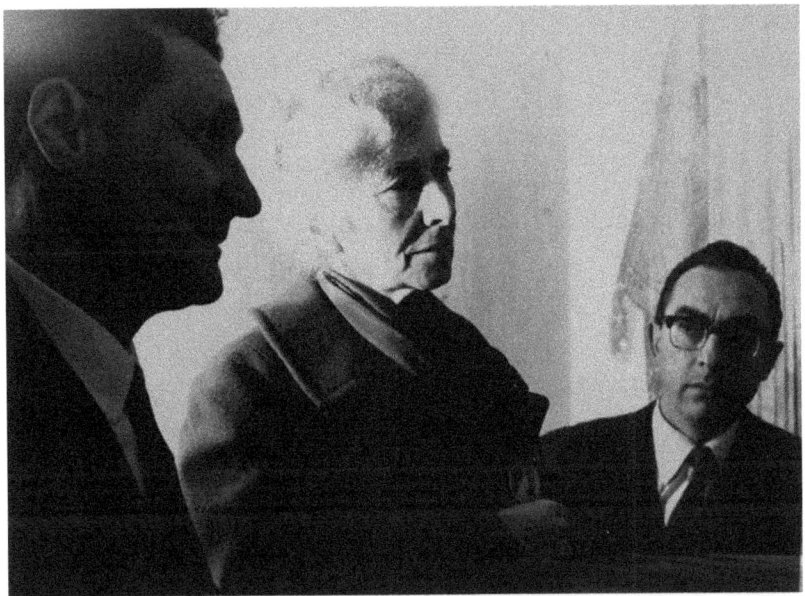

Professor Ugo Procacci, superintendent of fine art for the Florence region (left) with Luisa Becherucci, director of the Uffizi (middle), and Umberto Baldini, director of restorations (right). These institutional leaders met with Korab frequently to help direct his documentation of the restorations being undertaken by their respective institutions.

Conclusion

The story prevails in my approach to photography; the feelings, responses to a place, the message. . . . And photography is a very important way of creating a record of the transformations experienced throughout the cultural life of a place.

—Balthazar Korab[11]

As these proceedings aim to take stock of the progress made in the intervening decades, Balthazar Korab's photography is both visual evidence and illustrative context for the work of this important symposium. On November 4, 1966, in a matter of hours, the city of Florence and its inhabitants experienced one of the most sublimely horrific and transformative events in its millennia of existence. Today, fifty years on, the city and many of its most treasured artifacts still carry scars from the events of that fateful day.

Having lived a mostly transient life and borne witness to the ravages of war on the built environment, Balthazar Korab came to understand cities as much more than merely collections of static buildings, monuments, spaces, and artifacts. For him, cities made manifest the material, cultural, and historical circumstances that comprise the long arcs of history and the contingencies of the everyday. As his life and career progressed, Korab learned to redirect his technical capacities outward, beyond his personal interests and preoccupations, in order to help capture and understand the complex relationships between architecture and the human condition. In Florence, he broke through to produce images not just of the world but for the world.

Notes

1. For a detailed personal account of the details and events of the Florence Flood, see Kathrine Kressmann Taylor, *Diary of Florence in Flood* (New York: Simon and Schuster, 1967), 99–100. See also Victor Velen, "Ravaged Realm of Art," *Life*, November 18, 1966, 122–23; and Joseph Judge, "Florence Rises from the Flood," *National Geographic*, July 1967, 1–43, both of which feature photography by Balthazar Korab.

2. Monica Korab, interview with author, November 11, 2006.

3. For a more detailed biography on the life and career of Balthazar Korab, see John Comazzi, *Balthazar Korab: Architect of Photography* (New York: Princeton Architectural Press, 2012).

4. "Habits of depiction," as coined by Joel Snyder, are the means by which our pictorial vision is formed through a reciprocal relationship between what we see and the pictures we make. See Joel Snyder, "Picturing Vision," *Critical Inquiry* 6, no. 3 (Spring 1980): 499–526, quoted from 526.

5. Victor Velen, "Ravaged Realm of Art," *Life*, November 18, 1966, 122–23.

6. The commission by *National Geographic* culminated in a forty-three-page feature article in the July 1967 issue that included a broad sampling of Korab's photography. Joseph Judge, "Florence Rises from the Flood," *National Geographic*, July 1967, 1–43. In an interview with the author on November 11, 2006, Monica Korab indicated that it was rare at the time for *National Geographic* to commission work from nonstaff photographers for such a prominent assignment.

7. The Villa I Tatti had been renamed "The Villa I Tatti, the Harvard University Center for Italian Renaissance Studies" in 1961 after Bernard Berenson bequeathed the estate, his collections, and his library to Harvard University in 1959.

8. A double-page spread in *Life* magazine, for example, earned the Korab's roughly $2,500 and the *National Geographic* commission earned an estimated $3,000. Together, the earnings from these two commissions totaled roughly one half of their entire budget for a year in Florence. Monica Korab, interview with the author, June 6, 2006.

9. For more on Korab's portfolio from the Villa Gamberaia, see *Gamberaia: Photo Essay by Balthazar Korab and Text by Harold Acton* (Milan: Centro Di, 1971). In 1987, Korab also contributed images of Villa Gamberaia for a spread in *Casa Vogue*. See Paolo Pejrone, "Sotto un Manto di Neve," *Casa Vogue*, February 1987, 168–71.

10. Astra Zarina and Balthazar Korab, *I Tatti di Roma: Le terrazzo, le altane i belvedere* (Rome: Carlo Bestetti, 1970), 19.

11. Balthazar Korab, interview with author, November 13, 1997.

PETER WATERS AND THE ORIGINS OF LIBRARY CONSERVATION: A MEMOIR[1]

Sheila Waters

November 4, 2016, marks the fiftieth anniversary of the most devastating flood in Florence since 1333. The average person has never heard about it, even though at the time students and their professors the world over flocked to Florence to help in the initial rescue and cleanup. But those of us who were there and lived through the following months have indelible memories.

It is widely recognized that the vital and respected profession of book and paper conservation has its origins in the philosophy and treatments developed in the aftermath of the flood, in response to the immense challenge of dealing with so much damage to hundreds of thousands of rare books and documents in the libraries of Florence. I am a calligraphic designer, not a conservator, but I was there and have firsthand knowledge of how the huge restoration system was set up in the national library, the Biblioteca Nazionale Centrale di Firenze (the "BNCF"), during 1967. It is important for the profession to know its history, so the story needs to be told before it dies along with those who experienced it.

My late husband was the bookbinder and library conservator Peter Waters, who died in 2003. This is largely his story and that of his team

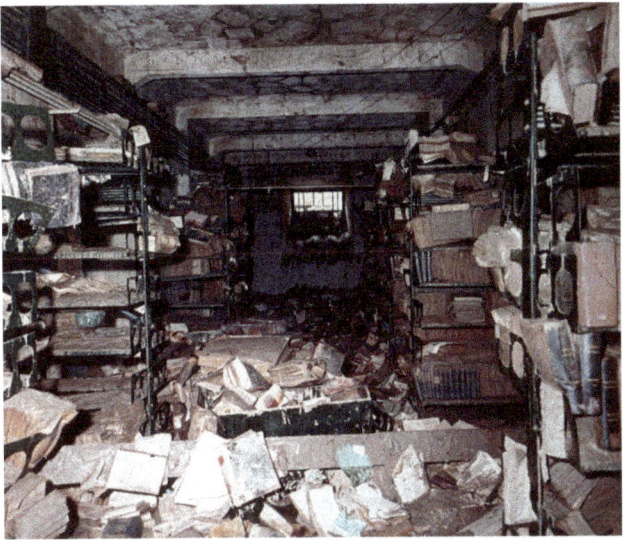

Fig. 1. Book "mono prints" on the ceiling.

members, who played a vital part in the restoration operations in the BNCF following the flood. In this talk, I will describe the setting up of that massive restoration system. It is impossible to cover this story adequately in a short talk, but it is covered in great detail in my new book called *Waters Rising: Letters from Florence.*[2]

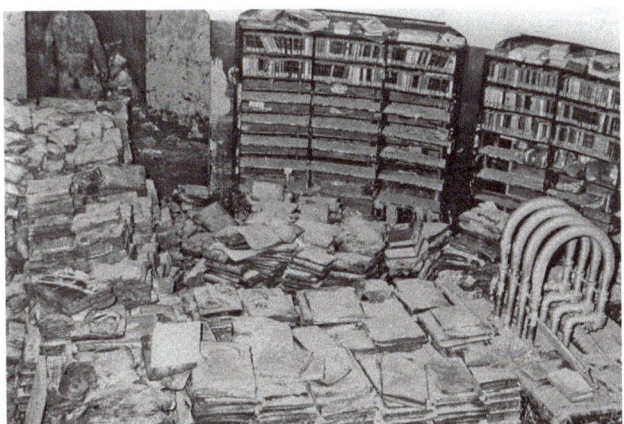

Fig. 2. Biblioteca Nazionale Centrale di Firenze basement, November 1966.

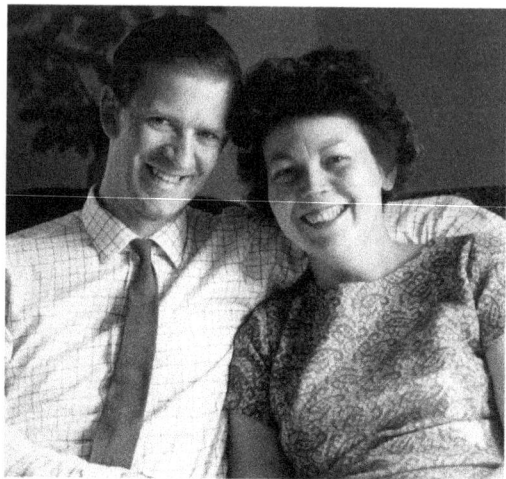

Fig. 3. Peter, thirty-six, on leave from Florence, at
home with Sheila, spring 1967.

Information about past events found in personal letters and eye-
witness accounts has powerful authenticity. At nearly five hundred
pages, my book contains all the letters Peter and I wrote to each other
during the months following the flood. Peter's letters, almost fifty
of them, were his chief diary. After his death, for easy reference, I
extracted all the relevant technical information from his letters and
notes for a "Narrative Diary" section. There are more than 280 photos,
mostly taken by Peter, of damaged books and the treatments devised
for them. Also included is a section of some of Peter's student book-
bindings, which he made before the flood, and his later commissioned
and exhibition bindings. I am very grateful to Cathleen Baker for the
huge amount of time she has so enthusiastically given to this project,
and to our eldest son, Julian Waters, her codesigner, for his immense
help in preparing visuals for this talk. I am also indebted to Randy Silverman for introducing us to Cathleen; for his masterful introduction
about Peter's life, work, and impact on the library field; and for naming
him the Father of Preventive Conservation. This presentation is but
a microcosm of the much bigger story told in the book. *Waters Rising*
comes with a remastered DVD of the forty-minute film about the restoration system made by Roger Hill and Peter in 1968.

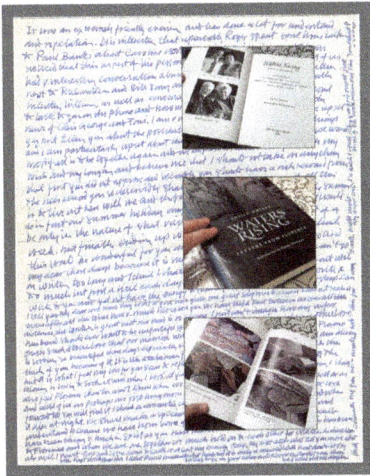

Fig. 4. *Waters Rising*, the book, and one
of Peter's letters.

I will use many of Peter's own words, taken not from his letters
but from his article in the 1969 edition of the *Penrose Annual*, a British annual review of the graphic arts since 1895, because his own
descriptions of the fully developed sections of the restoration system are so succinct that I cannot hope to improve on them.[3] I quoted
the same extracts in two previous overview talks, the first time in
2006 in New York University's fortieth anniversary symposium in
Florence. Those proceedings were published by Archetype Publications and entitled *Conservation Legacies of the Florence Flood of 1966*,
where more technical information can be found in the talks by Tony
Cains and Chris Clarkson.[4] The second time was at the National
Gallery of Art in Washington, DC, for the forty-fifth anniversary.
The Franco Zeffirelli film *Florence: Days of Destruction* was shown
on both occasions.

As a direct result of his pioneering work in Florence, Peter served
as chief of conservation at the Library of Congress in Washington, DC,
from 1971 to his retirement in 1995. He was the technical director for
the setting up of the BNCF's vast restoration system from the end of
November 1966 to October 1967. I became directly involved myself

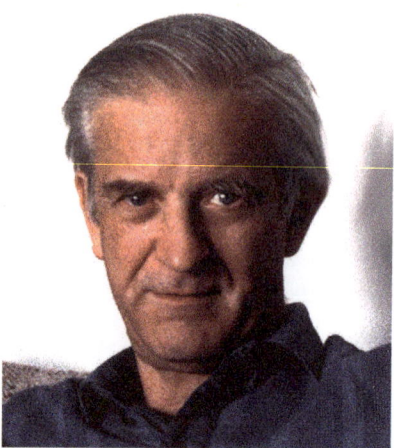

Fig. 5. Peter Waters when at the Library of Congress.

and spent a total of three months working with Peter in the BNCF during 1967.

Why Was Peter Chosen to Play a Leading Role?

Peter's work in England before he was forty is not as well-known as his time in the Library of Congress, so I will give a little of his background to explain why he was chosen to lead the British team. He had no experience dealing with damaged books on such a massive scale—who did?—but he had a reputation as an innovative designer-bookbinder and manuscript restorer in partnership with Roger Powell (who had restored and rebound the Book of Kells in 1953).

Peter and I met while we were master's degree students at the Royal College of Art (RCA), London, in 1949. He specialized in fine bookbinding, lettering, and typography and I in calligraphy, lettering, and typography, and Roger Powell was our bookbinding tutor. Peter had previously spent four years from the age of fourteen studying bookbinding with William Matthews at Guildford College of Art. We

Roger Powell & Peter Waters
Howard M. Nixon

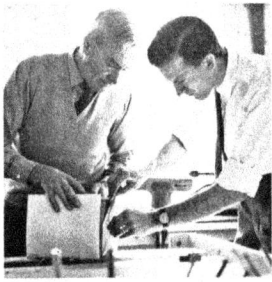

Fig. 6. Peter with his partner Roger Powell.

married in 1953 and ran our own businesses of commissions and part-time teaching. In 1957, we moved from Woking, Surrey, to Froxfield, Hampshire, for Peter to become Roger's full partner. From our college days, Peter and I collaborated on all our commissions, actively or with design critique, and I designed illustrations that were used on many of his and Roger's bindings.

The Call for Help

On Friday afternoon, November 25, 1966, Peter was phoned by Howard Nixon, keeper of printed books at the British Museum. Nixon had been contacted by Emanuele Casamassima, director of the BNCF, who needed advice on restoring at least 110,000 badly damaged, rare sixteenth- and seventeenth-century printed volumes. These included 90,000 from the Palatina and Magliabechiana collections, a primary source for Western scholarship and the nucleus of the library. Howard Nixon knew Peter's work well. When Peter was only twenty-one and still at the RCA, he was commissioned by Nixon to design a binding for *Le Livre Anglais* exhibition in

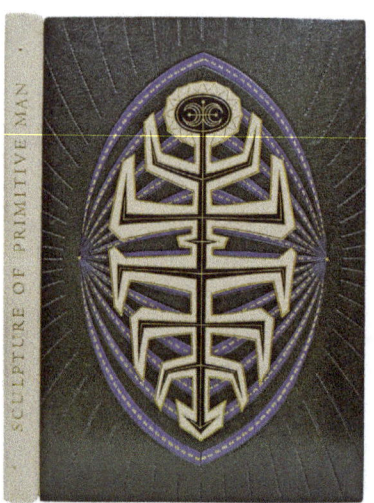

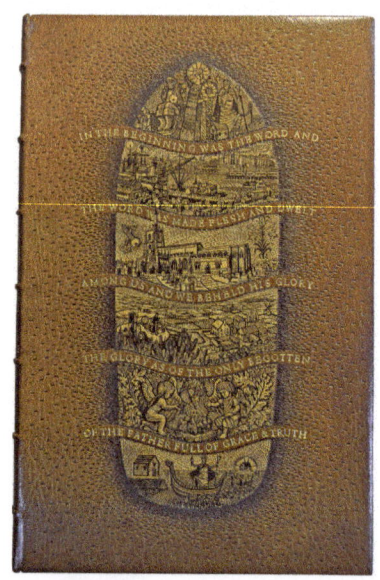

Fig. 7. Binding of *Sculpture of Primitive Man*.

Fig. 8. Binding of a book of donors for Chelmsford Cathedral, UK.

Paris in 1951. Peter revived the tradition of pre-1500 blind-stamped binding, and Nixon bought the book for the British Library's permanent collections. So Nixon had confidence in Peter's ability to assess the unusual and desperate situation at the BNCF and make recommendations.

Nixon asked Peter to choose two colleagues and fly to Florence the very next day. Tony Cains, a skilled private binder, and Dorothy Cumpstey, an expert teacher of binding, were able to drop everything to go with him. The three arrived in Florence, complete with gum boots, without any clear mandate and were set to work in the Forte di Belvedere to look for mold on dried books. These were arriving by the truckload every day from grain and tobacco drying facilities in Italy. Wet, muddied books had been dried en masse, and inevitably many had suffered further damage from the heat.

In the Forte, working conditions were uncomfortable with no heat and little water, and students were busy scraping dried mud off books.

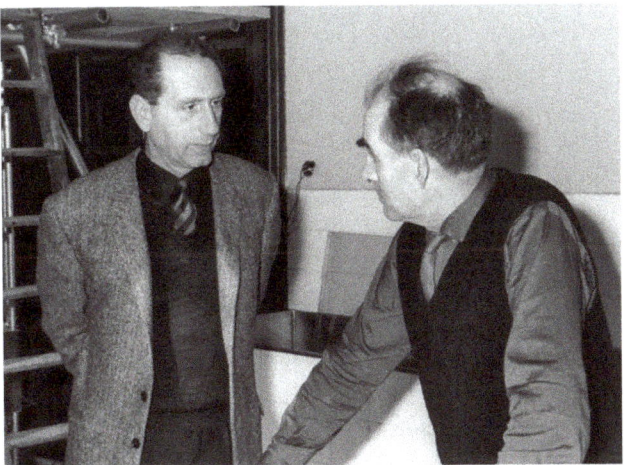

Fig. 9. Emanuele Casamassima with Sandy Cockerell.

Meanwhile, student volunteers were still digging books out of the BNCF basement, wiping off excess mud with wet sponges, and scattering sawdust over them to absorb some water. Three weeks after the flood, more than four hundred truckloads had already gone to drying plants.

Peter describes the state of the dried books in his *Penrose Annual* article:

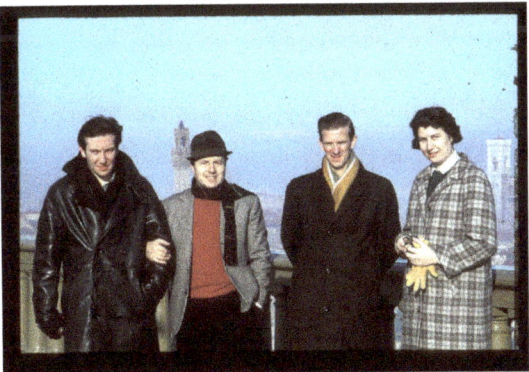

Fig. 10. Tony Cains, unknown, Peter, and Dorothy Cumpstey.

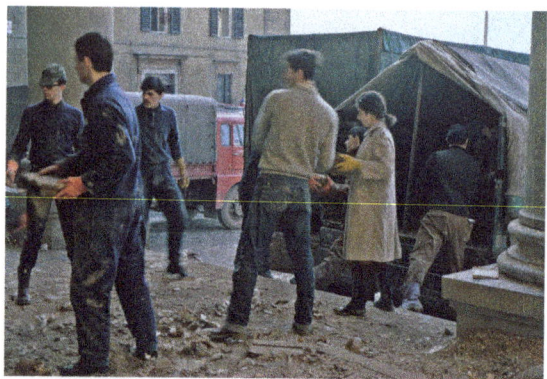

Fig. 11. Student volunteer Mud Angels loading trucks outside the BNCF.

Despite good superficial cleaning before drying and the wise rule by the Director at the beginning, that none of the books should be opened before arrival at the dryers, many of them, arriving at the Forte, resembled abstract sculptural forms. Vellum and leather covers were distorted and shrunken. Book stacks in the library have characteristic openings at each end and vellum bindings stored originally at the ends of the stacks had rotted where the water had run through these shapes, combining with the vellum to form a glutinous mass. Other covers were defaced with a combination of mud, sawdust, oil and mold and edges were badly stuck with gelatin, mud and sawdust.

The books had been stood upright to dry in the heated dryers, allowing water and gelatin to drain. The concentration of gelatin was greatest in the openings between the sections, leaving them brittle. Covers that had been too hurriedly ripped off had dragged the sewing through the backs of the sections. The water, combined with excessive gluing of the spine when originally bound, had accelerated the damage to the backs of the sections. Early 16th century spines suffered least because they had been pasted with starch paste rather than hide glue. The leaves of books bound in limp vellum withstood the flood better than most.[5]

This was a very important finding because it led to the later development of nonadhesive and limp vellum binding techniques.

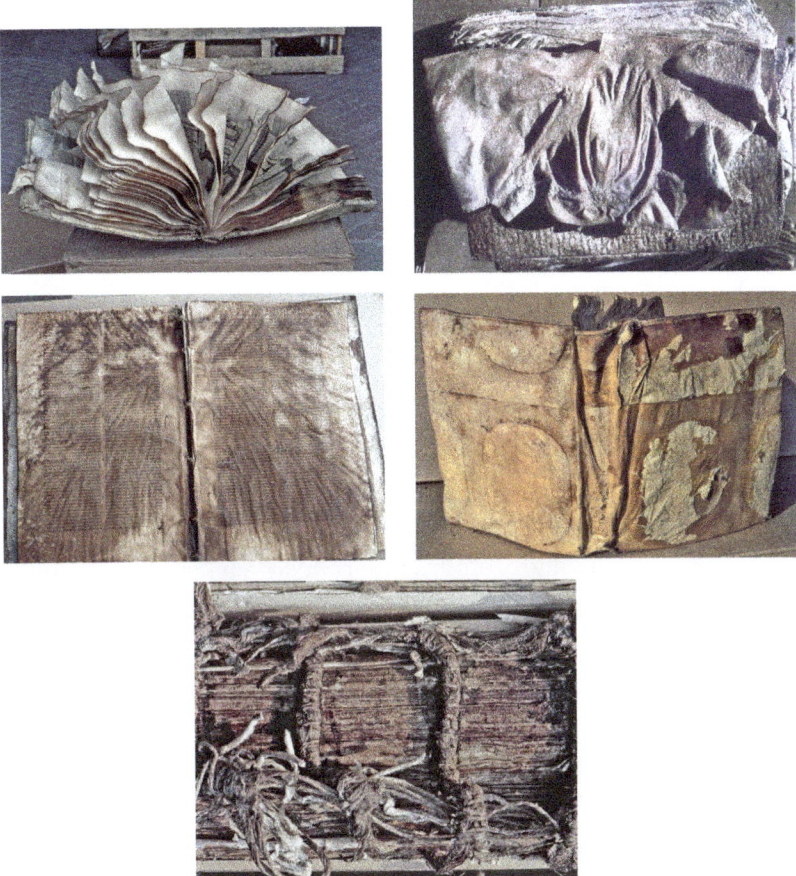

Figs. 12–16. Examples of damaged books.

Peter's Vision

Only four days after the team's arrival, a high-level meeting showed that there was no plan at all for the future beyond dry-cleaning, wrapping, and storing the often very badly distorted books. In that state, they would be unusable to readers, maybe indefinitely. Peter questioned this policy and suggested an outrageous idea: to set up a colossal dry-cleaning, washing, drying, and pressing plant to save and store the majority of the collections, wrapped but flat, to await mending and rebinding. The effect of this idea on Director Casamassima was dynamic, and from that moment, he supported the team and the implementation of Peter's plan, no matter any opposition. In fact, he cut through enough red tape to warrant a prison sentence in normal times.

It was decided that the whole series of operations would eventually be carried out in the BNCF itself. The Power Station had a large number of sinks and plenty of hot water, and during November, one hundred untrained students worked around the clock in eight-hour shifts. They were washing large books, causing even more damage by separating their leaves while wet, a technique normally requiring immense skill. The British pointed this out and so were asked to take over and train the students in their new system of washing, not in the wet state but after dried books had had their sections separated ("pulled") by the students working in the Forte. Tony Cains took charge at the Forte, and Chris Clarkson joined them to direct the students at the Power Station.

The original briefing had called for only an advisory visit to Florence by Peter, Tony, and Dorothy, but from November through April, Peter stayed there for most of the time. At home, I became the liaison between binders and restorers going out to help and the British Italian Art and Archives Rescue Fund. Peter describes that expansion of the team and the funding supplied:

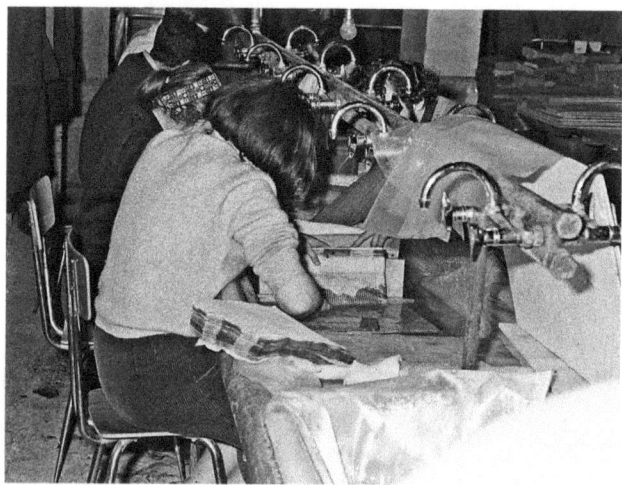

Fig. 17. Students washing books at the Power Station in the revised system.

It became clear that a great deal of additional help was needed and we appealed for more British restorers and binders, particularly those with teaching ability. In the following months over forty people worked for periods of from [*sic*] two weeks to several months developing the system and training volunteers. The team included members of the British Museum Stationery Office Bindery and the most distinguished private restorers, binders, and teachers of binding in Britain. This flow of help was organized by Howard Nixon and supported by the British Italian Art and Archives Rescue Fund, whose major effort in Florence became concentrated on the BNCF. From time to time the team was joined by restorers from many other countries. Guidance on chemical problems was given to the team by the British Museum Research Laboratory in collaboration with the Istituto di Patologia del Libro in Rome.[6]

Preparations to Move the Whole System to the BNCF

Peter then describes the preparations made from December through March for the move to the BNCF. Very early, it was clear that expert selection for appropriate treatment would be needed for each book on its journey through the system, and at Peter's request, Roger Powell, then seventy years old, arrived in early December to concentrate on

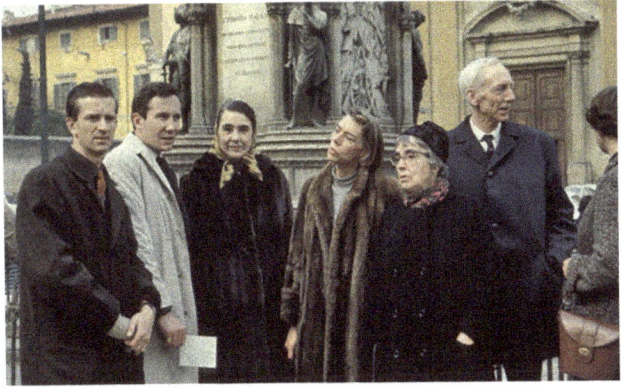

Fig. 18. Peter, Tony, Elizabeth Greenhill, Sally Lou Smith, Stella Patri, and Charles and Pamela Gott (née Fowler).

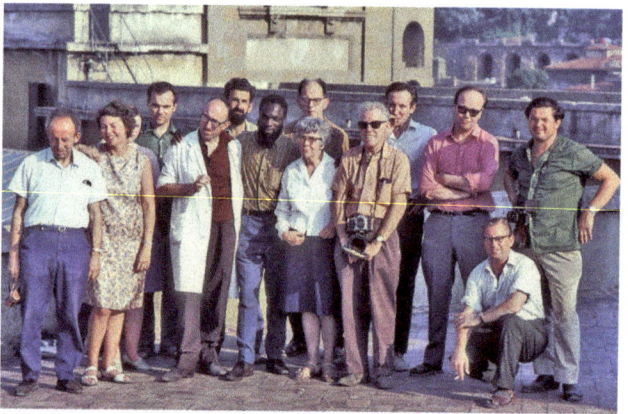

Fig. 19. Peter's photo of team members in May 1967.

this skilled work and to train more experts in selection. Peter describes this process:

> Before a book enters the restoration system, it has to be classified accord-
> ing to its value and the treatment it requires, and details of historical
> interest are recorded. Symbols were devised during our first week at the
> Forte to make international interpretation easier and designed to warn a
> student or worker of the state of the book and how it should be handled.
> For instance, OK indicated that a student could handle a book, whereas
> the international road "stop" sign showed that it was particularly valuable
> and should be reserved for specialist treatment. In the beginning, these
> signs were written on a slip of paper, but now a detailed printed restora-
> tion card and photographs of the original binding and any significant
> pages, accompany each book with classification and directions for treat-
> ment. The card also indicated the history of the original structure by
> means of an enlarged symbol system with other relevant details.[7]

He closes that paragraph with a very important sentence: "These symbols guard against the temptation to make the system more important than the books that are fed into it."

To add a personal note here, during the month of May 1967, while working with Peter, I designed these cards, drew the symbols,

LIB.			TITLE						VALUE
CAT NO.		SYM-BOLS	ORIGINAL STRUCTURE		REPAIR	25	Stabbed joint		COVERING
PHOTO			COVER		As necessary	26	Original holes	50	Full
5		⊞	Full	1	General dry cleaning	27	Alum-tawed thongs	51	Limp
C		⊖	Full	3	General mending	28	Vellum thongs	52	Yap edges
P		?	Stiff	4	Fold mending	29	Herring bone	53	Quarter and vellum tips
W		!!!	Limp	5	Reinforcement	30	Double cords	54	Case
FC		~~	Half	6	Swing plates	30	Single cords	55	Box
M		≈	Quarter	7	Do not trim edges	31	Single cords	56	Alum-tawed pig
Se		≋	Alum-tawed pig		SIZING & ADHESIVES	32	Staining cords	57	Vellum
For		R.	Vellum	8	Parchment size	33	Sawn-in cords	58	Calf
Fin		B.	Calf	9	Gelatine size	34	Linen tapes	59	Goat
WASHING YES NO		M	Goat	10	Starch paste	35	Linen braid	60	Native-dyed goat
OK		M	Sheep	11	Polyvinylacetate	36	Stab	61	Pulp
dk		X	Others	12	'Glutofix'	37	Link-sewing	62	Buckram
		△	SEWING	13	Methyl cellulose (Tylose)	38	Linked overcasting	63	Reback
S		△	Original	14	Soluble nylon	39	Machine	64	Refurbish
		₵	Thongs		TYPES OF PAPER	40	Stabbed joints	65	Restore as original
B		NT	Double cords	15	Handmade	41	As necessary		TITLING
T/4		₢	Herring bone	16	Mouldmade		BOARDS	66	Original
D		₢	Single cords	17	Machine-made	42	Laced-in	67	Manuscript
Ph Before After		₢	Sawn-in cords	18	'Japanese mending	43	'Split' ~	68	Tool
DEACIDIFICATION		—	Laced-in	19	Lens tissue	44	Original	69	Label
		—	Tapes	19	Heat-set tissue	45	Cased		TREAT WITH
		—	Two-on	20	ENDPAPERS	46	HEADBANDS	70	Saddle soap
REINFORCEMENT			HEADBANDS	21	'Italian'	46	Handsewn, laced-in	71	Potassium lactate
			Thread laced-in	22	'Made'	47	Handsewn, thread	72	Paranitrophenol
			Thread	23	'Library'	48	Handsewn, silk	73	Lanolin & neatsfoot oil
?			Silk	24	Tipped	49	Stuck-on		
!!!		OTHER INSTRUCTIONS							

Fig. 20. Record card for each book.

and wrote all the wording in plain, legible hand lettering, camera ready for printing by the thousands—one card in English, the other in Italian.

On his Sundays off, Peter photographed several hundred damaged books, his personal collection of slides finally numbering 1,100, and insisted that every book should be photographed before treatment. In less than two years, more than fifty thousand volumes were photographed to preserve their history.

Descriptions of Procedures for Treatment

Cleaning and Pulling

Next Peter describes the actual procedures of treatment in the present tense. The first was cleaning and pulling:

As much caked mud as possible is removed dry by flexing the edges of the leaves and the remainder is flaked off with spatulas and sharp blades. Then the book is collated and the sections are separated by careful cutting of the sewing from the spine. Covers, headbands, cords, threads, fragments and the record card etc. are placed in envelopes and catalogued. The sections are prepared for washing by interleaving with wet strength paper

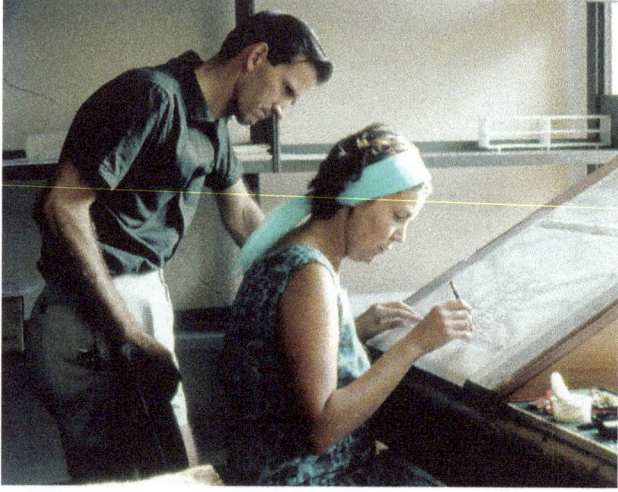

Fig. 21. Peter and Sheila working on the record card originals.

at frequent intervals. Hand-colored prints are protected where necessary with a 3% solution of soluble nylon in alcohol.[8]

Washing and Drying

Each leaf is supported on a floating wooden board and washed individually by soft brushing in warm water containing a saturated solution of Topane (2hydroxydiphenol). This is followed by gentle squeezing of the whole book which is then pressed to remove excess liquid. Bleaching, deacidification and re-sizing are done where necessary. At the Power Station the washing

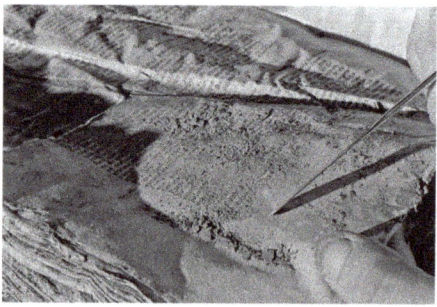

Fig. 22. Mud being scraped from a dried book at the Forte.

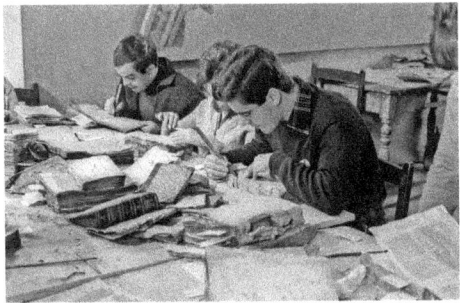

Fig. 23. Students pulling books.

was done in rusty sinks covered in polyethylene sheeting. In the library, there are multiple stainless steel sink units totaling forty compartments, and all are water-jacketed and thermostatically controlled. Random pH measurements are being taken with a Pye flat-head electrode pH meter before and after washing. At the Power Station, sections were hung to dry on terylene lines, but in the library they are laid flat on racked trolleys in purpose-made, electrically-warmed, automatically-controlled drying cabinets. A final collation is made by a librarian and the book is then wrapped for storage.[9]

I must add here that Sandy Cockerell, an engineer as well as a well-known private binder and manuscript restorer, was the prime advisor in the design and fabrication of these large drying cabinets, trolleys, and racks, and worked closely with Peter during several visits.

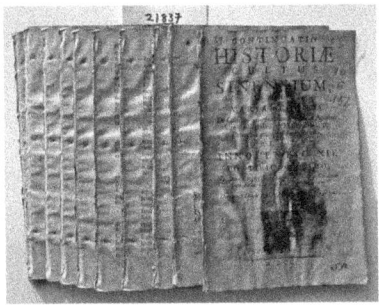

Fig. 24. A pulled book.

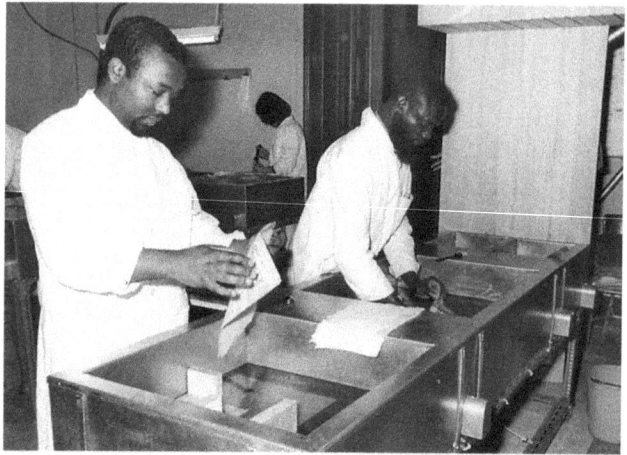

Fig. 25. Washing books in the new water-jacketed sinks

Mending of Tears and Lacunae

Peter's article continues with descriptions of the new mending and binding areas set up in the main reading room. This was unprecedented in a country's national library!

> Although the original intention was to send the prepared books to binderies throughout the world for mending and binding, by April 1967 it was apparent that this would be impracticable, mainly because of the wide diversity of standards and the impossibility of maintaining proper controls. It was therefore decided that mending, the most

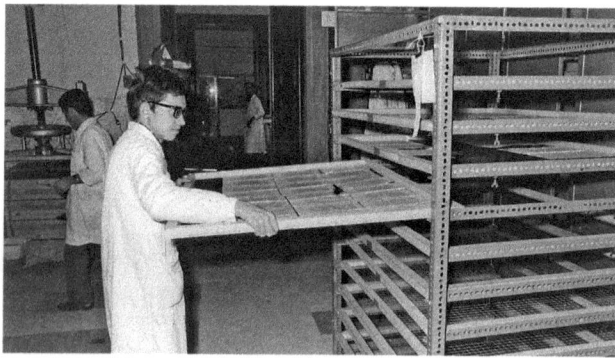

Fig. 26. A trolley being loaded with trays.

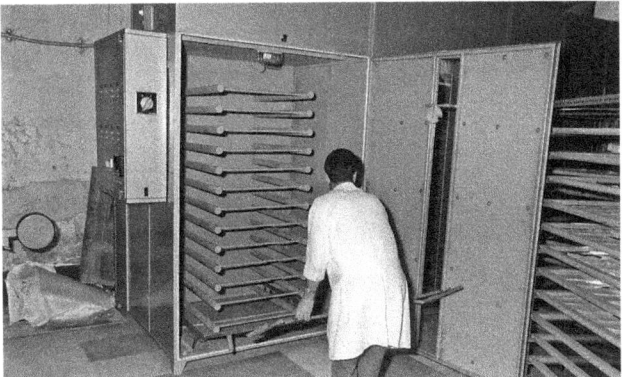

Fig. 27. A loaded trolley being pushed into a drying cabinet.

time-consuming operation of all, should be done in the library and that binding should follow. A mending department was designed for thirty workers (the maximum number for whom space and wages could be found), to be housed in the main reading room for at least a year or so. This was ready in August 1967, when the training of about five unskilled workers per week was undertaken until the room came into full operation.[10]

Mending methods had to be devised suitable for the scale of the operation and the condition of the paper. Long-fibered Japanese tissue paper

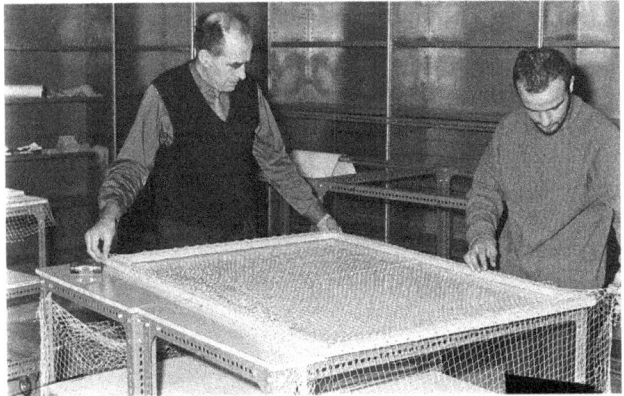

Fig. 28. Sandy Cockerell stretching olive netting for a drying tray.

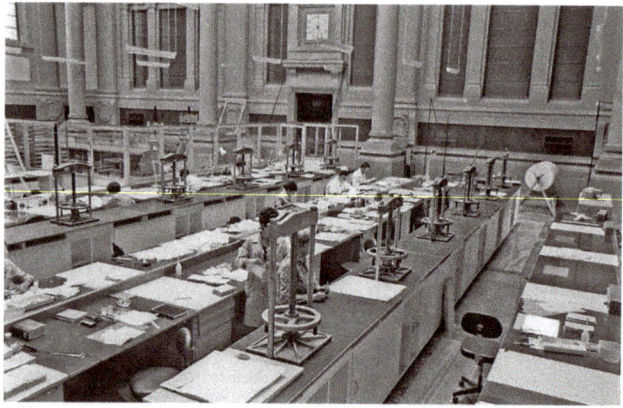

Fig. 29. The mending area in the converted main reading room.

is used to form patches, with adhesive designed to spread through to the area around the mend and remain flexible. A lens tissue is specially treated and used principally for the mending of tears. Many of the books have been reduced almost to single leaves and, on average, every section has at least two folds needing repair.[11]

When I worked in Florence for five weeks in the late spring of 1967, Peter designed the mending stations, and I drew plans and elevations for their construction. Each unit had a small light box inserted in the

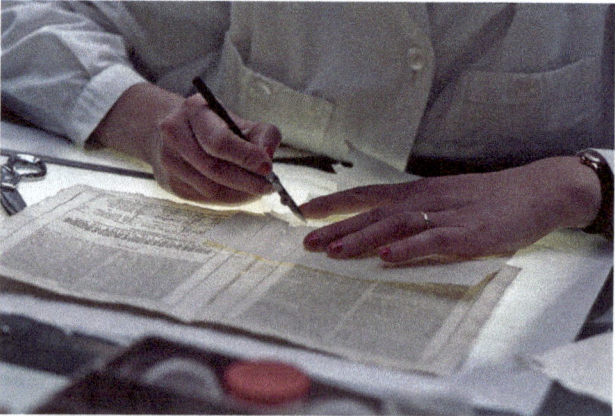

Fig. 30. Japanese tissue mending: cutting with a ruling pen.

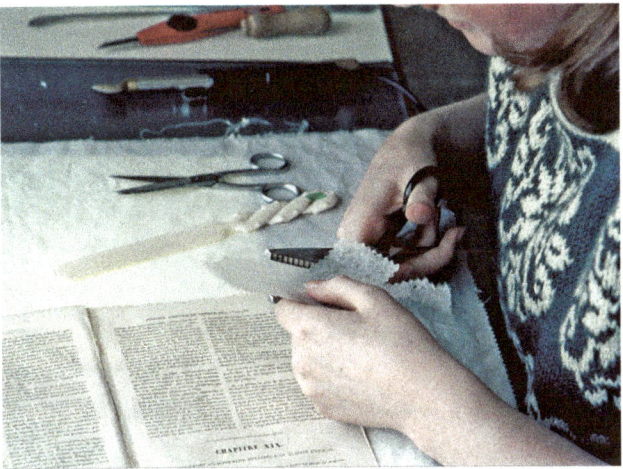

Fig. 31. Heat-set tissue: mending tears with a tacking iron.

desktop and plenty of storage space on either side. In the summer, we were in Florence for nine weeks, and I had the immense pleasure of watching the desks be carried in and installed in the reading room. We left our youngest son, Chris, in the care of our mothers but took Julian, age ten, and Michael, age seven, with us. They reveled in exploring the entire library and made special friends with the electrician they nicknamed Sparks.

The Final Stage of Rebinding
Peter wrote:

> A bindery was started in September 1967. Many of the smaller books will be rebound in limp vellum. A study is being made of the early Italian limp vellum structures as so many of the library's books are bound in this way. When the structure is sound, it is a long-lasting binding, strong and pleasant to handle and fairly quick to make. A limp vellum style, unique to the library, is being evolved, as, compared with the work of the 16th and 17th centuries, limp vellum binding of today has become decadent.[12]

In the DVD that comes with my book *Waters Rising*, Chris Clarkson, who has become recognized for his expertise on vellum structures,

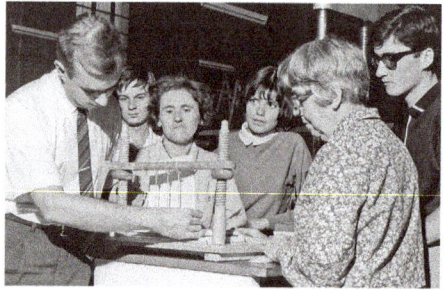

Fig. 32. Richard Young and Stella Patri teaching sewing.

makes a limp vellum binding from start to finish. Peter makes a leather binding. You see no faces, only their hands and arms.

Print Restoration

A print restoration department, with on-the-spot chemical analysis, was set up adjacent to the reading room by William Boustead, chief conservator to the National Art Gallery in Sydney, funded by the Australian government, and he trained a nucleus of workers in print restoration. It was later looked after by the chemist Joe Nkrumah, who stayed on for seven years.

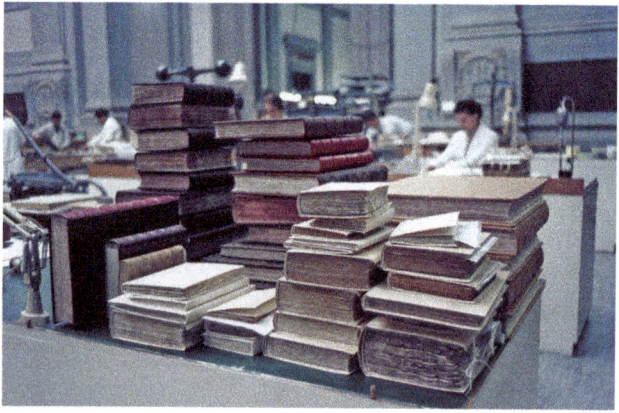

Fig. 33. Rebound books.

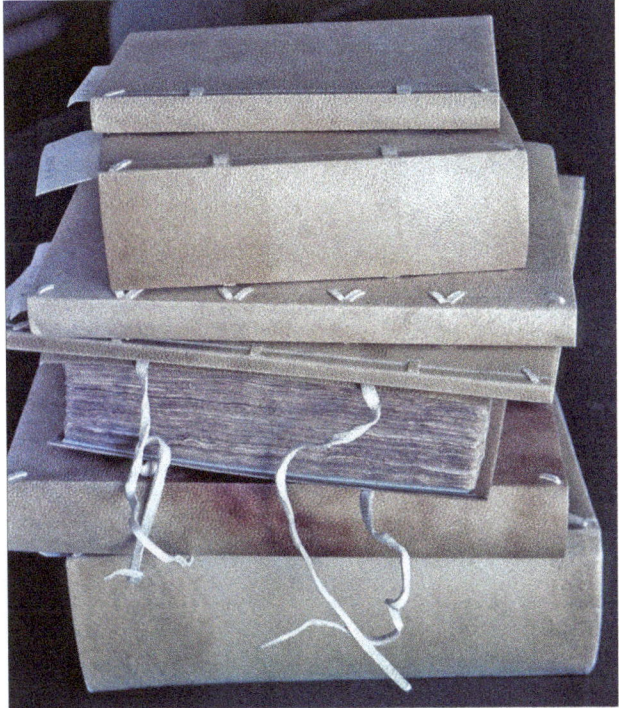

Fig. 34. Limp vellum bindings.

The Restoration System Post-1967

After October 1967, Peter left the technical direction of the restoration system to Tony Cains, the operation being funded for a further three years by the American Committee to Rescue Italian Art (CRIA). Mostly back in England, Peter resumed working with Roger Powell, teaching part time at the RCA. He also joined as codirector with James Lewis in a three-year program of backup research for the BNCF, overseen jointly by the Imperial College of Science and Technology and the RCA and funded by the American Council on Library Resources.

During 1967, the student labor force at the BNCF was gradually replaced by about one hundred Italian workers. The restoration was estimated to take about twenty-five years, though it still continues today, fifty years later. The whole system was gradually moved to basement rooms so the reading rooms could be reclaimed. Through the

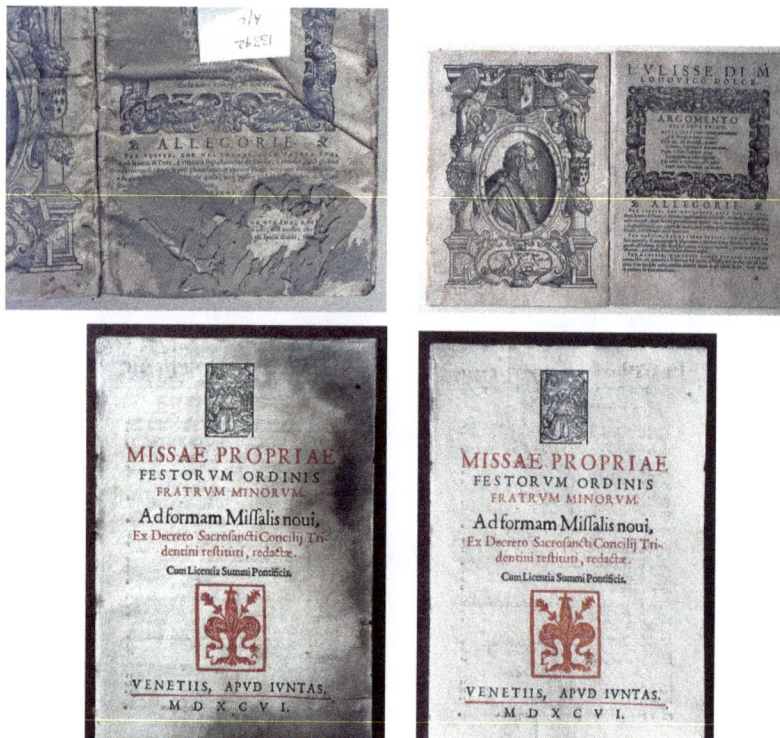

Figs. 35–38. Before and after treatment.

years, the workforce has dwindled through lack of financial support, and now it is down to about seven people in a lab outside the BNCF under the direction of Alessandro Sidoti.

International Training: The Future

The dream of setting up an international training center at the BNCF never materialized because of insufficient funding and too few expert restorers available to continue training. Even so, the legacies of the BNCF experience gave impetus to the new profession of library conservation, with the Library of Congress leading the way. Peter was given the task of designing its large comprehensive department from scratch, and from 1969 to 1971, he "commuted" from England ten times to the

Library of Congress until our family immigrated to the USA in 1971. During the following two years, he was able to persuade the curators to think more broadly in terms of what Peter called "phased conservation" (now termed "preventive conservation") instead of merely sending single items for repair to the library's bindery. Since then, conservation laboratories have been set up throughout the world, many of them directed and staffed by conservators trained at the Library of Congress and later at other centers too.

Summary

Tragedies and disasters often bring out the best in people involved, and the great Florence Flood certainly did that. So much good has come from its aftermath in the world of book and paper conservation. All who labored there will never forget the experience, and many of them have since taught and influenced countless others. Tragically, Peter died in 2003 at only seventy-three from mesothelioma, through exposure to asbestos in his twenties. I wish he could have been here to talk to you himself. He brought the skills of a designer-craftsman to the wider world of library conservation and used what he called "sideways

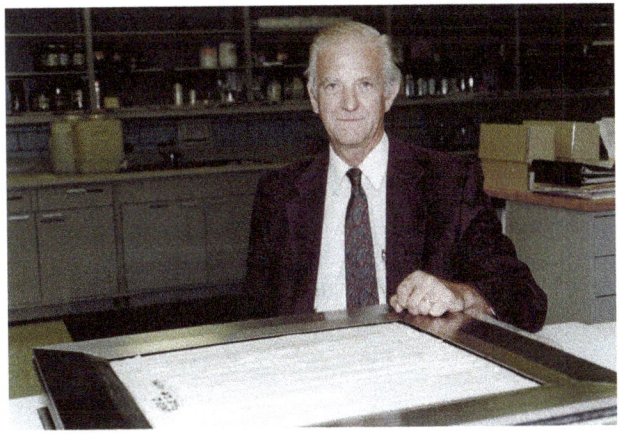

Fig. 39. Peter (retired) with one of the encased US Charters of Freedom, c. 2000.

thinking" to solve problems. He also felt that some treatments can cause more harm than good. I feel honored to have played a small part in the effort myself, as a support to Peter. By sharing these firsthand memories, I hope I have given you a feel for that momentous time after the flood and an appreciation for why the Florence experience was so pivotal.

Notes

1. Republished with permission. Waters, Sheila. "Post-Flood Development of Mass Treatments at the National Library of Florence: The Roots of Library Conservation." *Book and Paper Group Annual* 35 (2016): 109–19.
2. Waters, Sheila. *Waters Rising: Letters from Florence.* Ann Arbor, MI: Legacy Press, 2016.
3. Waters, Peter. "Book Restoration after the Florence Floods." *Penrose Annual: Review of the Graphic Arts* 62 (1969): 83–93.
4. Spande, Helen (ed.). *Conservation Legacies of the Florence Flood of 1966: Proceedings of the Symposium Commemorating the 40th Anniversary.* London: Archetype, 2009.
5. Waters, "Book Restoration," 84.
6. Waters, 86.
7. Waters, 87.
8. Waters, 87.
9. Waters, 88.
10. Waters, 88.
11. Waters, 88.
12. Waters, 89.

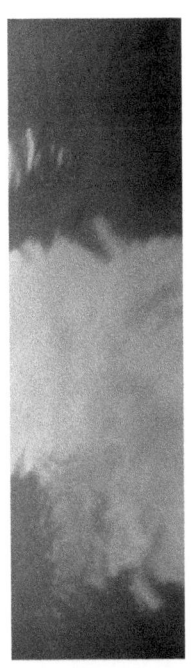

THEME PANEL: BOOK AND PAPER CONSERVATION

AFTER FLORENCE: DEVELOPMENTS IN CONSERVATION TREATMENT OF BOOKS

Don Etherington

A Fifty-Year Retrospective

The organizers of the symposium have asked me to reflect on my impressions of the conservation field over the fifty-year period since the flood. Most likely, I am one of the few still living who can give a few reasonable comments. First of all, I can claim that the restoration effort in Florence was the catalyst for many of us to change the direction of our careers. When I worked for Roger Powell and Peter Waters before and after the flood, they opened my eyes and helped me see structure and materials in a whole new light, as opposed to how, in my early training, I concentrated mainly on good technique and finish. Without realizing it at the time, through Florence and beyond, I went from being a bookbinder to a conservator.

The Florence Flood of 1966 was a milestone in the field of book conservation throughout the world. The aftermath of the Florence Flood was the point at which the word *conservator* entered the lexicon of our work. Until Florence, we were all restorers. I don't know if, in the other disciplines—painting, sculpture—the word *conservator* was used, but certainly for book restorers, the word *conservator* was not used before Florence. Also, for the first time, restorers from Germany, Denmark, Russia, and many other countries started to talk with each other about their work. Before, people who had some certain technique would hide it; nobody wanted to share. In Florence, talking about our individual techniques was like lifting a curtain. It was wonderful. For me it was one of the greatest events in my life to just sit over vino or coffee and discuss these things that had always been kept secret.

How I Got Involved

The scale of the disaster at Florence was enormous. There were about three hundred thousand volumes that suffered in the flood at the Biblioteca Nazionale Centrale di Firenze (BNCF), many not only sodden but covered in oil from broken heating systems.

After the flood, the Italian authorities reached out to the British Museum first. A British team was quickly assembled that included staff from the museum and a number of skilled workers from other parts of the country. These included Peter Waters, Roger Powell, Sandy Cockerell, and Tony Cains. Peter Waters headed up the team from the UK.

I came fairly early to the scene, in December of 1966—about a month after the flood. I was part of the British team. I had known Peter for a number of years. In fact, I worked for him and Roger Powell in the early 1960s. I was a twentysomething when I interviewed with Roger Powell to work at his studio. He asked, "What do you know about bookbinding?" I'd been doing it since age thirteen, so I had ten years of experience and I said, "Everything." For the next few years, he proved to me how little I really knew. But it was interesting to me because I was a bookbinder in those early years and the thought of conservation didn't really enter my head at the time. When the flood happened, I was teaching at Southampton College of Art as well as working with Roger and Peter. I will say this about Peter: I think we have lost a little bit of his skill in

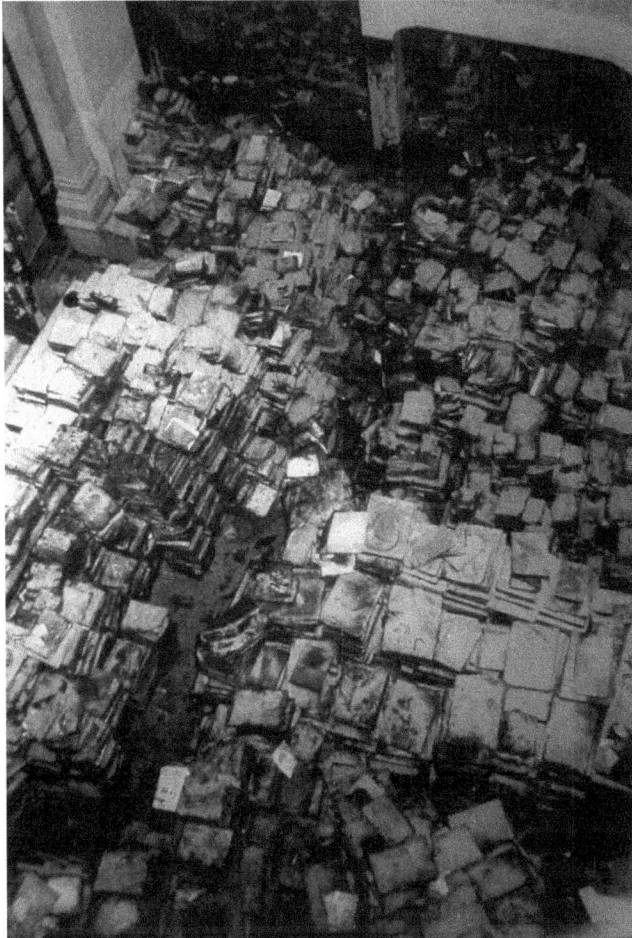

Fig. 1. Flood-damaged books piled up at the Biblioteca Nazionale.

our profession. He was one of the finest binders I've ever worked with. I used to use him as my personal standard. When I was working with him, if I could do the work as well as he could, I thought I was doing fine. Peter and I had a very good relationship over the years. I wouldn't be standing up here if it wasn't for Peter.

Some recovery activities had already begun before the British team arrived in Florence. The most significant of these was sending wet books to the tobacco kilns to be dried. To the untrained and inexperienced, the first thought would be to dry these wet, muddy, and oil-stained

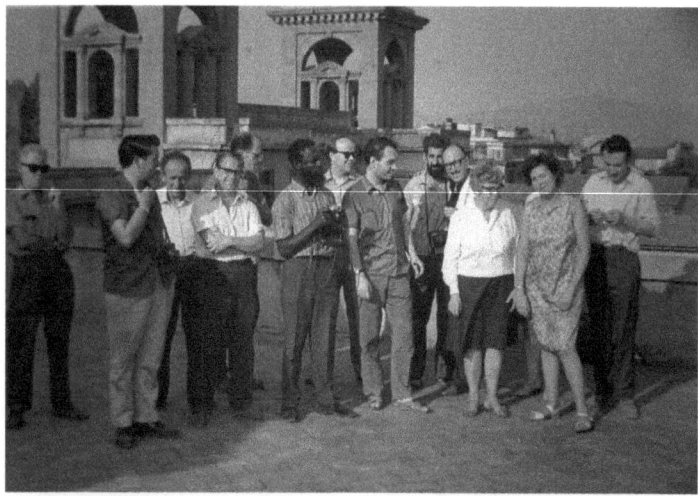

Fig. 2. International book restoration volunteers responding to the Florence Flood. From left to right: Bill Boustead, Don Etherington, Frank Tushingham, Desmond Shaw, John Corderoy, Joe Nkrumah, James Lewis, Chris Clarkson, George Jolly, Alfredo Cotogni, Stella Patri, Sheila Waters, and Tony Cains.

books, and that's what they did. But the drying process in the kilns did, in fact, cause a tremendous amount of extra work. It's sort of like the leather is burnt. Some of the books looked like pieces of roast beef. You would see marks on the fore edges of some of the books where they were set onto hot railings or metal rods in the kilns. There's nothing you can do with burned edges, so it was a major problem going in. In retrospect, I don't know what we would have done if we had been there up front before the books got dried like they did. I can feel sympathy for the Italian workers and students who thought they were doing the correct thing.

For many of us who arrived early on, the sheer size of the problem was a first. Some people would have come and seen three hundred thousand books soaking wet and covered in mud and oil, and would have lifted their arms and said, "This is impossible." Somehow I didn't go through that. I seemed to accept the challenge quite well, without feeling that the problem was too much that it overwhelmed my thinking. From the beginning we were all thinking, "What can we do?

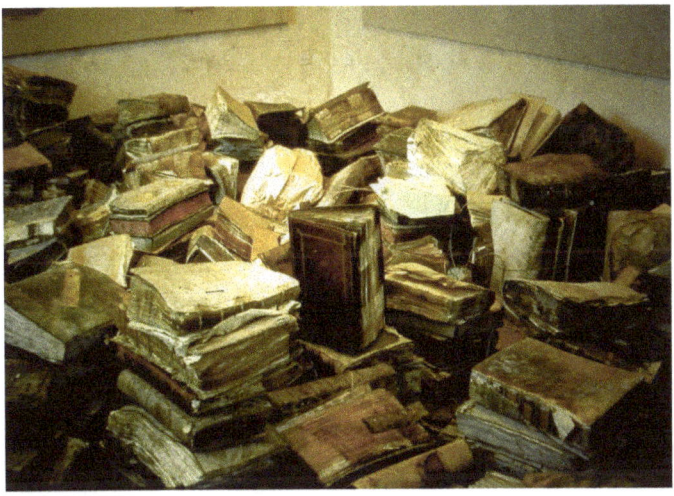

Fig. 3. Books damaged by heat-drying in tobacco kilns.

What's the best way?" We didn't think, "Oh, we can't do anything." That was the theme through Peter's and Tony's reigns there.

I traveled back and forth from England to Florence for various stints over a two-year period through 1967 and 1968. Southampton College was very generous in allowing me those extended periods of three to six weeks. My role was to train the new Italian workers in sound book conservation procedures. Some of the staff had some training and skills that were useful, particularly the leather workers from the famous leather trade in Florence. I had about three or four Italian men working with me on rebinding or repairing the books. There was a woman by the name of Barbara DeFreida who worked with us. She was from Florence, an American, and sadly she's not with us anymore.

What became very useful in this training was the specification card developed by Roger Powell and Peter Waters and designed by Sheila Waters. It was produced in both Italian and English, so it became very useful for the Italian workers.

One has to realize, too, that many of the books at the Biblioteca Nazionale Centrale di Firenze in those early years were rebound using, if possible, the original covers. The floodwaters had often washed the original leather covers off the text blocks nearly intact. The covers were treated, but I don't know what they were treating them with. One assumes it was some sort of oil to soften them. When you hear about soluble nylon being used, and benzene—we would never be allowed to do that today because of safety concerns. Workers rescued the covers and then hung them up on lines to dry, but a great deal of detective work was required after they were dry because in those early materials, books weren't titled on the spine. It took a team of experts to try to match covers with text blocks.

A new conservation workshop was designed by Sheila and Peter for the British team and housed in the main reading room of the Biblioteca Nazionale. It was truly a remarkable lab, with specially designed workbenches that had light tables inset flush with the working surfaces. The nipping presses also were installed flush with the bench. When you mended something, you just slid in the boards—you didn't have to lift them. There was good light for working.

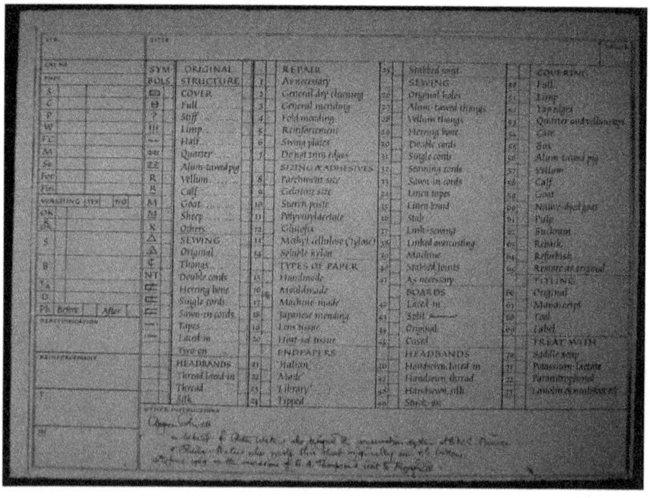

Fig. 4. Book examination and documentation form developed by Peter Waters and designed by Sheila Waters.

From Florence to the Library of Congress

My work in Florence led to my being asked to help Peter Waters establish a new conservation program at the Library of Congress in Washington, DC. Peter asked me to come over from London as the training consultant. I came in 1970, one year before Peter and Shelia moved permanently to the United States. I started by training the new people. We advertised a lot for people, and at the interview, prospective hires did a test in front of me and a couple of other people. It was a dexterity test, if you like, and it was pretty useful to see how people who've never done anything could deal with double-sided tape and polyester film or could judge the grain of paper. I would demonstrate a task and then give them ten samples, and they would see if they could do it. It was a relatively simple test. There was one test where we asked them to draw five lines an inch apart on a piece of paper. Now that's no big deal, but we watched what they did: whether they used a pencil like this or whether they did it lightly, and did they improve their spacing as they went down the five. Now, you might say that's a bit esoteric. Indeed, we received

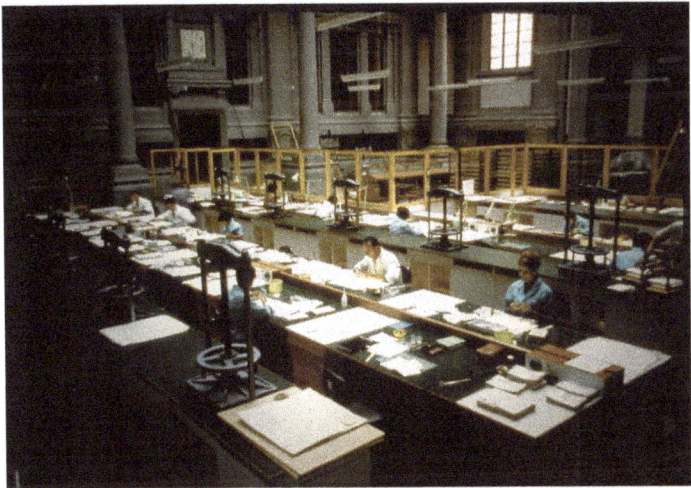

Fig. 5. Book conservation workshop in the reading room at the Biblioteca Nazionale in Florence, 1967.

some pushback from the employee's union. But we continued to test the manual dexterity of all our workers.

The recovery from the Florence Flood taught us about working at unimaginable scale. Before Florence, restorers were trained to do one book at a time. All of a sudden now, we were faced with three hundred thousand books. It takes a whole different mentality to think about solutions at that scale. When Frazer Poole brought us over to the Library of Congress, we saw thousands, even millions of books in the library's collections that needed work. Following our experience in Florence, our response was, "You can't treat one book at a time thinking of all the millions of books in the Library of Congress." The concept of designing mass preservation projects at the Library of Congress was a direct outcome of the Florence Flood experience.

One of the earliest mass treatments was the flood itself. It was the first mass deacidification project, because the Arno River had a lot of lime mud in the water. All the books got deacidified. That's a silly way to look at it, but that's what happened. A lot of the early books didn't need deacidification anyway, but there were a lot of twentieth-century materials that did.

One of the first things I did at the Library of Congress was design what I called the "phase box." Now we all know what the phase box is, but I designed it because I used to teach typographic design at Southampton College of Art. One of the things I had to teach there was how you lay out a cigarette package. It's in two parts: the outer part and the thing you pull in and out. You have to set up the type on the packaging so it is always aligned with everything—the folds and all that. But in doing that course, I learned about folding and cutting, because when you set up for printing cigarette packets, there's a cutter that's in between rubber. When you print it, it cuts as well as prints. It creates little segments of the box. That's where the phase box idea came from.

The first large phase boxing program was designed for the eight thousand books in the European Law Library collection, which were mostly vellum. Many of you know that a vellum binding gets distorted and it gaps at the fore edge, either because of the materials inside, which may be parchment, or because the covers themselves warp. We designed this phase box, but at first, we did it in one board. We soon realized that if you cut it out in one sheet of card, you have a tremendous amount of waste. It didn't take long for us to decide to cut in two pieces. We had two parts and then they were put together. These were constructed with buttons and ties so as to place a little pressure on the warped vellum covers. That was the phase box.

Also, just like the specification card for the Florence Flood books, we designed a card for the Library of Congress Law Library books. Every book was photographed and recorded on a different card showing all the deterioration. That card stayed with the book.

We didn't at first have skilled staff to do all this restoration on these early books. The idea was that after a number of years, we would have trained staff, able to restore the vellum-bound books in a professional manner. Carleton W. Kenyon, head of the European Law Library, thought of the phase boxes as "book coffins." He said once, "You make these boxes, nobody is going to see the book." It took six years to prove him wrong. We trained people, and after six years, we started work on the collection, as the conservation staff then had the skills to conserve them correctly. It was a big job, but working in stages could get it done.

When we arrived at the Library of Congress, they had two laminating machines working full time. Some of you most likely know these operate at 360 degrees Fahrenheit, with pressure, and they made all these manuscripts look like placemats. Thousands of documents from George Washington, Abraham Lincoln, and Thomas Jefferson at the Library of Congress still look like placemats, and it's deplorable. In those days when we first arrived, the people working at the Library of Congress in conservation were Government Printing Office people. They were working on these machines—about sixteen of them, I think, eight to a machine, maybe. Those numbers got diminished, and we got rid of the machines within a very short period of time. One of the major problems then became, What are you going to do now with the really fragile documents? What was the answer? Encapsulation. In those days, it was double-sided tape and polyester film. Later on, Bill Minter invented a machine—still in wide use—that uses ultrasound to "weld" two pieces of polyester film together. So the tape and all the risks of using it weren't needed anymore. (Except I would say if you don't have a machine, you can still use tape. Just be careful.) These mass projects were a continuum, as you like, from Florence.

After our very bad experience in Florence dealing with books dried in kilns, we worked with the Library of Congress research and testing lab and a number of companies to develop a freeze-drying technique for wet books. This work also included working with the National Aeronautics and Space Administration (NASA). Freeze-drying remains the standard practice for dealing with large numbers of wet books.

One important development that began in the Florence workshop early on was the discovery that limp vellum bindings seemingly flowed with the floodwaters and came out with only minor damage—a result of their nonadhesive binding form, as there was hardly any glue used in limp vellum bindings. The attachment of the covers to the text block was mechanical, with a thong or bands—it was a whole different way of binding than what we had experienced in England, where none of us encountered much limp vellum binding. Christopher Clarkson decided he would like to take the bull by the horns and study the whole issue of limp vellum binding and some stiff board vellum bindings. Chris was learning on the spot. He then showed me and we worked together to perfect our limp vellum binding technique. Chris, Desmond Shaw, and I all worked to understand these vellum binding structures. We produced a number of various styles of vellum and paper bindings for use as training aids for the staff at the library. I know if you're not a book conservator, you may not think it's such a big step, but for us, one of the major impacts of the Florence Flood was the still ongoing study of limp vellum and its adoption in the conservation studio. Chris wrote extensively about the technique, so now many conservators are using nonadhesive structures in their rebinding of early books, including the use of concertina guards.

Another really important outcome of the experience of conservators in the Florence Flood is the knowledge and availability of high-quality materials for treatment. The extensive use of Japanese paper for mending early books was developed in Florence. The Japanese paper manufacturers have likely benefitted from the now normal conservation practice of using Japanese paper throughout the world.

Now, I'm treading on somewhat tenuous ground here, but I don't think Japanese paper was used in the repair of early printed materials until Florence, because prior to Florence, we were always trained in mending Western papers with Western papers. Nearly every restorer I knew, particularly Bernard Middleton, would have drawers and drawers of old paper that they saved from end papers and so on, which they then used to match the original. That repair technique is called "scarfing." When you scarf the original, you take away some of the thickness of the paper at the edge with a knife or sandpaper, and then you "scarf" the edge of the repair paper, and you overlap and paste the edges together—it was a very effective method. In fact, I can tell you there are some papers I've seen that I treated but I didn't know they had been scarfed and mended—they were that good.

By way of example, Harold Tribolet in his shop in Chicago was famous for making up damaged-looking replicas of the Declaration of Independence using paper that matched the original, printing with broken type to match the broken type that was on the original, and inserting it in the document to make a damaged Declaration look like new. It was a very good method, but what are you doing when you do that? You actually are damaging the original by sanding some of it off. The conservators at Florence felt it was awful to do that. But I know we all did it prior to Florence.

The use of Japanese paper and the long fiber technique was very important because one of the golden rules of mending and filling in losses is that the mend must be weaker than the original. If you always go by that as a golden rule, you won't go far wrong in mending. That's why the practice now is that the long fibers along the torn edge of the Japanese paper are the only thing that overlaps the original. Japanese papers can be a problem, however, if used to mend or fill original papers that are weak. If strong Japanese paper and paste are used on brittle materials, the strength is in the mend now: if the paper is stressed, the mend holds, but the original breaks again.

Heat-set tissue was also invented in Florence by Sidney Cockerell. Heat-set papers were produced by coating sheets of glass with an acrylic adhesive and then dropping lens tissue on top. When dry, the sheets of tissue could be removed safely. Heat-set tissue was used for twentieth-century and nineteenth-century material; we never used it for the early materials and still don't. Now various companies produce and market a variety of heat-set tissue.

Another positive outcome of the restoration effort in Florence was the development by Italian paper makers of some really fine paper for end papers and for limp paper bindings. Also, we managed to per-suade an Italian company to produce some really fine cord for sewing supports—it was wonderful to work with; it's nothing like what you see in the store now or what you can get from supply houses. Another company produced some good-quality alum-tawed leather based on our specifications.

Not everything worked out as we had hoped. The wonderful pro-gram in the Biblioteca Nazionale Centrale de Firenze started by Peter Waters and Tony Cains never really got off the ground. An international center for the book, which could have had a wonderful home in Italy, never materialized. I think it's pretty sad, and I'm a little upset that the International School for Book Conservation that Peter envisioned and we all supported never came to be. It was the one time, if you can imagine, when all this equipment, all these wonderful benches that Sheila helped design, drying cabinets, everything, were there. If there was ever one chance to have done that—not in the reading room of course, I know they would've moved it from the reading room—with a little ingenuity, you'd think the Italians could've worked it out. I don't know what happened, but the opportunity was lost.

The impetus for conservation treatment that the Florence Flood disaster spawned in the United States—and, to a certain degree, in Europe—reached its peak in the 1980s and 1990s with new labs open-ing in various parts of the country. Since the turn of the twenty-first century, we have seen a marked decline in the field of book conserva-tion. Many institutions have closed or downsized their conservation labs. The advent of digitization and scanning has contributed to this decline. I personally worry that we are slowly losing a skilled workforce in the conservation of rare books and archives. The current conservation degree-granting programs are starting to develop book conservation programs, and hopefully these programs will begin to develop skilled book conservators.

FROM THE MASTER'S ELBOW TO THE INTERNET: THE CHANGING NATURE OF THE TRANSMISSION OF KNOWLEDGE IN BOOK CONSERVATION

Beth Doyle

Introduction

The purpose of my commentary following Don Etherington's theme paper is to focus on how knowledge is transmitted through the conservation profession and how that transmission has evolved over the past fifty years. I admit up front that my viewpoint is decidedly United States–focused, collections-conservation centric, and not at all comprehensive.

It is important to note that book "restoration" has been around since shortly after the first codex was created and, shortly thereafter, started falling apart. For generations, book restoration was learned at the master's elbow. The apprenticeship model, where information is passed directly from instructor to student, is a one-to-one mode of knowledge transmission. "Learn one, do one, teach one" was a routine training method for generations.

Florence disrupted that training model. The sheer scale of the damage caused many bookbinders to rethink not only their methods and materials but how best to teach and transmit that knowledge to a larger audience.

Modes of Transmission

As we know, collections conservation theory started well before Florence.[1] However, Florence brought attention to the complications of working with large collections in a very dramatic way. As Don Etherington mentioned, the young men and women returned home from Florence and started working with vendors and each other to develop new products and repair methods. They also created new ways to share their knowledge more broadly and collegially. Many national, regional, and state-wide professional organizations started forming shortly after Florence. Each of these organizations gather together at least once a year in person, and many host in-person training opportunities. The formation of so many groups around this time period may be a coincidence. However, I believe we saw the influence of the Florence conservators in the development of these groups either directly or indirectly:

- The American Institute for Conservation of Historic and Artistic Works (1972; known as the AIC)
- The Preservation Section of the Society for American Archivists (1978)
- ALA-ALCTS Preservation Section (1980; merged with the Reformatting Section in 1994)
- Western Association of Art Conservation (1975)
- Midwest Regional Conservation Association (1980)
- North Carolina Preservation Consortium (1990)

During the 1970s and 1980s, we also saw an explosion of publications focusing on library and archives conservation. Conservators were now sharing their research and techniques in a much broader way through

print publications. At this time, subscriptions to newsletters and journals were an excellent way to disseminate and receive new information:

- In 1974, the AIC started publishing the *Bulletin of the American
  Institute for Conservation*, which changed its title to the *Journal of
  the American Institute for Conservation* in 1977.
- Ellen McCrady started the *Abbey Newsletter* in 1975 and the *Alka-
  line Paper Advocate* in 1984.
- Robert Hudson Patterson created *Conservation Administration
  News* in 1979.
- The first AIC *Book and Paper Group Annual* was published in 1982.

Then came the internet. In 1987,[2] Walter Henry began an email distribution list, *Conservation Online*, the first online preservation publication focusing on libraries, museums, and archives. Our inboxes are
a good indicator of just how popular this mode of transmission has
become.

Training Conservators

A disruption to the apprenticeship model for training conservators
came in the early 1980s. In 1981, Paul Banks developed the first graduate-
level library and archives conservation training program at Columbia
University. That program moved to the University of Texas at Austin
in 1992. Now instead of a one-to-one transmission of knowledge, we
have a one-to-many model, which has a much wider educational reach.
"Learn one, do one, teach ten" became the new model for conservation
education. The establishment of the Columbia program signaled not
only a shift from one mode of knowledge transmission to another; it
very significantly acknowledged book conservation as a distinct profession from craft bookbinding and restoration, a direction we're still
moving in today.[3]

With the advent of the internet, training ten students per graduate class has turned into training potentially hundreds online, at the
place and time of the student's choosing. Never before have we had

the opportunity to share knowledge on as large a scale as we do now. Search "book repair" in Google and you get more than fourteen million hits that include blogs, websites, webinars, YouTube videos, and, of course, ads. For better or worse, everyone on the internet is now a conservator.

While it has been incredibly beneficial to have so much knowledge at the click of a button, this convenience comes with some very long strings attached. For a layperson, it is increasingly difficult to discern good advice from bad. I would argue that information literacy has never been a more important issue for us as a profession.

The More Things Change . . .

None of these transmission models have truly disappeared. We have not stopped collaborating, teaching, taking classes, or reading and writing. We are all consumers, contributors, and transmitters of the knowledge base of our profession. These transmission models are multidimensional across time and space; they feed into and inform each other; and they are in fact often imbedded in our job descriptions. We are never *not* consuming and transmitting knowledge. No wonder we are all tired.

Looking Ahead

We seem to have more avenues for transmitting knowledge than ever, yet we still worry about the future of our profession and how we will train new conservators. Conservation has become the Schrödinger's cat of professions, both alive and dead at the same time. We are at a critical juncture where we need to reembrace and build upon the lessons we learned in Florence and ask ourselves, "Where do we go from here?" Let us think boldly and be optimistic. How do we again accelerate progress and forge new directions as we did immediately after Florence? Where should our focus be as we move forward, and how do we communicate those things that should be passed down? These are a few themes that I am personally interested in: information literacy, partnering with allied organizations, funding, outreach, open access advocacy, and diversity.

What are your "blue sky" ideas of how we can share knowledge? Do you want live broadcasts of AIC talks? What about an American Library Association podcast on preservation issues? Could there be an accredited online book conservation degree? Leaving technical and funding issues aside, where can we imagine going from here?

Notes

1. Harris, Kenneth E., and Susan E. Schur, "A Brief History of Preservation and Conservation at the Library of Congress," https://www.loc.gov/preservation/about/history/pres-hist.pdf (October 2006).
2. American Institute for Conservation of Historic and Artistic Works, "Conservation DistList." To subscribe via the World Wide Web, visit http://cool.conservation-us.org/mailman/listinfo/consdistlist.
3. Banks, Paul N., "Education in Library Conservation," *Library Trends*, 189–91 (Fall 1981), https://www.ideals.illinois.edu/bitstream/handle/2142/7200/librarytrendsv30i2d_opt.pdf?sequence=1.

THE 1966 FLOOD IN FLORENCE: CHANGING CONCEPTS OF BOOK CONSERVATION AND ETHICS

Sherelyn Ogden

The Flood in Florence of 1966 influenced the development of book conservation in the United States in several important ways. It energized the field and accelerated its development. It contributed to changes in the way practitioners conceptualize conservation and approach the care of library materials. It stimulated creativity and innovation and promoted the sharing of information. These effects were realized through the practitioners who were called to Florence to assist with the salvage of books. They saw the enormous nature of the task before them and developed methodologies to deal with it. The experience they gained provided them with the foresight to lead the field forward.

Book conservation always has had a strong sense of ethics. I trained with Paul Banks, an early leader in the field. Banks participated in the salvage operations in Florence, and that experience reinforced his unwavering commitment to high standards, best practices, and education. One of the first things he impressed upon me when I began my training was that library materials are our cultural heritage. They belong not only to the current owners but to all humankind, both present and future. These materials must receive proper conservation treatment if they are to remain available for future generations. Because the consequences of inadequate treatment may not become apparent for years, a long-term perspective involving a sound ethical and philosophical basis for decision-making in the treatment of books is important.[1]

Before the flood only a few practitioners brought a long-term perspective to their work. Tom Conroy aptly refers to them as "protoconservators." Unlike most practitioners at the time, who were restorers or trade bookbinders, the protoconservators took a more mindful approach, seeing the book as an artifact and being selective in their choice of techniques and materials, particularly papers, adhesives, and leathers.[2]

When I became interested in book conservation in 1970, it was not a recognized profession like painting or art on paper conservation. Formal training programs focusing on books did not exist in the United States, and only a few on-the-job opportunities for learning were available. Most conservation practitioners in libraries were referred to as book restorers or bookbinders, and they tended to be seen as nonprofessionals rather than as professionals equal to librarians.

This, however, was beginning to change. To improve their status and more accurately reflect their attitudes, some practitioners referred to themselves as conservators and modeled their work after that of art conservators. They placed an emphasis on written and photographic documentation, reversible treatments, and the use of materials that were chemically stable. Work was done in conservation laboratories rather than in commercial or in-house binderies and was performed on one book at a time rather than on stacks of books in an assembly-line setting. Conservators worked only on high-value books of special significance, and treatments tended to include washing, deacidification, sizing, mending, and rebinding. The goal was to carry out the best possible treatment on a book unless historic and bibliographic significance dictated that the book should remain unchanged. In that case, the best treatment was simply boxing.

By 1972, Peter Waters, Donald Etherington, and Christopher Clarkson, British book conservators instrumental in the salvage operations in Florence, had relocated to the United States from England and were being employed by the Library of Congress.[3] They had been hired to establish the institution's first conservation laboratory and to introduce new standards of practice and methods of care based on the lessons they learned in Florence. Waters soon recognized that elaborate, time-consuming, physical treatment was not a realistic way to preserve the vast amount of materials that required attention. Financial and human resources were not available to accomplish this. As in Florence, the magnitude of the problem at the Library of Congress required pragmatic new approaches.

In response, Waters developed the concept of phased conservation, a progressive, holistic approach to stabilizing large collections in stages. The first phase was to provide physical protection for items in disrepair. Books were prioritized according to vulnerability and historic or cultural value, and the high-priority ones were individually boxed rather than treated. The reasoning behind this approach was that providing protective housing, such as chemically stable boxes, for many books in need of repair made better use of limited resources than complex treatment of just a few. Boxing was seen as the first "phase" in the care of collections, with treatment occurring at some appropriate time in the future.[4] Waters had taken a similar approach at the Biblioteca Nazionale Centrale di Firenze, where books were disbound, cleaned, washed, and then wrapped in fungicide-impregnated brown paper for temporary storage until they could be bound.[5] Phase boxing, as the practice is commonly known, is now a widely accepted preservation strategy in institutions in the United States.

Boxing rather than treating books marked an important change in attitude in the field. Conservation was shifting from all-inclusive, invasive treatment to minimal, noninvasive treatment. Conservators were shifting their focus from individual books in a collection to entire collections. This in turn led to a change in the approach to book conservation as a whole. Less emphasis was placed on single-item treatment and more on measures that mitigated deterioration and damage.

The concept of phased conservation broadened and eventually became known as preventive conservation. Preservation practitioners had been aware of the harmful effects of poor environmental conditions, and they had been focusing for years on controlling levels of temperature and relative humidity to slow the rate of deterioration. Gradually, environmental control came to include improvement in light levels, storage practices, and handling and maintenance procedures, as well as emergency management and integrated pest management. These measures benefitted every item in the collection, not just the special, high-value volumes. Today the concept of preventive conservation is accepted across the heritage preservation profession and is a standard component of preservation practice.

These changing attitudes, along with experience gained in Florence, paved the way for the development of new techniques, materials, and mass treatments. Heat-set tissue for paper repair, in limited use prior to the flood, was developed further and improved upon to meet needs in Florence and has become accepted practice today. Cellulose acetate lamination, shown to be potentially damaging, has been displaced to a large extent by the noninvasive, reversible process of polyester film encapsulation. With the introduction of chemically stable double-sided tape and ultrasonic and heat welders, encapsulation has become a universal means of protecting fragile paper. Mass deacidification, in development before the flood, underwent extensive research and testing. It gained in acceptance and now is in regular use for certain types of books.

Conservation-quality materials were hard to obtain before the flood. The availability of handmade rag papers and machine-made acid-free and buffered papers was limited. Suitable enclosures were difficult to find, and folders, pamphlet binders, and storage boxes of permanent-durable materials often needed to be made in-house. Now rag papers of the sort used in books that survived the flood are reproduced regularly in mills in Europe and the United States. Acid-free and buffered machine-made paper is the standard paper used in book publishing. Enclosures of permanent-durable and acid-free materials are sold in an array of types and standard sizes. The commercial availability of custom-sized boxes for the storage of fragile books is an especially valuable development, an outstanding example being affordable clamshell boxes produced by the automated corrugated box-making machine invented by Waters and his son Michael.

Research into historical binding structures became more prevalent. Based on the study of structures that survived the Florence Flood conducted by Christopher Clarkson and his colleagues, experimentation with nonadhesive and paper case bindings has led to innovative and minimally invasive conservation binding techniques.

These changing attitudes and approaches to book conservation are reflected in the field's ethics and standards, which are the hallmarks of a mature profession. A code of ethics and standards of practice both define and guide a profession and provide the basis for its decision-making. The first attempt at standards for conservators in the United States was the "Murray Pease Report" produced in 1963. It dealt with the treatment of individual works of art, and it was based on the single-item treatment approach. It included four important principles. First, all actions of the conservator must show respect for the integrity of the artifact. Second, the methods and materials used in treatment must be permanent and durable and must not adversely affect the artifact. Third, treatment should be reversible if possible, implying that the conservator can undo a treatment and is using materials that will not damage the artifact if removed in the future. Fourth, all treatment must be documented and all original parts of an artifact retained if not reused.[6]

These principles formed the basis of the "Code of Ethics and Guidelines for Practice" of the American Institute for Conservation of Historic and Artistic Works (AIC), the leading organization for conservation professionals in the United States.[7] The AIC code has been updated regularly over the years, and changes in the field have been incorporated into it. For example, books and electronic media are listed along with other specialties. The conservation of historic as well as artistic works, nonartifact materials as well as artifacts, entire collections as well as single items, and preventive conservation are included. Even though these changes have been substantial, the early principles are still a fundamental part of the code.

The Florence Flood of 1966 was a calamitous event that shocked the world. It forced us to realize how important our cultural heritage is and how quickly it can be lost. In the years since the flood, book conservation has changed, in part because of this realization. It has become a recognized profession with hundreds of trained professionals working in a variety of influential positions. Education for book conservators has been incorporated into graduate conservation training programs. Attitudes regarding what constitutes preservation have changed, leading to more emphasis on measures that mitigate deterioration and damage. New concepts have emerged, such as phased conservation and preventive care. New techniques and materials have been developed to support these concepts, and mass treatments have gained in acceptance. Perhaps most important for the field as a profession is that these changing attitudes and concepts have been incorporated into the AIC "Code of Ethics and Standards for Practice."

More, of course, needs to be done as the field continues to grow and change. Integration of the care and handling of digital formats into the preservation paradigm is one example. I keep returning to Banks's statement that it is important to develop a long-term perspective involving an ethical and philosophical basis for decision-making in both treatment and, I might add, nontreatment. As situations change and the field develops, preservation practitioners will need to continually change the way they conceptualize conservation and approach the care of all library materials, including digital data. Sound and informed judgment, based on experience, a strong sense of ethics, and respect for our cultural heritage, will lead to the basis for decision-making to which Banks referred.

Notes

1. P. N. Banks, "The Preservation of Library Materials," in *Encyclopedia of Library and Information Science* (New York: Marcel Dekker, 1978), 217.
2. Tom Conroy, "Binding at Midcentury: The *Rivers of America* Competition of 1946," in *Suave Mechanicals: Essays on the History of Bookbinding*, volume 2 (Ann Arbor, MI: Legacy Press, 2015), 84–85.

3. Sheila Waters, *Waters Rising: Letters from Florence* (Ann Arbor, MI: Legacy Press, 2016), 114.

4. Randy Silverman, "Peter Waters: Father of Preventive Conservation," in *Waters Rising*, 10–11.

5. Restoration Department of the Biblioteca Nazionale Centrale di Firenze, "The Restoration System of the Biblioteca Nazionale Centrale di Firenze" (Florence: Biblioteca Nazionale di Firenze, 1970), 9.

6. Murray Pease et al., "The Murray Pease Report," *Studies in Conservation* 9, no. 3 (London: International Institute for Conservation, 1964), 116–21.

7. American Institute for Conservation of Historic and Artistic Works, "Code of Ethics and Guidelines for Practice," October 15, 2015, http://www .conservation-us.org/our-organizations/association-(aic)/governance/code -of-ethics-and-guidelines-for-practice#.Wdz-L1tyKM8.

ANOTHER FLOOD? RESEARCH AND PUBLISHING ON HISTORICAL BINDINGS SINCE FLORENCE

Julia Miller

In his opening remarks for this theme panel, Don Etherington summed up the changes in thinking among many bookbinders during and after the flood. This happened through the sharing of techniques and knowledge and by embracing the crucial idea that an understanding of historical structures and materials has to be considered when deciding on treatment. My remarks focus on how this change in thinking has played out in some of the published literature since the Florence Flood and the continuing need for conservators to publish their accumulated knowledge.

The Flood in Florence and the many years of recovery efforts in its aftermath contributed a great deal to the development of modern disaster planning, the recognition that some types of binding have greater survivability in certain conditions, and bench practices that continue to apply some of the lessons of Florence. Florence also has had an influence on some scholarly aspects of the history of the book, most notably, early on, the body of work by Christopher Clarkson, much of it the result of his observations during the Florence recovery effort. Though sporadic, there has also been an increase in general knowledge about historical book materials and book structures, the documentation of more types of historical structures, and concern for the preservation of original or notable bindings as well as the layers of evidence and cultural information bindings and texts carry.

The Mud Angels of Florence, who did the tedious work of item-by-item rescue and recovery, accomplished a huge task under the great leadership of knowledgeable and flexible thinkers. The combination of this leadership and determination under pressure led to the atmosphere of experimentation at the bench; the search for viable, high-quality materials; and the development and use of equipment that allowed conservators to take on ever more challenging problems.

In spite of everything good that happened in book conservation in the years after the Florence Flood of 1966, most of us still do not have all the historical information we need to make informed decisions about whether or how to treat a historical exemplar. We have not encountered such books before, or we do not take the time to think about what we are seeing, or we have not read what is already written about such structures. We are still trapped within our professionalized competencies (conservator, curator, cataloger), and we can do more to make wise decisions in some cases if we collaborate.

The lessons of Florence both informed us and blinded us. Looking back, it might be argued that the development of "conservation bindings" based on the structures of the historical exemplars encountered in Florence has had a negative effect. When conservators use these bindings to rebind books from completely different eras and binding traditions, they often erase the books' original structural elements.

The work carried out in Florence planted the idea that more treatment is better than less. Intensive and irreversible interventions practiced on text papers (wide-scale washing, deacidification, resizing) and wholesale rebinding projects grew to be two parts of the same destructive spectrum of thinking, and when those two things both happen to one historical book, we have destroyed what we set out to save. We must learn our materials, our structures, and our binding types, and we must apply what we know to treatment decisions. We must accept stabilization as our professional norm and be less eager to seek the complete "cure." We must make and remake the case to preserve our history *and* maintain it in a useable way. It is the first and most important imperative of our professional ethics.

There is solid evidence of an increase in publishing activity since the Florence Flood. J. A. Szirmai's comprehensive bibliography *The Archaeology of Medieval Bookbinding*, which was published in 1999, itemizes 601 reference works published between 1530 and 1999.[1] Of this total intellectual output, 262 books or articles appeared in print between 1530 and 1966—a period of some 436 years. In the three decades following the Florence Flood (1967 to 1999), an additional 339 books or articles were published. These figures represent a twentyfold increase in the annual rate of publishing and demonstrate an intense and highly focused level of research and analysis on what is arguably the rarest and most valuable corpus of books subject to conservation treatment in Florence.

A closer look at the broad characteristics of research on bindings prior to and following the Florence Flood highlights major differences in emphases. In the four centuries of writings before the flood, authors tended to focus on the age, rarity, association, and decoration of individual volumes, with some marginal interest in physical structures. Research and publishing on rare bindings were often by scholars who were not binders, with some notable exceptions: Sandy Cockerell, Roger Powell, and Peter Waters, all of whom wrote on early bindings. In the pre-flood era, binders published manuals on historical practice whereby they applied some of the same or modified techniques in restoration work. Some of these same techniques have passed on to conservators through these published works.

In the decades since the Florence Flood, publications on medieval books demonstrate some of the same focus as before but with a notably increased attention to materials, structures, and a richer range of binding types. Book conservators have researched and published comparative studies of groups of similar bindings, turning particular attention to best and worst practices from the past. Documented conservation treatment work is informed by this research into historical structures, with new attention given to imitating historical materials. Since the flood, articles have appeared that emphasize the preservation of original bindings, binding evidence, and stable earlier repairs. This attention to the life of the artifact has had a big impact on how we conservators assess and handle old bindings.

Book conservators who treat historical bindings try to assign the book on their bench to a place in the history of hand bookbinding. Some books are puzzles and do not fit, but each one is a piece of evidence. Questions arise, and in trying to answer them, new knowledge is acquired and sometimes shared. The best outcome in good treatment decisions is action that is based on sound knowledge, combined with a commitment to the preservation of evidence that has been lost or changed, through documentation by images, drawings, and written descriptions. Book conservators are ideally suited to add to research and writing on historical bindings in their normal, everyday work of treatment documentation. We spend a great deal of time surveying collections. We spend even more time with individual historical exemplars during our years at the bench. We develop a broad idea of the physical qualities represented by our collections, and we certainly benefit from our own research and the writing of others on historical structures.

We will comprehend the material qualities of our historical bindings *before* we treat them; this is an ethical issue, perhaps the most important issue in our profession today and in the future. Knowledge of materials, structures, and binding types fosters our ability to research suitable repair materials and develop appropriate treatments. Our knowledge and our experience help us notice, identify, and describe nontypical historical binding structures; documenting these understandings then adds to our knowledge base. In the past, we looked to a few scholars to research and write the history of bookbinding for us, many of whom were preoccupied by external qualities: decoration, association, rarity, market value. The complexity and variety of binding history have become steadily more apparent since Florence. And in response, there is a new "flood" of thinking, lecturing, teaching, and publishing about historical bindings, their structures and materials; book conservators are key to this.

How do we learn to identify and describe historical bindings in our collections? It begins with curiosity and ends with recognition and connection. Combining condition surveying in book stacks with binding description is a great way to learn about the rich variety of bindings. We tend to bury our acquired knowledge about bindings in our collections in treatment files. It is important that conservators share binding descriptions with librarians and collaborate with catalogers on catalog descriptions. Publish your acquired knowledge; the profession needs it. The time for us to share our insights on physical description is now: interest is high, we have new tools to help us assess physical properties, and interdisciplinary conferences are planned that will foster increased attention to physical descriptions of the book and heightened focus on bindings.

Here are some suggestions for increasing the level of recorded knowledge about conservation bench training and practice. Our best instructors are the books in our collections. Although knowledgeable guidance is invaluable, simply paying attention is a key skill worth nurturing. Our best technique for learning from our books is the condition survey, combined with historical description and accompanied by photographic documentation. Historical binding surveys can be designed to focus on specific historical periods or specific structural elements. The surveying of conditions in collections of historical books should be a prerequisite for all conservation and preservation training programs, and for those already at the bench who have not had that experience. For book conservators, the most important outcome of studying historical bindings is knowledge of what has worked over a long period of time in terms of material and structure and the translation of that knowledge to create a sympathetic repair when there is a problem. The wholesale application of unsympathetic repair regimens across binding traditions or the acceptance repair materials just because they are "reversible," "conservation quality," or the hot new treatment can have serious long-term pitfalls. The history of book treatment is full of misapplied methods.

Pairing bench conservation technicians with senior conservators around particular types of binding and text structures will spread knowledge and will spare time spent on redundant experimentation. Pairing junior conservators with master conservators would pay off in two ways: in informed treatment and in another practitioner with good sound knowledge of these particular structures, which the practitioner can use and pass along. We can team up with our colleagues who have need of some of the same material and structural information as book conservators do: the most obvious team is the book conservator/rare book cataloger; others include the book conservator/curator and the conservator/book historian. A good example of the value of pairing is described by Arielle Middleman and Todd Pattison.[2]

Although learning from your own collection and from your colleagues is important, so is attending Rare Book School (RBS) courses. Take as many as you can. Rare Book School offers a series of excellent in-depth seminars on many topics valuable to book conservators. It is of some concern that only twenty-three conservators attended RBS courses in 2015, spread among nine of the thirty-three courses offered that year. One suggestion for a future class is a seminar designed to pair book conservators and catalogers to develop crossover consultation on identification and description of historical bindings. This could be a course or a series of courses that develop collaboration, determine terminology, and arrive at descriptive templates to aid both conservation and cataloging.

Finally, encourage conservation staff, as well as curatorial and cataloging professionals, to engage in research either on their own or through work release time. Encourage them to publish. Too much of our experience and knowledge of historical book structures—gained from years at the bench or as rare book curators, librarians, or catalogers—is lost to us because it has never been written down.

Notes

1. Szirmai, J. A., *The Archaeology of Medieval Bookbinding*. London: Aldershot, 1999.
2. Middleman, Arielle, and Todd Pattison, "Benjamin Bradley and the 'Profitable Stroke': Binding *Six Months in a Convent* and the Need for Copy-Specific Cataloging of Nineteenth-Century Publishers' Bindings." *Suave Mechanicals: Essays on the History of Bookbinding*, volume 3. Legacy Press, 2016.

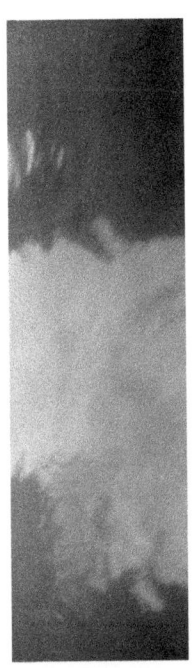

THEME
TALK: ART
CONSERVATION

THE FLORENCE FLOOD: AN ART HISTORICAL PERSPECTIVE

Megan Holmes

When I set off for Florence in 1989 to conduct my doctoral research on the Florentine Renaissance painter Fra Filippo Lippi, I was of a generation of American graduate students who had had limited exposure to the 1966 flood. I had only vague childhood memories of seeing the *Life* and *National Geographic* magazine features on the flood. The Florence with which I was acquainted and my art historical orientation were at a remove from the heroic international effort to save invaluable artistic patrimony in the aftermath of the Florentine flood. I was riding the wave of the "new art history" movement, where 1968 was a more resonant date than 1966. We were a determined cohort of American graduate students based in Florence, positioning ourselves against "traditional" connoisseurial valuations of "great masters," pressing for more historical, social contextual approaches that were grounded in period discourses, critical theory, and interdisciplinary methodologies. I had no inkling (and it probably would not have interested me to know) that a key altarpiece that I intended to feature in one of my dissertation chapters, the *Coronation of the Virgin* by Filippo Lippi, had narrowly escaped being damaged by the flood: it was removed from the ground floor of the Uffizi early in the morning of November 4, 1966, as the floodwaters rapidly rose.

Conservation issues, on the other hand, were center stage in my field at this time, during the ongoing, controversial restoration of Michelangelo's Sistine Chapel ceiling (1980–90), with James Beck, the Columbia University art historian, one of its most vocal critics.[1] In response to the negative coverage in the media, the Vatican conservators extended themselves to the scholarly community in an effort to explain and defend their methods. One of the highlights of my first year in Italy was an hour spent up on the scaffolding with my advisor and a fellow graduate student, talking with the conservators, directly beneath Michelangelo's *Creation of Adam*.

The flood did surface on occasion in "my Florence"—the city where I ended up living for more than ten years. I marveled at the extreme height of the high-water markers posted throughout the central urban area. In the Archivio di Stato, where I conducted research, the request forms that I submitted for fifteenth-century ledgers would, on occasion, come back with the word *alluvionato* written across them—indicating that these volumes had either been irreparably damaged by the flood or were still awaiting restoration. Later in my career, working on a book on miraculous images in Florence, I became more attentive to the earlier flooding of the Arno, since a number of the miraculous images in Florentine nunneries that I was studying were initially activated during the 1557 flood, when they were considered to have performed miracles or saved communities.[2]

While I am of a generation of historians of Florentine Renaissance art at a remove from the flood, my predecessor at the University of Michigan, Marvin Eisenberg, was not. Marvin died recently, on May 18, 2016, and while I missed the opportunity to speak with him about the flood, among the materials that I consulted in preparing this essay are critical early publications related to the flood that Marvin gave to me when he broke up his personal library.[3] Marvin, like so many scholars of Italian Renaissance art of his generation, was active in the aftermath of the flood. He was the Ann Arbor regional representative of the American Committee to Rescue Italian Art (CRIA). In this role, and as chair of the Department of the History of Art at the University of Michigan, he sent out an "urgent call for help" through the University newspaper, soliciting donations and keeping people informed.[4] As a specialist in early Italian gold-ground panel painting, he followed the art recovery and conservation efforts attentively.

My own scholarship, over time, has evolved to embrace the kind of intimate engagement with Italian panel painting characteristic of Marvin. I also have come to share his interest in the conservation history of the works of art that I study, as well as in the history of art conservation, and the critical role of the Florentine flood of 1966 in this history. I will take up my symposium mandate now and offer an art historian's perspective on the flood damage, the initial conservation interventions, and the subsequent exhibition initiatives that have kept the memory of the disaster and recovery alive over the intervening decades.

The flooding of the Arno on November 4, 1966, in Florence affected certain areas of the city more extensively than others. The Uffizi is located very close to the river, and while most of the works of art in the museum galleries were displayed on the upper levels, the ground floor was the site of storage rooms and a conservation facility, where paintings by Giotto, Masaccio, Botticelli, and Filippo Lippi, among others, were awaiting or undergoing treatment. While no public warning was issued about the rising floodwaters on the night of November 3, the director of Florentine museums, Ugo Procacci, was on hand at the Uffizi, and he and his colleagues were able to carry many paintings from the conservation laboratory and storage rooms to safety.[5] Procacci also had the foresight to consider the fate of the glass negatives in the major photograph archive on the ground floor of the Uffizi, which reproduced works of art located in the province of Florence.[6]

There were choices made that first night and again during subsequent years, as the salvage work continued, about which works of art to save and conserve. Should, for example, Botticelli's *Coronation of the Virgin* have been transported from the ground floor of the Uffizi, where it awaited restoration, on the night of November 3, or Neri di Bicci's *Madonna and Child with Saints?*[7] These choices made by administrators, curators, and conservators were responsive to the multiple and competing systems of valuation that grade works of art according to their relative merits—like artistic quality, association with named masters, cultural capital, exhibition potential, worth on the art market, physical condition, and historical value.[8] While I, too, probably would have saved Botticelli's painting, and certainly Filippo Lippi's *Coronation of the Virgin*, I did cut my art historian's teeth on Neri di Bicci, writing my "qualifying paper" in graduate school on his remarkable surviving account book and eventually publishing an article on what I called "the commodification of artistic values" in his paintings. For the social history of art, Neri di Bicci is a practitioner of considerable interest.[9] These triage choices that were made during and after the flood should, thus, be acknowledged. The *Coronation of the Virgin* by Botticelli was carried to safety on the night of the flood and is now on exhibit in the Uffizi. The altarpiece by Neri di Bicci remained behind. It was consequently badly damaged by the flood and later painstakingly restored by Italian and Scandinavian conservators, and now appears to have been consigned to storage.[10]

The Arno overflowed its retaining walls and swept into the city on November 4, reaching its highest point around midday, with waters rising up to twenty feet above street level in parts of the city. The raging waters carried an unsavory mixture of mud, raw sewage, and the *nafta* heating oil that had leaked from tanks just recently filled in anticipation of the coming winter. The flooding inundated the Piazza del Duomo, forcing open Ghiberti's *Gates of Paradise* on the Baptistery and dislodging a number of the gilded bronze relief panels. Within the Baptistery Donatello's polychrome wooden statue of *Mary Magdalene* was partially submerged. The main sculpture museum in Florence, the Museo Nazionale del Bargello—which, like the Uffizi, was close to the river—was thoroughly flooded. Works of sculpture that were completely underwater, like Michelangelo's *Bacchus* in the Bargello (fig. 1), were less affected than those that were only partially submerged but stained by the "high-tide mark" of the black *nafta* oil floating on the surface of the water.

It was the Santa Croce quarter of the city where the damage to visual art and buildings was the most extreme, and where the flood impacted the lives of residents to the greatest extent. Six of the seventeen deaths

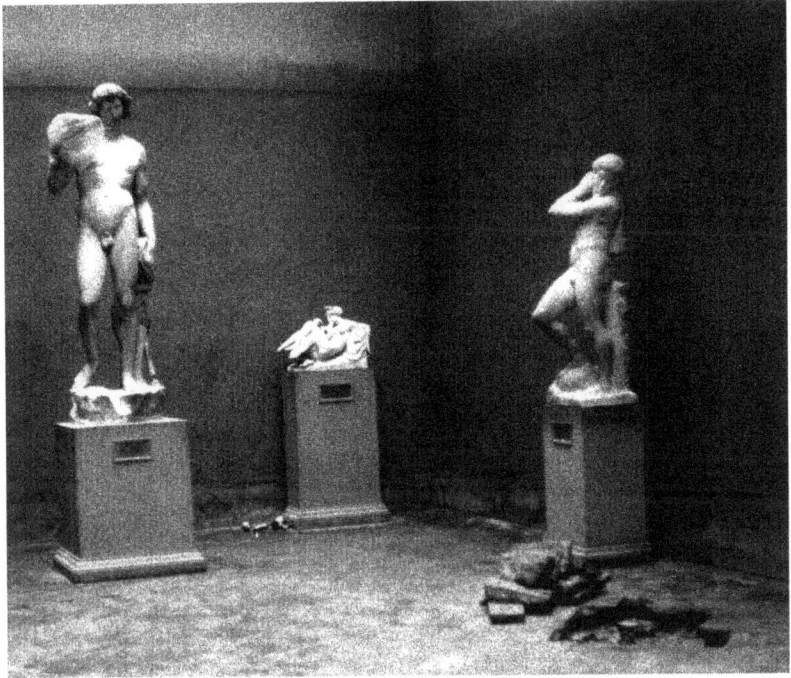

Fig. 1. Bargello Museum with Michelangelo's *Bacchus* and *David/Apollo*, with the high-water mark visible on the wall, 1966. Photo by Swietlan Nicholas Kraczyna.

in the city took place in this neighborhood.[11] Anger erupted in the quarter over how the city administration was handling the relief effort, with frustration also over the channeling of international aid toward the recovery of works of art rather than urgent humanitarian needs. Photographs document the distribution of food by inflatable dinghy to residents stranded on the upper floors of buildings. The polemical signage in a photograph taken by Nicholas Kraczyna reads, "The best mud cure for those sick from rheumatism on Via Anguillara" and "Money, now, otherwise a second drowning for artisans and others" (fig. 2).[12] The Franciscan church and monastic buildings of Santa Croce, with a museum on the site, located just behind the Biblioteca Nazionale, was among the hardest hit areas in the city.[13] David Lee's dramatic photograph for *Life* magazine of the interior of the church, taken just after the floodwaters receded, leaving mud and devastation, was used by the newly formed American Committee to Rescue Italian Art—known as

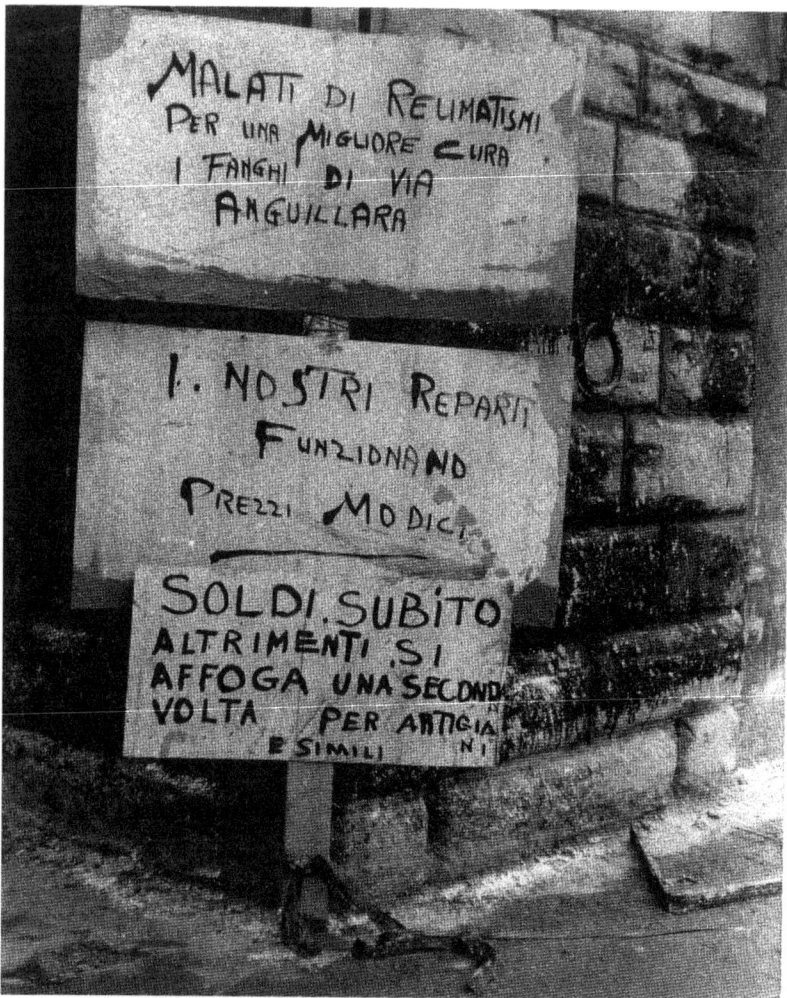

Fig. 2. Via Anguillara in the Santa Croce quarter of Florence, 1966. Photo by Swietlan Nicholas Kraczyna.

CRIA—in their campaigns to raise money. Public attention became riveted, in particular, on the monastic refectory. It was here that Cimabue's monumental late thirteenth-century *Crucifix* was affixed to the wall, and at the peak of the flood, the water rose above the head of the figure of Christ. Over the next days, weeks, months, and years, the Passion narrative of Cimabue's *Crucifix* was told episodically through media coverage,[14] from its descent from the wall, to a lamentation over the

supine image as it rested on benches in the refectory during initial drying (fig. 3), where it was blessed by the pope during his Christmas visit
to the devastated city, to a kind of entombment following transport
by motorcade to the painting restoration facility, to its gradual resur-
rection in the new conservation center at the Fortezza da Basso, with
a triumphant Ascension in the form of a world tour in 1982, when the
restored crucifix journeyed to New York, Paris, London, Madrid, and
Munich. (This Passion drama does not, however, neatly accommodate
the criticism levied against the restoration itself, as we shall see.)

Damaged works of art were quickly evaluated, separated according
to their media, and treated in provisional facilities set up in the city by
a combination of Italian and international conservators and scientists,
young trainees, and Mud Angels. Ugo Procacci, as the head of the Florentine museums and artistic patrimony, coordinated the efforts, rely-
ing on the specialists from many countries who had quickly assembled
in Florence and the funds raised by various international organizations

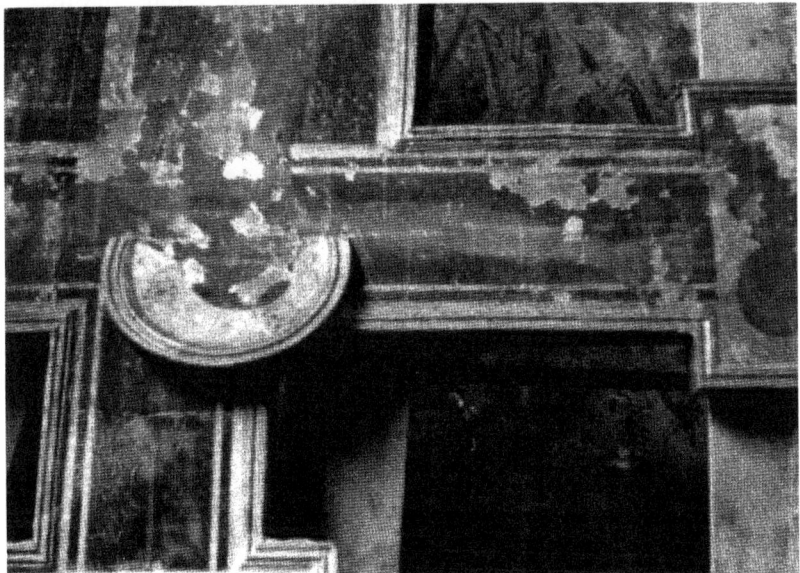

Fig. 3. Cimabue's *Crucifix* from Santa Croce, after removal from the wall, during
initial treatment, 1966. Photo by Swietlan Nicholas Kraczyna.

like CRIA in America and the British Italian Art and Archives Rescue fund.[15] Art historians and historians, particularly specialists in the Renaissance, like Marvin Eisenberg, were active in these international organizations. The number of damaged works—in public and private collections, in churches, antique shops, and the flea market—will never be known. The official figures for the flood-damaged works of art located within institutions administered by the state are 734 paintings, 11 fresco cycles and 70 individual frescoes, and 144 sculptures.[16]

Conservation interventions were media specific. The treatment of damaged sculpture was among the more positive and successful endeavors, similar in the effective international collaboration and the revolutionization of conservation procedures characteristic of the manuscript and book recovery described by Shelia Waters in these symposium proceedings. Prior to the flood, there had not been a professional Italian specialization in stone restoration, and the conservation of sculpture and the applied arts in Florence was not as advanced as that of painting. The introduction of new conservation approaches to the various sculptural media marks one of the ways in which the initial crisis intervention had a major impact on conservation training and media specialization afterward. Furthermore, Italy was somewhat behind in the integration of scientific techniques for analyzing and treating works of art, and this, too, would change during and after the flood.[17]

A site for treating sculpture was initially set up in the Bargello museum, with treatments coordinated by the sculpture conservator from the Museum of Fine Arts in Boston, William J. Young, one of twenty conservators who came over from the United States in the days immediately following the flood. Soon afterward, a restoration laboratory was established in the Palazzo Davanzati, with funding and supplies provided through CRIA, as well as English and German aid organizations. In this laboratory, international conservators worked alongside their Italian counterparts, with contingents from England, Germany, Holland, Scandinavia, and the United States.[18] Equipment and supplies were quickly assembled from various sources and transported to Florence. Scientists joined the conservators, and photographers were hired to document the conservation progress. Some of the treatments were overseen by Kenneth Hempel, a sculpture conservator from the Victoria and Albert Museum in London.[19] The Victoria and Albert Museum had a state-of-the-art facility at that time, and Hempel had experience working with the museum's extensive Italian sculpture collection. The museum was also on the vanguard of incorporating scientific techniques into conservation practice. While Hempel waited in London for his leave papers to be processed, he experimented, creating what eventually became known as the "Hempel pack"—a poultice of sepiolite and Shellsol A used to extract stains from marble. In London, he approximated the oily filth of the flood stains by inserting a core of freshly drilled Carrara marble into a mixture of soil, crude oil, and urine for a number of days. After arriving in Florence, Hempel operated out of the Palazzo Davanzati and also dispatched crews to work on marble paneling and statuary on-site in churches. The writer Katherine Kressmann Taylor, in her published journal *Diary of Florence in Flood*, describes one of the British Mud Angels assigned to work with Hempel, on the verge of a nervous collapse over the slow and meticulous process required to clean stains that could penetrate up to an inch into the marble: "It takes so long. We aren't getting anywhere! . . . Nobody knows anything," she lamented.[20]

Once again, triage determinations were made, and not always on the basis of the extent of the damage and the possibility of recovery, with the need now to appeal to international donors contributing funds to organizations like CRIA. Donatello's *Mary Magdalene* was one of the poster children in this regard, appearing in photographic essays on the flood, and in one instance, beside the head of Florentine conservation operations, Umberto Baldini. Triage decisions were also made in a manner that privileged works of art from the Renaissance period. In a fascinating volume of essays that came out in 2006 to commemorate the fortieth anniversary of the flood,[21] Kirsten Aschengreen Piacenti, who worked in the Palazzo Davanzati facility with Hempel, notes with pride her persistence in restoring a wooden relief which she herself had recovered from a flooded restoration facility, recognizing it as an important seventeenth-century carving by the British sculptor Grinling Gibbons. She writes, "Professor Procacci and [Otello] Capara did not want to have anything to do with it—'it is nineteenth century,' they said—and left it there. They would not listen when I told them that it had been commissioned from the artist by King Charles II [of England as a gift for] . . . Grand Duke Cosimo III [de' Medici of Florence]."[22]

If we turn to fresco paintings, the challenges in conserving the flood-damaged wall paintings were extreme. Even when the water level did not reach the paintings themselves, humidity seeped into the walls and caused salt deposits on the surface. The solution used in many cases was to remove the frescoes from the walls. This technique, known as *strappo*, was already in practice before the flood but was used energetically during the two years immediately following, with more than 3,000 square meters of fresco detached.[23] In a quite extraordinary technical feat, Taddeo Gaddi's *Last Supper* from the refectory of Santa Croce, measuring 122 square meters, was removed in one piece. The results of fresco removal often yielded hitherto unknown underdrawings on the rougher plaster layer below, known as *sinopie*, and these discoveries were featured in a widely circulating *Life* magazine feature on the flood.[24] Greater insight into the fresco process became available to art historians by virtue of the exposure of so many preparatory drawings. *Strappo*, as a conservation practice, has since gone out of fashion and is now avoided if possible, since the most stable condition for frescoes is considered to be the original plaster and wall support on which they were made. There are also now available less-invasive techniques, although somewhat controversial, for removing humidity and consolidating plaster.[25]

One striking art historical result from the fresco recovery following the flood was a remarkable exhibition (fig. 4) that brought seventy of these once immobile objects, affixed to buildings in Florence, to international museums between 1968 and 1971, sponsored by the Italian corporation Olivetti. "Birnam Wood has come to Dunsinane," wrote Millard Meiss, quoting from Shakespeare's *Macbeth*, in his "Preface" to the catalog.[26] One hundred and eighty thousand people attended the exhibition at the opening venue, the Metropolitan Museum of Art in New York, during the first month and a half. The exhibition, both spectacular and spectacularly received, then traveled to Amsterdam,

London, Munich, and other European cities.[27] There was a notable appreciation of the *sinopie*, displayed alongside the finished frescoes, which were considered from a somewhat distorted modern perspective to manifest the personal style and spontaneous creativity of the Renaissance painters.[28] The glossary of fresco terms in the catalog—*giornata*, cartoon, *secco*—and the procedures described are the foundation of what I, and my fellow historians of Renaissance art, teach in the classroom about fresco painting. An exhibition of this scale and ambition, involving such a number of a single city's most celebrated and extremely fragile works of art, would be inconceivable today. It must be understood as a direct consequence of the 1966 flood and was framed in the catalog as a one-time, unique opportunity that was both a gesture of reciprocation by the custodians of the frescoes and a demonstration of the "universal significance of Italy's cultural heritage."[29]

In the restoration of panel paintings damaged by the flood, Ugo Procacci and the head of his painting conservation unit, Umberto Baldini, were apparently less inclined to give autonomy to conservators coming from outside of Florence or to work with them in a productive, collaborative manner.[30] There had been a state-sponsored painting restoration facility in Florence since 1932, founded by Procacci. By 1966, however, the Florentine facility had a somewhat strained relationship with the major Italian conservation center in Rome, the Istituto Centrale di Restauro (ICR), where the influential figure Cesare Brandi had presided for years.[31]

In the treatment of paintings immediately following the flood, panel paintings posed the most significant challenge. Marco Grassi, a young conservator trained in Rome who had worked for some years in the Florentine restoration laboratory, describes how each painting was given "a 'rating' according to historical significance, state of conservation, age, and size. In effect, it became a kind of artistic triage whereby certain works, such as the Cimabue, went to the head of the line while many others languished in the dangerous limbo of the Boboli greenhouses."[32] With no precedent for this kind of extensive water damage, some choices were made during the "first-response moment" that proved, with hindsight, to be highly problematic. The panels were

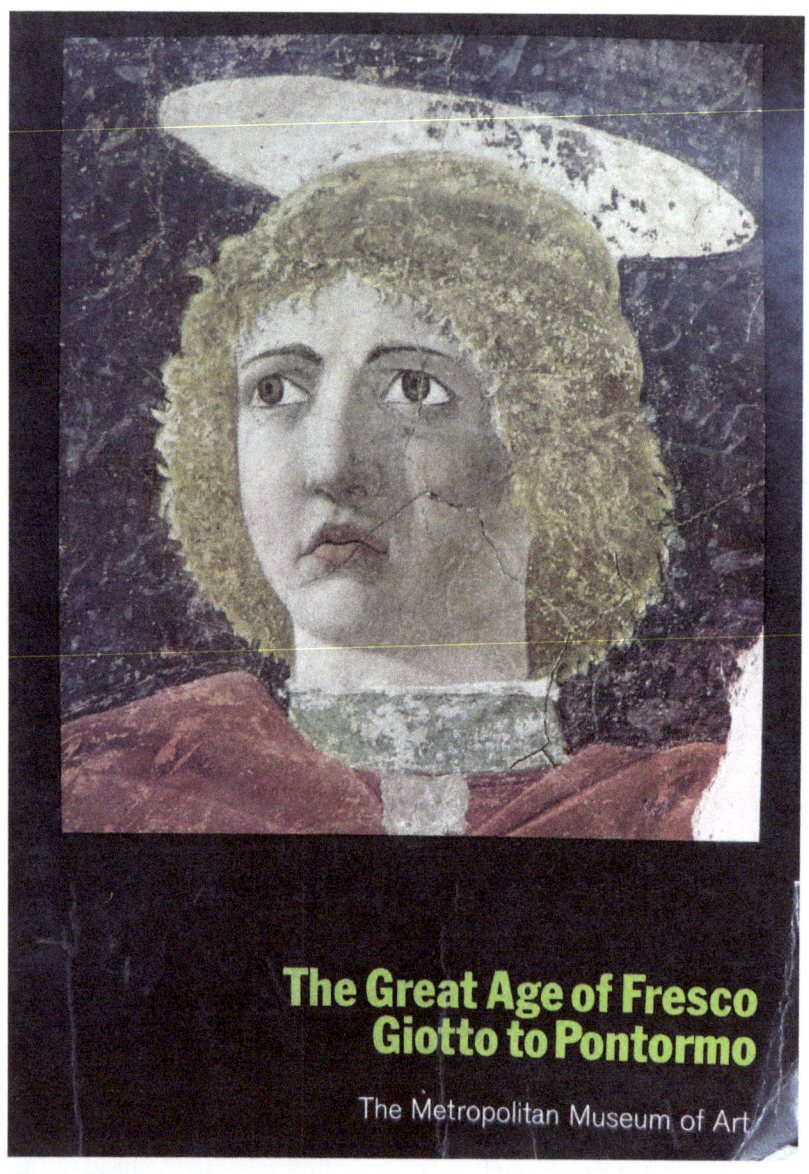

The Great Age of Fresco
Giotto to Pontormo

The Metropolitan Museum of Art

Fig. 4. Catalog for the exhibition *The Great Age of Fresco: Giotto to Pontormo*, 1968, in the Metropolitan Museum of Art, New York (Marvin Eisenberg's copy). Photo by Megan Holmes.

treated in a systematic manner, first while still in situ and then in a facility set up for painting restoration. They were laid flat and coated with the synthetic acrylic resin Paraloid B-72, diluted in a toluene solution, and covered with pieces of fine Japanese paper to consolidate the paint, creating a protective covering known as a *velinatura*. Conservators, trainees, and Mud Angels were sent out with buckets of Paraloid B-72 and mounds of Japanese paper—until supplies in Italy of the latter were exhausted and a variety of tissue papers were substituted.[33] When it became apparent that mold was beginning to form on the panels, the conservators began to spray them systematically with the fungicide nystatine.[34] The panels were then taken to the Limonaia, a complex of greenhouses above the Pitti Palace, which was used in the winter months to house the citrus trees from the Boboli Gardens. A decision was made to dry the panel paintings gradually, and using CRIA funds, a climate-controlled environment was devised in the Limonaia for this slow process of dehumidification.[35]

Years later, Marco Grassi commented, "Ever since those fateful days, legitimate questions have been asked: were these the *only* solutions possible and with the *only* material possible."[36] The gradual drying of the panels led to the continual formation of mold as well as cracks in the wood. Later, when restoration was attempted, it turned out that the *velinatura* of acrylic resin and paper adhering to the paint layer was rigid rather than elastic and had not dried in sync with the wood and gesso ground, with the wood actually shrinking to smaller dimensions than its preemersion state. The natural animal glues in the gesso had dissolved, leaving the gesso layer compromised. The *velinatura* also proved to be much more difficult to remove than had been anticipated on account of the unexpected hardening of the Paraloid B-72. Repeated applications of caustic solvents were necessary, causing some damage to the paint layer and exposing the conservators to the solvent. Grassi noted that in the 1960s, there had been an enthusiastic embrace of new synthetic materials that were being developed by chemical companies like Dow, which introduced Paraloid B-72, without knowledge of the behavior of these materials over the long term and under varying conditions.[37] In retrospect, the painting conservator Andrea Rothe reflects

that the panels should not have been covered with Paraloid B-72 and
paper and that the paint surface should have been left exposed.[38] The
drying of the panels should have been rapid rather than slow, with
the consolidation of the lifting paint undertaken progressively during this shorter drying time. Whether this would have been possible
given the great number of damaged panels is difficult to say.

Perhaps, too, in the two years that the Limonaia operated, before
painting conservation was shifted to new facilities in the Fortezza
da Basso, the conservation of paintings might have benefited from
more open debates about procedures and from the sharing of experiences and technologies among the international group of restorers, akin
to that in the manuscript and book recovery field and in the laboratory
in the Palazzo Davanzati. Robert Clark, in researching his book *Dark
Water: Art, Disaster, and Redemption in Florence* (2008), consulted the
archives of CRIA, which was footing the bill of much of this early conservation of panel paintings in the Limonaia. He found a confidential
report written to CRIA during the summer of 1967 indicating that the
Limonaia was dirty, insect-infested, and without temperature regula-
tion; people were suffering from respiratory ailments and low morale;
and it was an increasingly difficult working environment unless one
showed loyalty to what was referred to in the report as a "troika" consisting of the head conservator, Umberto Baldini, and his two chief
assistants.[39] The narratives that one reads of in other domains of flood
conservation—recounting knowledge gained about historical craft
materials and production techniques and effective new methods of
conservation—contrast with the accounts of treating panel paintings,
which tend to be about the extreme difficulty of removing the *velinatura*
with the least damage to the paintings.[40]

Many of the international conservators and scientists continued
to work in Florence for a number of years until their financial support dried up or their home institutions called them back. The Nordic
Center of Restoration, accommodated in the Palazzo Davanzati restoration facility, for example, operated for three years, with the participation of more than one hundred conservators during that time, from
Sweden, Denmark, and Finland, specializing in different branches of

conservation.[41] The Florentine administrators, with still much flood-related conservation work left to coordinate, and with new and more scientific approaches to treating different media put into practice, inaugurated a new conservation system in 1970 known as the Opificio delle Pietre Dure (OPD), with the primary laboratories in the Fortezza da Basso, an old Medici military fortress in the north of the city.

What we have seen emerge in this narrative about the energetic first response to the flood damage to the visual art in Florence is an interesting relationship between crisis interventions and established standard operating procedures. On the one hand, crisis interventions, in their most positive manifestations, foster international collaboration, generosity, unprecedented measures, herculean effort involving human energy and synergy, creative solutions, the use of new technologies, heightened media attention, and extraordinary allocations of funds and resources. But crisis responses are, necessarily, short term. A key question is how to hold on to at least some of these positive features after the fact, once standard quotidian operations resume. In the words of one of the people involved in coordinating the restoration work in Florence in 1966, "When disasters occur, it is best to accept them as portents, and to adopt the target, not of restoring the status quo, but of improving on it."[42] On the other hand, crisis interventions, particularly on account of the need for quick and often drastic solutions, can also have a high risk factor and can lead to mistakes. The challenge is how to minimize the potential for damaging mistakes through the participation of qualified specialists and capable managers and the sharing of expertise, dialog in decision-making, good record-keeping, and, in the case of art conservation, practices that, to the extent possible, are reversible, noninvasive, and respectful of the original materials.[43]

Some of the ways that Ugo Procacci attempted to support and sustain the energetic international relief effort were to keep the Florentine museums open, to celebrate the recovery and renewal of the city's visual art, and to share the experience of art restoration with the public.[44] I have already mentioned the 1968–71 international exhibition of detached frescoes from Florence, which Procacci authorized. But there were other key initiatives. The Uffizi—which, in the days immediately after the flood, served as an improvised repository for resituated works of art and as the operational headquarters for coordinating art preservation—quite remarkably was reopened to the public just a little more than a month after the flood. In addition, in late December 1966, a small exhibition, *Dipinti salvati dalla piena dell'Arno, 4 Novembre 1966* (*Paintings Saved from the Flooding of the Arno, 4 November 1966*), was mounted of those works that had been safely moved from the ground floor of the Uffizi during the night of November 3 and the early morning of November 4, as the floodwaters were rising. I have Marvin Eisenberg's copy of the brochure (fig. 5) that was printed to accompany the small exhibition (in which Ugo Procacci's foreword is dated December 21, 1966).[45]

This process of commemoration and memorialization through exhibition continued. A year later, in December 1967, Procacci mounted an exhibition at the Bargello museum dedicated to works of sculpture and decorative art that had been physically compromised by the flood and subsequently cleaned or restored.[46] The catalog (fig. 6) is a tribute to the restoration efforts. The entries describe the extent of the damage and the restoration procedures, and rather extraordinarily, they list the individual conservators. Under Michelangelo's *Bacchus*, for instance, is listed "restauro William Young"—the Museum of Fine Arts conservator who treated the *Bacchus*, which apparently required only a fairly superficial cleaning.[47] Special mention is made in the catalog, too, of the professionals and student helpers who worked on-site in the churches and whose efforts were therefore not visible in the exhibition itself.[48] This catalog is an important public record that both documents and brings some transparency to a process involving the modification of the physical integrity of highly valued cultural patrimony in the name of flood restoration.

Five years later, in 1972, a landmark exhibition was held in Florence, in the Fortezza da Basso. This exhibition, entitled *Firenze Restaura* (fig. 7), was unprecedented in taking restoration itself as its principal subject matter, with 355 works of art, as well as photographs and didactic panels, displayed in sixty-one galleries.[49] The exhibition included triumphant flood recoveries, like Donatello's *Mary Magdalene*,

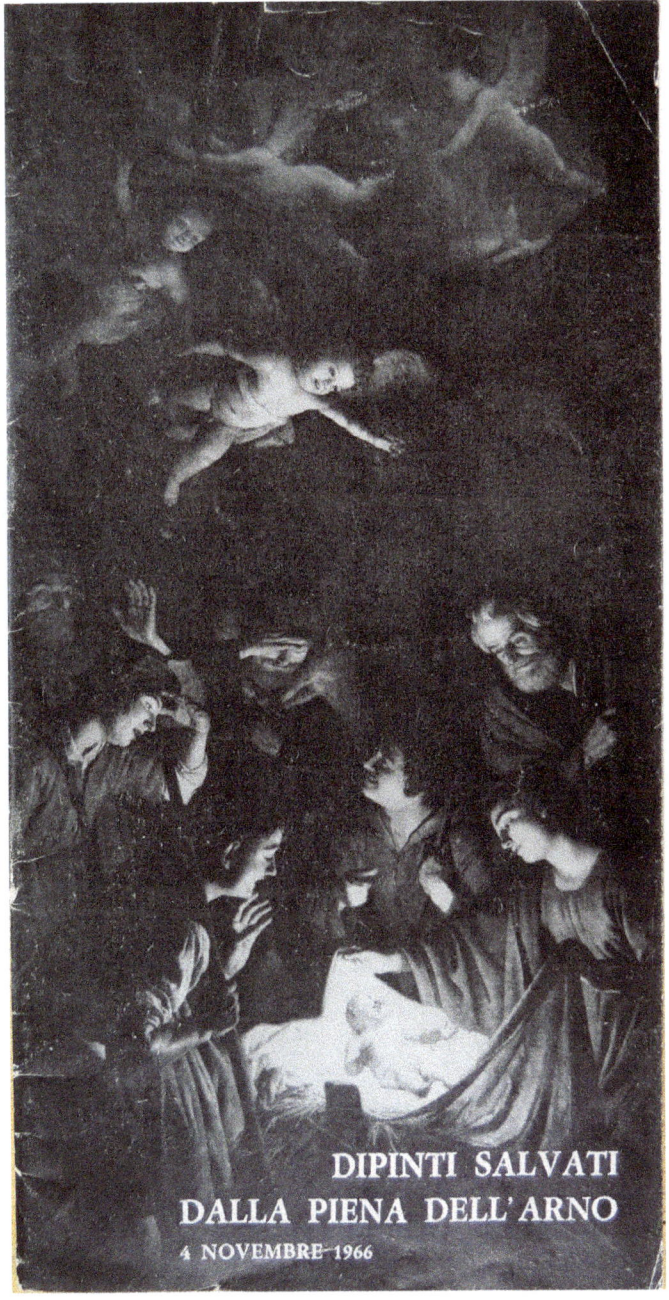

DIPINTI SALVATI
DALLA PIENA DELL'ARNO
4 NOVEMBRE 1966

Fig. 5. Brochure for the exhibition *Dipinti salvati dalla piena dell'Arno: 4 novembre 1966*, which opened late in December 1966 in the Uffizi, Florence (Marvin Eisenberg's copy). Photo by Megan Holmes.

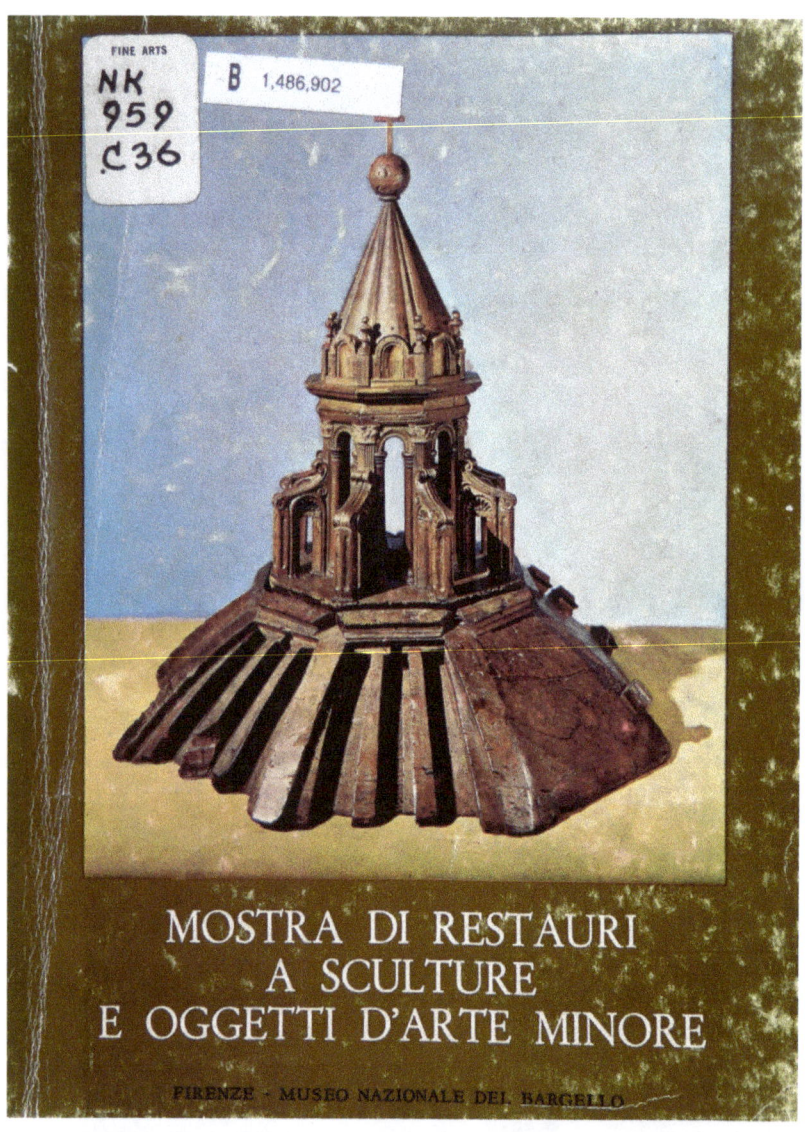

MOSTRA DI RESTAURI
A SCULTURE
E OGGETTI D'ARTE MINORE

FIRENZE · MUSEO NAZIONALE DEL BARGELLO

Fig. 6. Catalog for the exhibition *Mostra di restauri a sculture e oggetti d'arte minore*, 1967, in the Museo Nazionale del Bargello, Florence (University of Michigan Fine Arts Library's copy). Photo by Megan Holmes.

but also presented the flood interventions within a broader history of Florentine restoration. Earlier examples were included, which demonstrated changes in the definition of and approach to restoration, from the renewal of cult images, to the remaking of figuration and settings through extensive repainting, to the recovery and consolidation of the surviving original paint and composition. Across the galleries the exhibition visualized the historical shift and reformulation from "restoration" to "conservation."[50] Cimabue's *Crucifix*, still a work in progress at the time, made an appearance, with the wooden cross present but denuded of its painting and the painting itself displayed on an adjacent wall, rather disconcertedly, as detached body parts on fragments of newly reinforced canvas.

The catalog is not quite as generous as the 1967 Bargello exhibition catalog to the many conservators who labored on the works of art damaged in the 1966 flood, listing them en masse in the preface. There is also a marked parochial emphasis on, and celebration of, Florentine restoration history. This 1972 exhibition date marked the fortieth anniversary of the founding in 1932 of the restoration laboratory in Florence by Ugo Procacci and thus chronicled forty years of Florentine restoration activity. In the last gallery, the curator Umberto Baldini offered his unabashed homage and thanks to Ugo Procacci. Procacci had appointed Baldini as the head of the new Florentine conservation center at the Opificio delle Pietre Dure two years earlier, and a decade later, Baldini was to pull off a rather incredible coup in becoming the director of the rival Roman conservation institution, the Istituto Centrale di Restauro.

There are two further 1966 Florence Flood–related restoration events that I will briefly mention here before concluding. One of these was the completion of the restoration of Cimabue's *Crucifix* in 1976, followed by an ambitious world tour of five exhibition venues, authorized by Umberto Baldini and once again sponsored by Olivetti.[51] The reception of the restoration was mixed. Some critics objected to the innovative striation technique used to fill in the extensive areas of loss, which was a modification of Cesare Brandi's widely used *tratteggio* technique. The restorers called their in-painting "chromatic abstraction"—an

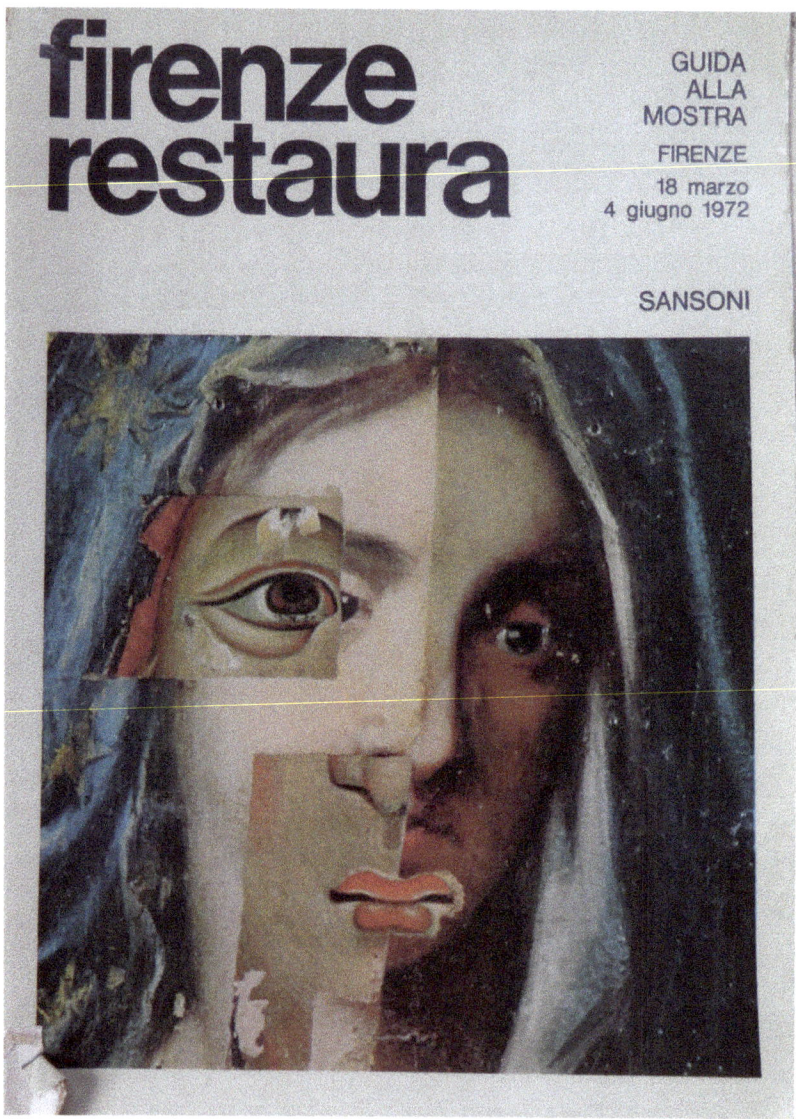

Fig. 7. Catalog for the exhibition *Firenze Restaura*, 1972, in the Fortezza da Basso, Florence (Marvin Eisenberg's copy). Photo by Megan Holmes.

intentionally scientific-sounding term that they linked with both color theory and optics.[52] Critics felt that the chromatic abstraction problematically drew attention away from the surviving areas of original paint so that the restored composition failed to cohere (which was the overriding objective of Brandi's *tratteggio* technique). The Frankensteinian

dismembering and resuturing to which Cimabue's *Crucifix* was sub-
jected has also become a vivid demonstration of extreme measures that
are to be avoided, if possible, in the conservation of Italian panel paintings, where every effort is now made to respect the structural integrity
of the work, with reversibility and the possibility for future interventions also objectives.[53]

A final major flood-related event brings us up to date with the
anniversary occasion of this symposium. Giorgio Vasari's monumental *Last Supper* panel painting, which had been submerged under
floodwater for twelve hours in Santa Croce in 1966, has been restored
in a collaborative venture between the Florentine Opificio delle Pietre
Dure and the Getty Conservation Center, overseen by the conservator
Cecilia Frosinini.[54] The official unveiling was planned for November 4—coinciding with the day of the flood, fifty years ago. This venture participated in a practice that evolved in Florence and beyond of
marking each successive ten-year anniversary of the 1966 Florentine
flood with an exhibition or symposium—just as we have done here at
the University of Michigan.[55] This practice has generated a productive
combination of retrospective and forward-looking reflection about
art conservation and historic preservation, recognizing the 1966 flood
as a critical catalyst.

The restoration of Vasari's *Last Supper* is a conservation project that
nicely encapsulates a number of the conservation and art historical
themes addressed here. There is, for starters, the interesting issue of the
amount of money and expertise allocated to remove the resistant *velinatura* that covered the five sections of the dismembered panel painting
and to restore a work of art that has effectively accrued value as a flood
victim and memorial to the 1966 flood.[56] At a time when resources for
conservation work are limited, one hopes that high-profile endeavors
like this one will ultimately serve to draw public attention to the value
of conservation and will benefit the wider practice and less sensational
projects.[57] The international collaboration between two conservation institutions is encouraging and is in the spirit of the 1966 flood
response. It is also healthy to have the financial support of the well-
endowed Getty Foundation so that the funding is not directly domi-
nated by commercial contributors from outside the conservation and

art historical domains, which can, even in the best of circumstances, have certain negative consequences for conservation projects.[58]

There was an interesting development over the ten-year period in which the active restoration on Vasari's *Last Supper* transpired, supported by both changing approaches to conservation and new technologies. It was originally assumed that the paint layer would have to be detached from the wooden support, as had been done with Cimabue's *Crucifix*. This would have been a particularly tricky prospect in the case of Vasari's *Last Supper* since, by the mid-sixteenth century when the painting was made, canvas was no longer used to cover panels. This makes the transfer process more complicated, since the wood must be laboriously planed down from the back. Furthermore, after the *Last Supper* was immersed in the floodwater and initially kept upright, the gesso ground between the wood support and paint layer apparently shifted and settled down toward the bottom of the panels. The conservators, in the end, were able to save the original wood support and consolidate the gesso and paint layers.[59]

I would like to conclude with some forward-looking reflections about the historic preservation of cultural artifacts, mindful of the lessons learned from the Florentine flood of 1966. During the symposium, we saw a screening of the University of Maryland's copy of Franco Zeffirelli's film *Per Firenze* (*Florence: Days of Destruction*), made in collaboration with Radiotelevisione Italiana (RAI) and narrated by Richard Burton. We appreciated the impact of this film that was shot during and immediately after the flood and then aired on television in Italy and abroad just over a month after the event. We have also been moved by the evocative, powerful photographs of the flood taken by Balthazar Korab, David Lees, and Nicholas Kraczyna, among others. With these demonstrations of the critical role of film and photography in mind, we want to be mindful of how media and the web operate in the domain of historical preservation at this time and also consider how they might be more productively harnessed in the future. We want to consider the impact on our practices of new technologies, science, and the global reach and rapidity of internet exchanges. As we are all going more "digital"—our files and resources stored on our personal computers and our interactions with colleagues and opinions recorded in personal emails—we need to be sure that there are backups and analog records that document our work and professional activities.

Another subject that I would like to address is disciplinarity and interdisciplinarity in relation to historic preservation. The impressive demonstrations in the symposium papers of collaboration during first-response efforts and longer-term preservation initiatives give rise to reflections about how we operate within our different domains of practice and through our institutional affiliations. In our various endeavors to support the preservation of valued cultural heritage, we need to be mindful of our evolving disciplines and missions, to operate with historical awareness, to exercise self-critique and transparency, and to share our technologies and data. At a time when broad support for our costly and time-consuming work as scholars, conservators, scientists, librarians, and educators is in question, and we are being pressured continually to demonstrate and measure our productivity and utility, we must find ways to work against the potential for isolation, ossification, and compromise, as well as against the unreasonable hierarchies and gatekeeping within our respective fields and institutions. We also need to operate with an awareness of how our respective disciplines are organized across a network of institutions and independent practitioners. Within these networks, the organizations that have more funding and resources—certain museums, libraries, universities, conservation centers, and research institutes—have a responsibility to act on behalf of the wider domain, extending themselves to and involving practitioners from outside. And finally, in the spirit of both the Florentine flood relief and the pedagogy and mentorship of Marvin Eisenberg at the University of Michigan, we want to collaborate and exchange across national boundaries, institutions, disciplines, and generations.

Notes

1. Douglas C. McGill, "Scholars Warn Vatican of Dangers of Frescoes," *New York Times* (Nov. 6, 1986); Kathleen Weil-Garris Brandt, "Twenty-Five Questions about Michelangelo's Sistine Ceiling," *Apollo*, vol. 126 (Dec. 1987), pp. 392–400; James Beck and Michael Daley, *Art Restoration: The*

Culture, the Business, and the Scandal (London: John Murray, 1993). In 1992, Beck founded ArtWatch International, an organization that brought attention to art restoration projects that it considered problematic.

2. On image cults in Florence that started up in relation to the 1557 flooding of the Arno, see Megan Holmes, *The Miraculous Image in Renaissance Florence* (New Haven: Yale University Press, 2013), pp. 40 (Table I), 74, 94–95, 124, and 169.

3. I have Marvin Eisenberg's copies of the following: Franco Nencini, *Firenze: I giorni del diluvio* (Florence: Sansoni, 1966); Thomas Hoving, Millard Meiss, and Ugo Procacci, eds., *The Great Age of Fresco: Giotto to Pontormo* (Florence: The Metropolitan Museum of Art, 1968); *Firenzo Restaura: Il laboratorio nel suo quarantennio* (Florence: Sansoni, 1972) (inscribed on the title page: "Marvin Eisenberg, Florence, July–August, 1972").

4. CRIA Archives, Harvard University, Villa I Tatti, Florence, http://cria .itatti.harvard.edu/area_chairmen (consulted 7/14/2017). The University of Michigan donated one thousand dollars, and Marvin Eisenberg placed advertisements soliciting individual donations in the *Michigan Daily* on Nov. 16 and 17, 1966. An article in the *Michigan Daily* on Nov. 22, 1966, described Marvin's role, the damage and relief efforts, and the University of Michigan's donation. Bentley Library, University of Michigan, *Michigan Daily* Archives, https://digital.bentley.umich.edu/midaily (consulted 7/14/2017).

5. Nencini, *Firenze*, pp. 13–14; Robert Clark, *Dark Water: Art, Disaster, and Redemption in Florence* (New York: Anchor Books, 2009), pp. 139–40, 148, and 153.

6. Procacci contacted the art historian Eve Borsook, who was instrumental in transporting circa thirty thousand wet negatives to high ground for drying at the Villa I Tatti, the former home of Bernard Berenson and study center run by Harvard University. In the aftermath of the flood, Borsook operated as a liaison between I Tatti (where many of the foreign scholars assembled), the foreign conservators who had come to assist in the restoration work, and the Italian museum and conservation personnel. Interview with Eve Borsook, "4 Novembre 1966: 50 anni fa l'alluvione di Firenze," in *Opera Magazine* (Opera di Santa Maria del Fiore, Nov. 4, 2014), https://operaduomo .firenze.it/blog/posts/4-novembre-1966-48-anni-fa-l-alluvione-di-firenze (consulted 7/13/2017). See photographs of the glass negatives drying at I Tatti on the CRIA website: "Role of I Tatti," http://cria.itatti.harvard.edu/ exhibits/show/the-committee/role-of-i-tatti (consulted 7/13/2017).

7. Clark, *Dark Water*, p. 140; on the *Madonna and Child with Saints* by Neri di Bicci, see Erling Skaug, "Transfer of Panel Paintings after the Flood," in *Conservation Legacies of the Florence Flood of 1966: Proceedings of the Symposium Commemorating the 40th Anniversary*, ed. Helen Spande (London: Archetype Publications, 2009), pp. 141–46 and 149, n. 4.

8. Cathleen Hoeniger, "The Restoration of Early Italian 'Primitives' during the 20th Century: Valuing Art and Its Consequences," *Journal of the American Institute for Conservation*, vol. 38 (1999), pp. 144–61. See also Marco Grassi's account of the "rating" system used in the aftermath of the flood in the conservation of panel paintings, discussed below.

9. Bruno Santi, *Neri di Bicci: Le Ricordanze (10 marzo 1453–24 aprile 1475)* (Pisa, Italy: Marlin, 1976); Anabel Thompson, *The Painter's Practice in Renaissance Tuscany* (Cambridge: Cambridge University Press, 1995); Megan Holmes, "Neri di Bicci and the Commodification of Artistic Values," in *The Art Market in Italy (15th–17th Centuries)*, eds. Marcello Fantoni, Louisa Chevalier Matthew, and Sara F. Matthews Grieco (Ferrara, Italy: Pannini, 2003), pp. 213–23. In my article I argue that art historians can benefit from engaging to a greater extent with Neri di Bicci's paintings, not just his account book.

10. While Erling Skaug notes that Neri di Bicci's painting was in the Pinacoteca in Siena in his article on the restoration published in 2009 ("Transfer of Panel Paintings after the Flood," in *Conservation Legacies*, p. 146), the painting is not currently in the galleries or listed on the Pinacoteca website, or on that of the Polo Museale Fiorentino. On the restoration of Botticelli's *Coronation of the Virgin*, see Marco Ciatti, *L'Incoronazione Della Vergine del Botticelli: Restauro e ricerche* (Florence: Edifir edizioni, 1990).

11. "L'elenco ufficiale delle vittime dell'Alluvione 1966," *Associazione Firenze Promuove* (May 15, 2016), http://www.firenzepromuove.it/?p=1684 (consulted 7/13/2017); Clark, *Dark Water*, pp. 149–52.

12. Clark, *Dark Water*, pp. 160–61 and 182–90. See Swietlan Nicholas Kraczyna, *The Great Flood of Florence, 1966: A Photographic Essay*, ed. Dorothea Barrett (Florence: Syracuse University Florence, 2006), p. 78.

13. On damage to works of art at Santa Croce, see Marco Ciatti, Cecilia Frosinini, and C. R. Scarzanella, *Angeli, santi e demoni: Otto capolavori restaurati: Santa Croce quaranta anni dopo [1966–2006]* (Florence: Edifir, 2006).

14. Clark uses a Passion metaphor in describing the dismounting of the waterlogged *Crucifix* from the walls of the refectory of Santa Croce as a "deposition" (Clark, *Dark Water*, p. 169).

15. See Millard Meiss's account of CRIA's role in the efforts to save and conserve works of art during the year following the flood, "Report on Scholarship in the Renaissance: Florence and Venice a Year Later," *Renaissance Quarterly*, vol. 21, no. 1 (1968), pp. 103–18. The CRIA archives are now housed at the Bernard Berenson Center for the Study of Renaissance Art at the Villa I Tatti, outside of Florence.

16. *Rapporto sui danni al patrimonio artistico e culturali* (Florence: C. E. Giunti, 1967), p. 10.

17. See Giorgio Bonsanti's assessment of Italian conservation at the time of the flood in "Restoration in Florence Following the Flood," in *Conservation*

Legacies, pp. 111–12. On the history of art conservation in Italy, see Alessandro Conti, *History of the Restoration and Conservation of Works of Art*, trans. Helen Glanville (Oxford: Elsevier, 2007); Massimo Ferretti, "La storia del restauro e il mestiere di storico dell'arte, da Alessandro Conti a Roberto Longhi," in *La cultura del restauro. Modelli di ricezione per la museologia e la storia dell'arte*, eds. Maria Beatrice Failla et al. (Rome: Storia dell'arte, 2014), pp. 555–68. Marco Ciatti, the director of the OPD in Florence, has also written on the history of conservation in Florence and at the OPD; see, for example, his "Dall'alluvione al moderno OPD," in *Firenze 1966–2016: La bellezza salvata*, eds. Cristina Acidini Luchinat et al. (Livorno: Sillabe, 2016), pp. 33–41.

18. On the restoration center in the Palazzo Davanzati, see William J. Young, "The Florentine Flood, November 4, 1965," *Boston Museum Bulletin*, vol. 66, no. 345 (1968), pp. 101–15; Kirsten Aschengreen Piacenti in *Catalogo della mostra di restauri a sculture e oggetti d'arte minore* (Florence: Museo Nazionale del Bargello, 1967), pp. 5–7; and Kirsten Aschengreen Piacenti, "The Flood and the Palazzo Davanzati Laboratories," in *Conservation Legacies*, pp. 134–40.

19. Kenneth Hempel, OBE, "The Rescue of Statues and Sculptures in Florence and Venice," in *Conservation Legacies*, pp. 116–28.

20. Katherine Kressmann Taylor, *Diary of Florence in Flood* (New York: Simon and Schuster, 1967), pp. 148–49.

21. Helen Spande, ed., *Conservation Legacies of the Florence Flood of 1966: Proceedings of the Symposium Commemorating the 40th Anniversary* (London: Archetype Publications, 2009).

22. Aschengreen Piacenti, "The Flood and the Palazzo Davanzati Laboratories," in *Conservation Legacies*, p. 137.

23. Bonsanti, "Restoration in Florence," p. 113. For a perspective on the use of *strappo* and the study of detached frescoes prior to the flood, see three exhibitions, and related catalogs, held in Florence at the Forte di Belvedere in 1957, 1958, and 1959, each entitled *Mostra di affreschi stacatti*, in which Ugo Procacci, Umberto Baldini, and Luciano Berti were involved.

24. *Life*, June 30, 1967.

25. The new technique involves the use of barium hydroxide (Bonsanti, "Restoration in Florence," *Conservation Legacies*, p. 113). For criticisms of these new techniques, see Alessandro Conti, "Attenzioni ai restauri," *Prospettiva*, vol. 40 (Jan. 1985), pp. 3–9.

26. Millard Meiss, "Preface" to *The Great Age of Fresco: Giotto to Pontormo*, eds. Thomas Hoving, Millard Meiss, and Ugo Procacci (Florence: The Metropolitan Museum of Art, 1968), p. 15.

27. The exhibition, funded by Olivetti, was shown at the Metropolitan Museum of Art, New York (*The Great Age of Fresco: Giotto to Pontormo*, Sept. 28–Nov. 15, 1968); the Rijksmuseum, Amsterdam (*Fresco's uit Florence*,

Dec. 19–March 9, 1969); the Hayward Gallery in London (*Frescoes from Florence*, Apr. 3–June 15, 1969); and the Haus der Kunst in Munich (*Fresken aus Florenz*, July 11–Aug. 24); extending its tour to Brussels (1969), Lugano (1970), Stockholm (1970), Copenhagen (1970), Paris (1970), Milan (1971), and, on a reduced scale, Mexico City (1979).

28. See, for example, the reviews by Juergen Schulz and Anne Markham Schulz in *Burlington Magazine*, vol. 111, no. 790 (Jan. 1969), pp. 50–55; Ernst Gombrich in *New York Review of Books* (June 19, 1969); Henk van Os in *Simiolus: Netherlands Quarterly for the History of Art*, vol. 4, no. 1 (1970), pp. 6–12.

29. Millard Meiss, "Preface" to *The Great Age of Fresco*, pp. 12–15.

30. For a somewhat negative assessment of the restoration of panel paintings, see Clark, *Dark Water*, pp. 234–36; Andrea Rothe, "New Methods of Paintings Conservation Developed in Response to the Flood," in *Conservation Legacies*, pp. 129–33; Marco Grassi, "The Florence Flood: Some Personal Recollections," in *Conservation Legacies*, pp. 102–10. Cristina Acidini presents a rosier picture in her article "Recovery of the Panel Paintings of Florence" in this same volume, pp. 168–77.

31. On the Florentine painting conservation laboratory, see Giovanni Gronchi, *Firenze Restaura: Il laboratorio nel suo quarantennio* (Florence: Sansoni, 1972), pp. 9–13 and 126–27; Marco Ciatti, "Il gabinetto di restauro a la pulittura," in *Ugo Procacci a cento anni dalla nascità*, eds. Marco Ciatti and Cecillia Frosinini (Florence: Edifir, 2006), pp. 153–72. On Brandi's theory and methods of restoration, as director of the ICR in Rome from its founding in 1939 to his retirement in 1959, see the essays in Cesare Brandi, *Teoria del Restauro* (Rome: Edizioni di storia e letterature, 1963). On the participation of the ICR in conservation efforts in the aftermath of the Florentine flood in 1966, see Pasquale Rotondi, *Firenze 1966: Appunti di diario sull'alluvione* (Lugano, Switzerland: Edizioni San Lorenzo, 2013); and "L'Istituto Centrale di Restauro e l'alluvione di Firenze del 1966" on the ICR website, http://www.icr.beniculturali.it/pagina.cfm?usz=1&uid=182& idnew=412 (accessed 7/20/2017).

32. Marco Grassi, "Letter from Florence: After the Great Flood of Florence," *New Criterion*, vol. 35, no. 5 (Jan. 2017), p. 55.

33. Marco Grassi, "Letter from Florence" and "The Florence Flood: Some Personal Recollections," *New Criterion*, vol. 35, no. 5 (Jan. 2017), pp. 102–10; Rothe, "New Methods of Paintings," pp. 129–33.

34. On the use of nystatine, see Rothe, "New Methods of Paintings," p. 130. On the repeated applications of nystatine to Cimabue's *Crucifix*, see Clark, *Dark Water*, pp. 215–24.

35. On the painting restoration facility in the Limonaia, see Acidini, "Recovery of Panel Paintings," pp. 171–74; and Harold J. Plenderleith, "The Paintings Hospital in the Lemon Grove," *UNESCO Currier* (Jan. 1967), pp. 24–34.

36. Grassi, "The Florence Flood: Some Personal Recollections," p. 109.

37. Ibid., p. 104.

38. Rothe, "New Methods of Paintings," pp. 129–33.

39. Clark, *Dark Water*, pp. 233–34. Umberto Baldini's assistants were Edo Masini and Gaetano Lo Vullo.

40. Skaug, "Transfer of Panel Paintings," pp. 141–46; Roberto Bellucci, Marco Ciatti, and Cecilia Frosinini, *Dall'alluvione alla rinascita: Il restauro dell'Ultima Cena di Giorgio Vasari* (Florence: Edifir, 2016).

41. On the *Centro Nordico di Restauro* in the Palazzo Davanzati, see Leif Einar Plahter, "Nordisk center for restaurering i Firenze," in *Conservare necesse est: For Leif Einar Plahter on his 70th Birthday*, ed. Erling Skaug, with an English summary (Oslo: IIC Nordic Group, 1999).

42. John Pope Hennessy, quoted in Hempel, "Rescue of Statues," p. 117.

43. See Cesare Brandi's principles of conservation, in *Restauro: Teoria e practica* (Rome: Editori Riuniti, 2005), particularly the essays in the section "Il restauro: Teoria e practica, 1939–96," pp. 1–60.

44. Clark, *Dark Water*, p. 210.

45. I found the brochure for the exhibition slipped into one of the books that Marvin Eisenberg gave me—Franco Nencini's *Firenze: I giorni del diluvio* (a photo essay on the flood that was, quite remarkably, published in Florence on November 30, 1966, a mere twenty-six days after the flood).

46. The Bargello exhibition ran from December 1967 through February 1968. *Catalogo della mostra di restauri a sculture e oggetti d'arte minore* (Firenze: Museo Nazionale del Bargello, Dec. 1967).

47. Ibid., no. 19, p. 18.

48. Ibid., p. 50.

49. *Firenze Restaura* ran from March 18 to June 4 at the Fortezza da Basso in Florence. *Firenzo Restaura: Il laboratorio nel suo quarantennio* (Florence: Sansoni, 1972). *Firenze Restaura* was reassembled as a virtual exhibition in 2012 for the forty-fifth anniversary of the flood, with a website with photographs of the galleries and a searchable database for the works displayed. Opificio delle Pietre Dure, "'Firenze Restaura,' quaranta anni dopo," http://www.firenzerestaura1972.beniculturali.it/ (accessed 7/14/2017).

50. On this shift, see Conti, *History of the Restoration*, pp. x and 327–55, with emphasis on the role of Giovanni Battista Cavalcaselle in the mid-nineteenth century.

51. Cimabue's *Crucifix* was exhibited in New York, at the Metropolitan Museum of Art (Sept. 6–Nov. 11, 1982) in Paris, at the Louvre (Dec. 7, 1982–Jan. 17, 1983); in London, at the Royal Academy (Feb. 12–Apr. 4, 1983); in Madrid, at the Prado (May–June 1983); and in Munich, at the Alte Pinakothek (Sept. 29–Oct. 30, 1983), with a catalog, issued at each venue, written by the conservators Umberto Baldini and Ornella Casazza, and published by Olivetti.

52. Umberto Baldini and Ornella Casazza, *The Crucifix of Cimabue* (New York: Olivetti, 1982). See Robert Clark's account of the criticism of the restoration in *Dark Water*, pp. 252–55, citing Alessandro Conti's article in the Florentine newspaper *Paese Sera*, "Cronaca Firenze," Aug. 29, 1977 (n. 231).

53. Alessandro Conti, *Restauro* (Milan: Editoriale Jaca, 1992), p. 24.

54. On the restoration of Vasari's *Last Supper*, see Clark, *Dark Water*, pp. 266–70, 275–80, 285–86, and 309–12; Bellucci, *Dall'alluvione*; Getty Foundation website (with a publication forthcoming), http://www.getty.edu/foundation/initiatives/current/panelpaintings/panel_paintings_vasari.html (consulted 7/14/2017).

55. Here is a list of the major art exhibitions, with their catalogs, held in Florence on decade anniversaries of the flood: thirtieth anniversary (1996), exhibition at the Palazzo Vecchio (Monica Bietti, ed., *Salvate dalle Acque: Opere d'arte e da restaure a trent'anni dall'alluvione* [Florence: Centro Di, 1996]); fortieth anniversary (2006), exhibitions in Santa Croce (Marco Ciatti, Cecilia Frosinini, and C. R. Scarzanella, eds., *Angeli, santi e demoni: Otto capolavori restaurati: Santa Croce quaranta anni dopo (1966–2006)* [Florence: Edifir, 2006]) and San Marco (Magnolia Scudieri, ed., *Picoli grandi tesori alluvionati* [Florence: Sillabe, 2006]); fiftieth anniversary (2016), unveiling of Vasari's *Last Supper* in Santa Croce (Bellucci, *Dall'alluvione*) and an exhibition in the Palazzo Medici Riccardi (Cristina Acidini Luchinat et al., eds., *Firenze 1966–2016: La bellezza salvata* [Livorno: Sillabe, 2016]).

56. Vasari's *Last Supper* was not included on the trimmed down "adoption list" drawn up by CRIA in April 1967 of flood-damaged works of art that CRIA funds could be spent on. Clark, *Dark Water*, pp. 230–31, records that in 2000, the estimated cost for the conservation, prior to the undertaking, was assessed by the conservator Giovanni Cabras at circa four hundred thousand dollars. Ibid., p. 268.

57. In regard to works of art damaged by the 1966 flood that have yet to be restored, see Marco Ferri, *L'Eredita' di Fango: Cosa rimane da restaurare a Firenze 40 anni dopo l'alluvione* (Florence: Societa' di Toscana Edizione, 2006). See also Clark, *Dark Water*, pp. 268–69; Magnolia Scudieri, "L'Ufficio Restauri della Soprintendenza per 'gli alluvionati,'" in *Firenze 1966–2016*, pp. 43–49.

58. An example where the commercial financier influenced critical decision-making is the Sistine Chapel ceiling, where the Japanese firm Nippon Television Network Corporation maintained exclusive rights to the photographic reproductions of the restored frescoes, making it extremely difficult for scholars and conservators to study the results. One wonders, in the case of the two Florence Flood exhibitions supported by Olivetti (the detached Florentine frescoes in 1968–71 and the restored Cimabue *Crucifix* in 1976–77), whether the ambitious geographic footprint and the extended duration of the multicity Euro-American tours were negotiating points for

the corporation, designed to maximize the publicity aura around their financial support for the art restoration. On the controversy of corporate sponsorship and support of art restoration projects, see Roberto Suro, "Saving the Treasures of Italy," *New York Times*, Dec. 21, 1986.

59. Getty Foundation, http://www.getty.edu/foundation/initiatives/current/panelpaintings/panel_paintings_vasari.html.

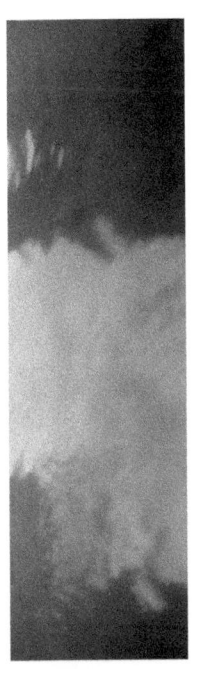

THEME PANEL: DISASTER PREPAREDNESS AND RESPONSE

THE UNLUCKY DITCH: FORWARD
THROUGH PREPARATION
FOR DISASTER

Jeanne Drewes

It seems to be a rule in life that it is through remembering, and not forgetting, that we can improve the likelihood of reducing loss. In my brief opening remarks for this session on the technologies of preventive conservation, I will argue that disaster preparedness and mitigation constitute an umbrella of aptitudes, perspectives, and technologies. These ideas, and the actions that they motivate, have emerged since the Flood in Florence as one of its most lasting impacts. Not all the changes in conservation are a result of the events of 1966, because there have been many advances in technology since then that have had a major impact on how we respond to disasters. But the impact of the Florence Flood continues to resonate. The three panelists who follow me do an admirable job of fleshing out the details through their case studies.

The 1966 Florence Flood was horrendous and inspiring all at once. Horrendous in its damage and destruction and inspiring in the solutions, many devised on the spot, for saving the treasures of Western civilization. The world responded to that imminent loss of Western culture; the young and old from countries far flung came to help. College students, professional conservators, art historians, and people who had visited and loved Florence were moved to go there to work, to send money, to be part of the tremendous effort to save as much as possible. The Arno River was nicknamed the "Unlucky Ditch" because of the many floods that had occurred. Not remembering the past can lead to disasters that might have been avoided. That was certainly true in Florence, where the Arno had flooded many times before. It's the forgetting that leaves cultural institutions ill prepared when disaster strikes, and one of the differences today is the strong preparedness efforts that have grown since that fateful event in 1966.

The broad effects of the Florence Flood from 1966 to the present, fifty years later, are perhaps not clearly measurable. But it is intuitively evident that in the fifty years since the Arno flooded its banks, many changes in professional practice can be attributed to the work of recovery. Included on my list of changes are advances in book conservation techniques, the professionalism accorded conservation after the event, the interconnectedness of the international conservation community, the development of partnerships across preservation communities to support training and recovery strategies, the use of images and communication technologies for raising support for recovery, and the development of commercial recovery services for disaster response.

The aftermath of the Flood in Florence had a quite direct impact on the Library of Congress. Some of the bookbinders who were on-site at Florence working to recover the thousands of books damaged by the flood and now thinking of themselves as conservators were hired to apply their expertise to save deteriorating collections at the library. Peter Waters and Don Etherington came to America from the United Kingdom after they had returned from their flood recovery to start a conservation program at the Library of Congress. Some of the methods they developed in Florence to deal with the unprecedented number of materials to be restored were instituted as the "phased" process for the collections at the library. That idea was also adopted by many other libraries. The Library of Congress also recognized the need to train staff for the new conservation lab, so part of the mission to care for the library's collection was the development of the training program. Part of that training was in disaster recovery techniques and batch processing of large amounts of materials to be treated.[1]

The timing of the flood coincided with the growth of the research collections in the United States and the need for conservation and preservation programs to care for those collections. Indeed, collections care as a new focus came about in the 1980s both in museums and in libraries.

Hands-on experience with disaster recovery is one of the continuing "opportunities" starting most notably with the Florence Flood; one becomes "expert" through the actual experience of recovering materials. The flood at the Colorado State University Library in 1997[2] and the fire at the Los Angeles Central Library in 1985[3] became hallmarks where individuals learned through doing and so became the experts and authors of books and articles about disaster planning and recovery. This followed in the tradition of those who saved materials after the Florence Flood writing and teaching about the methodologies they had developed.

In the United States, there have been and continue to be efforts, funded through the National Endowment of the Humanities (NEH) and the Institute of Museum and Library Services (IMLS), that provide training in the preparation of disaster plans, hands-on recovery, and risk management. Wide participation in these programs ensures that there is a cadre of knowledgeable professionals who know what steps to take and which resources to employ and can assist at the institutional or regional level when disaster strikes. Newly chartered regional preservation groups, such as the Northeast Document Conservation Center (NEDCC) as well as state libraries and archives, received funds for some of this training. National organizations such as the American Library Association (ALA), the Society of American Archivists (SAA), the American Institute for Conservation (AIC), and the nonprofit Heritage Preservation (now the Foundation of the American Institute for Conservation of Historic and Artistic Works) all provided and continue to provide programming and preconferences on the topic. Publications through these organizations and the publishers who sell to these sectors also found experienced experts to write manuals on disaster planning and recovery.

The same focus exists in the international community through the work of the International Federation of Library Associations (IFLA), the International Council of Museums (ICOM), and the International Centre for the Study of the Preservation and Restoration of Cultural Property (ICCROM).

Communication technology in 1966 ensured that the Flood in Florence was a watershed moment in the popular imagination. Television images and breaking news on radio broadcasts made such a difference in the response and donations received to support recovery. Additionally, a documentary film produced by Franco Zeffirelli, *Florence: Days of Destruction*, reached a worldwide audience with a direct appeal for recovery funds.

In Florence, books were dried in the tobacco barns, but later scientists and technologists working with the Library of Congress developed technologies to freeze-dry wet books and remove moisture through sublimation for disaster recovery of paper materials. Freeze-drying has now been embraced by commercial companies that have international reach and the resources to dry out entire buildings using warm, dry air, along with their contents of books, papers, films, and artifacts.

Even though the Arno River flood was a localized event, the shocking scope of damage to internationally valued cultural heritage attracted people from all over the world to volunteer. Today, wealthier individual countries are more likely to have their own national resources to respond to natural and human-made disasters that clearly affect cultural heritage sites. In the United States, National Heritage Responders (NHR) provides unified training and a twenty-four-hour call center staffed by volunteers to assist when disasters happen both nationally and—occasionally—internationally, as in the case of Haiti.[4] There are a variety of groups that help with cultural heritage devastation when it occurs, including IFLA. That said, cultural heritage disasters in war-torn countries such as Syria and Iraq remain an overwhelming challenge for the conservation profession.

One of the many impressions made by images from the Florence Flood recovery effort, a particularly striking one, is the clear lack of any personal protective equipment for responders. Today, due in part to research completed in the wake of the catastrophe of 9/11, the health dangers inherent in natural disasters are well documented and understood, so it is much more likely that appropriate action will be taken to protect responders from mold and other chemical pollutants that result from fire and water events. Today staff and responders use protective gear to avoid personal injury.

Other writers have documented associations and organizations that have been important contributors to the literature and training in disaster preparedness around the world. Beginning in the early 1980s, with the growth of preservation librarian positions and the establishment within ALA of a Preservation of Library Materials Section, now the Preservation and Reformatting Section (PARS), ALA-based resources that provided information about and training for disaster preparedness, response, and recovery began to be available. Today, these and many other resources are widely accessible on the web, significantly increasing awareness across libraries of all types and sizes.

The example set by the Peace Corps, created in 1961 by President John F. Kennedy, played out in the volunteer response to the Flood in Florence. The Peace Corps codified an ethic of volunteerism. The youthful and positive "can-do" energy marshaled in the 1960s was represented well in the outpouring of Mud Angels who descended on Florence from many countries, including the United States, and whose volunteered labor proved essential to the initial recovery efforts.

In spite of decades of devastating natural and human-made disasters, disaster planning is far from a ubiquitous activity of individual organizations or national governments. We know through the Heritage Health Index[5] that too many cultural institutions do not have disaster plans, even though more and more organizations are realizing the short- and long-term monetary value of assuming that damaging disasters are not a matter of "if" but rather a matter of "when."

Natural disasters are about far more than the damage that might happen to cultural heritage sites and resources. Disasters also test the varieties of human responses in a crisis. Among writings about disasters, of particular interest for our consideration of the aftermath of the Florence Flood is the work of Amanda Ripley. In *The Unthinkable: Who Survives When Disaster Strikes—and Why*, Ripley analyzes how people survived disasters such as 9/11, airplane crashes, and earthquakes.[6] For example, Ripley interviews people who survived a plane crash. They said they knew where the exit was before the crash, so it took them less time to escape. From a host of specific examples, Ripley suggests that people who experience a major disaster fall into three different types of disaster personalities: First, there are the people who freeze, whether in shock or not, and are incapable of acting without direction. Then there are people who rush in and act without thinking through an appropriate path forward. Finally, a third type of person shows the presence of mind to take in a scene and exercise a type of leadership that can find momentum in the face of chaos. The actions of restorers/conservators such as Peter Waters and Don Etherington displayed the third and most effective personality type.

As we have learned in this symposium, Waters was a consummate and experienced professional, while Etherington at the time served in an apprenticeship role, at least initially. Both shared a propensity to look beyond the problem at hand and chart a course ahead. In disasters in cultural institutions, there are the people who freeze or rush in, and there are the people who have already made a backup plan and are thinking about how best to execute that plan. There are people who take charge in a situation that requires someone to lead. When disaster strikes libraries, archives, and museums, it is the professional who must think about what needs to be done, analyze the situation, and step forward. This is the true legacy of the Florence Flood. Disasters by their nature cause disruption and loss, but the best recovery for disasters comes out of being prepared to act, not forgetting how loss can happen.

Notes

1. For Preservation Week 2016, Andrew Robb summarized the history of disaster preparedness at the Library of Congress. Robb, Andrew. "Emergency

Management since the Florence Flood: Federal Programs and National Initiatives." Library of Congress, April 28, 2016. http://www.loc.gov/preservation/outreach/tops/robb/index.html.

2. See Colorado State University. "Guide to the Records of the Library Flood, 1987–2008." http://lib.colostate.edu/archives/findingaids/university/ulif.html. Accessed on March 19, 2018.

3. See Los Angeles Public Library. Central Library Blog, "April 29 Marks 30th Anniversary of 1986 Fire." April 29, 2016. https://www.lapl.org/collections-resources/blogs/central-library/april-29-marks-30th-anniversary-1986-fire.

4. National Heritage Responders. https://www.conservation-us.org/emergencies/national-heritage-responders#.WdkxgVtyKUk. Accessed on March 18, 2018.

5. Heritage Health Index. "A Public Trust at Risk: The Heritage Health Index Report on the State of America's Collections." 2005. https://www.imls.gov/publications/heritage-health-index-full-report. Accessed on March 18, 2018.

6. Ripley, Amanda. *The Unthinkable: Who Survives When Disaster Strikes—and Why*. New York: Three Rivers Press, 2009.

BRIDGING THE RIVERS

Nancy E. Kraft

Kevin Driedger at the Library of Michigan once dubbed me the "Queen of Disaster," but sometimes I think when it comes to disasters, I'm the character in Al Capp's *Li'l Abner* comic strip—Joe Btfsplk, the jinx who brought disastrous misfortune to all around him! We have nine major rivers in the state of Iowa, and so the odds of flooding are high. This contribution to the symposium proceedings is an overview of my experiences with cultural heritage disasters since 1993 and a reflection on some of the changes I have seen in that time.

Two weeks after I became preservation librarian for the State Historical Society of Iowa (SHSI) in 1993, Iowa rivers and creeks started flooding, and high water continued until mid-August. That was my first disaster response experience. SHSI pulled together an assessment team and traveled around the state providing training and advice to the small institutions that had been impacted. In 1996, SHSI conservator Jane Meggers and I wrote a disaster plan and conducted training for our staff. Three weeks later, a pipe broke on the top floor, and the entire building took on water. In 2001, after just a few months at the University of Iowa Libraries, the Old Capitol dome in Iowa City burst into flames during renovation. Then, just to reinforce my hands-on experience, we had a major mold outbreak on campus in 2003. On reflection, I think all this was just training, because in 2008, we had massive flooding in Iowa. Both the Iowa River in Iowa City, where I work, and the Cedar River in Cedar Rapids, where I live, flooded. Those events were followed by some minor experiences in 2010 with the Skunk River, and then again this year, 2016, in Cedar Rapids—the second-highest flood level we've ever had. Throw in a few tornadoes along the way, and I feel like I have been dealing with disasters most of my career. So what has changed over these twenty-five years?

The ways we communicate during disasters have changed tremendously. In 1993, we communicated by fax machine. National organizations, including the Federal Emergency Management Agency (FEMA) and the American Institute for Conservation of Historic and Artistic Works (AIC), faxed masses of information to affected Iowa institutions. University of Iowa Libraries preservation librarian Cathy Larson and I had a horrible time trying to sort out what information would be pertinent to us. We picked out the most practical and useful and created the *Flood Recovery Booklet*. The state printer printed and distributed the booklets. Today we have the World Wide Web, email, and cell phones. Moreover, we have standardized the way to handle flood recovery for the various types of materials we have in our cultural collections. Now we can focus on getting the job done instead of sifting through reams of advice and information.

Our understanding and use of personal protection equipment have changed dramatically. In 1993, we had no idea that we needed to protect ourselves during a disaster response. No one on the team used protective gear. We went into buildings covered with bird droppings, mold, and gunk from rivers. I don't like to remember what we encountered. By 2008, we understood the kinds of protection we needed. Ellen McCrady and her *Mold Reporter* publication[1] and Mary Lou Florian's research on mold and heritage collections[2] made a significant difference to our understanding and ability to deal with mold safely. Since the 1990s, too, more and more training has become available on staying mentally healthy as responders, and we have a better understanding of the emotional impact disasters have on those dealing with the loss of collections. These developments are a good thing; over and over again in the field, I have seen the importance of recognizing our mental responses and adjusting for them.

Public awareness has also come a long way. In 1993, one of our biggest problems was that the rain continued the whole summer. It seemed as if we were flooding all the time. But temperatures never went above eighty degrees or so. In frugal Iowa, we didn't use our air conditioners, and we didn't use fans. As a result, we experienced a series of mold outbreaks. We did not know that we needed the air conditioners and fans to prevent mold. By 2008, even the general public knew to put things in freezers. This became apparent that year when I met a woman who had one book survive the flooding of her business, but she knew to put it in the freezer. Later she brought it to University of Iowa Libraries, where we salvaged it for her.

Early on, I focused my training on library material—books, photographs, microfilm—with the thought that this area of expertise would be most needed in a disaster. I did not think initially that the entire built environment of the library is impacted in a flood. For example, during stabilization of the SHSI whole-building incident of 1996, I learned about wood swelling and the importance of opening wooden drawers quickly lest they swell shut. That's when I started concentrating on really learning about the building itself, as well as the materials in it. My experiences gave me a broader understanding of disaster planning and recovery: to respond effectively, you cannot just have a specialized understanding of the objects collected, but you also must understand the whole system and environment in which they are kept.

Methods for drying out buildings have changed. In 1998, we used turbo fans, turned up the heat in the building, opened windows—anything we could do to get the building dried out. By 2008, it was common practice to contract with a commercial company to use venting tubes or flex ductwork along with a desiccant system.

Another big change is environmental monitoring. By 2008, we were routinely monitoring our environment with data loggers. By the time of the Iowa City flood, we knew what the building environment could and could not do because we had the charts documenting our temperature and humidity over a number of years. Soon after the flood, our insurance company brought in a team of people to walk around the library with their temperature and humidity sensors. They kept telling us, "We still have to keep these vents going because you're not down to 50 percent relative humidity yet." I responded, "We're never down to 50 percent. This is Iowa in summer; 65 percent is normal." We saved a lot of money and completed the remediation process much more quickly because we had information on our environment ahead of time and could pull the evidence when we needed it.

We've learned to use triage methods in a number of different ways, not just to identify things that are most valuable. Adapted from the experience of battlefront medics, triage quickly separates damaged materials into three categories: safe for now, hopeless, and salvageable with immediate attention. Disaster response focuses particularly strongly on the third category. For example, in 2008, we could leave in place items that were dry; they were shelved above the eight-foot flood mark. We put our volunteers to work evacuating those materials that wouldn't get damaged by the handling. Meanwhile the disaster response team met to decide how to deal with the other more seriously damaged materials, making decisions about who should do what and what we were not going to try to salvage. We were able to act more efficiently by applying triage to the collection on the macro level even before we had a detailed plan in place.

In the beginning, I never thought about disaster response as an evacuation process, but if you're in a flood situation, you hope to get your collections out before the water gets there. And not just collections. It was in the 2000s that we started thinking, talking, and seeing literature about Continuity of Operations (COOP) plans. In 2008, as we were moving our collections from the basement, we were also taking out our equipment—book repair presses, computers, and servers—so we could stay in business as a library and keep staff employed while safety authorities kept us locked out of our buildings. Continuity of operations planning is now standard operating procedure in the threat of disaster, recommended by FEMA for agencies at all levels of government.[3] Of course, we don't think about our servers as much anymore because many of us are following best practices and keeping digital records in multiple sites or in the cloud.

One lesson I've learned about disaster preparedness and mitigation is that politics can work either against you or for you. We were so lucky in 2008. One of our county superintendents was a former museum curator, and one of our state senators was keenly aware that the flooding had not only damaged and destroyed homes in the area but also caused major losses to our community culture. Salvage teams for our museums were the first ones the authorities allowed past safety barriers because the community leaders understood the importance of saving our cultural heritage resources. What a refreshing change from typical past practices!

Cultural heritage responders are increasingly collaborating with other disaster response professionals. Together, we are advancing, experimenting, and learning better ways to respond to disasters and to prepare ahead of time. In 2008, flood control was all about sandbags, and we had very short notice of an impending disaster. By the time of the 2016 Cedar Rapids flood, advance notice gave us time to put up ten miles of HESCO barriers, a sophisticated alternative to sandbags, borrowed from the United States Army. Since HESCO barriers have to rest on a flat surface, some buildings still ended up in the river, but we saved the majority of them. The city experienced little damage because of these barriers and the advance warning afforded by improvements in medium-term weather forecasting.

The establishment of disaster response networks among cultural institutions has become more common in recent decades. Networking can make a big difference. In 2008, we had five professionals ready at the gate waiting for authorities to give permission to enter the flood area. That's when I learned that having an outside professional is a huge asset, even if the institution's own curators are well trained. Someone on-site who is not emotionally invested in the materials can see problems and solutions more objectively. The curator of the African American Museum of Iowa in Cedar Rapids estimated that because we were there with her, we were able to save 90 percent of those collections from the 2008 flood.

Other reminiscences of the Florence Flood at this symposium mention batch work. I can confirm that batch work is a good practice for disaster recovery and salvage. At the University of Iowa Libraries, we converted part of our conservation lab into a disaster salvage workshop after the 2008 floods. We asked staff from each of the three museums we assisted to identify the most important types of material from their collections. If they said phonograph records were really important, we would focus just on those materials for a block of time. We worked out protocols for phonograph records and ran the protocols by the curators; they'd sign off on them. After the initial consultation, we only contacted them when we encountered exceptions. This methodology allowed the curators to get back to the work of recovering the building and getting the museum back in business. The African American Museum of Iowa was open within six months—and they had taken in seven feet of water!

Finally, there are the disaster plans themselves. I suspect that these past few decades could be called the era of the disaster plan for cultural heritage institutions. Not everyone has a disaster plan, and I doubt everyone ever will. But the profession certainly has simplified and codified the process. We have countless new tools at our disposal, including our cell phones and specialized apps for them. Training has become widely available. The curator at the African American Museum of Iowa took a training course just a couple weeks before the 2008 flood. When the waters hit, she didn't have a written plan in place, but she had the Emergency Response and Salvage Wheel[4] with her. She consulted it religiously, and it helped her. The wheel was her lifeline, and holding on to it got her through the event.

When sifting through my own files to prepare this paper, I found a report that I had written in 1993, as a total beginner. I had forgotten how we'd had to work around all kinds of institutional grandstanding and politics. Different heritage organizations in the region—museums, libraries, archives—did not have a way to work together. In the report I recommended that in the future, we should work with the Department of Emergency Management, continue training, and maintain networks. Twenty-four years later, those recommendations still hold true. When it comes to preparing for the inevitable waterborne disaster, perhaps there are some universal laws that we should all heed.

Notes

1. McCrady, Ellen (ed.). *The Mold Reporter*. Newsletter. Austin, TX: Abbey Publications, 2001–4.
2. Florian, Mary-Lou E. *Fungal Facts: Solving Fungal Problems in Heritage Collections*. London: Archetype Publications, 2002.
3. Federal Emergency Management Administration. "Continuity of Operations (COOP)." https://www.fema.gov/media-library/assets/documents/72598.
4. Emergency Response and Salvage Wheel. Washington, DC: National Institute for the Conservation of Cultural Property, 1997. Reprinted in 2016 for Friends of the American Institute for Conservation of Historic and Artistic Works (FAIC). http://www.conservation-us.org/emergencies/aaslh-technical-leaflet-resources#.WT5y_3XytIp.

THE FLORENCE FLOODS OF TODAY

Doris A. Hamburg

In November 1966, news reports and dramatic images vividly captured the raging, swollen Arno River as it engulfed the city of Florence. Upon receding, the river torrents left in their wake massive destruction and damage to the city and the beautiful art and historical treasures for which Florence is so well known—paintings, sculptures, books, manuscripts, archives, monuments, buildings—as well as personal and commercial property and more. The flood was like an assault, not just on Italy's patrimony, but on Western culture and perhaps all civilization.

The relatively fresh memory of World War II's destruction twenty years earlier to both material culture as well as intangible cultural heritage[1] across Europe and Asia intensified the blow of seeing the flood's impact and contributed to the immediate international response and outpouring of financial and other aid and support to address Florence's loss and destruction. Conservators gathered from many different countries to develop and implement strategies on behalf of the muddy, damaged artifacts. In addition, volunteers, dubbed "Mud Angels," came from around the world to help as much as they could.

Renaissance historian Myron Gilmore wrote shortly after the floodwaters receded about how Florence's libraries and archives were especially hard hit: "What happened to archives and libraries, . . . means the interruption of the life of the Florentine scholarly community. . . . The Biblioteca Nazionale suffered a disaster such as few libraries, if any, in history have encountered."[2] The conservation methods and strategies implemented in order to recover from the Florence Flood have long been viewed as the beginning of modern-day library and archives conservation.

The Florence Flood was a seminal event in the development of cultural heritage conservation and emergency preparedness, as well as recovery and response strategies for cultural heritage. Many significant disasters have occurred since 1966, and more will take place in the future. This paper investigates the current state and outlook on what we could call the Florence Floods of today—what we can expect to face in the future and how we will be able to meet those challenges. While our primary focus pertains to tangible cultural heritage, there are parallels and interdependencies related to intangible cultural heritage that are critical to address in any disaster.[3]

Natural Disasters

Florence had flooded many times prior to 1966, although it had been more than four hundred years since a flood of similar magnitude had engulfed Florence. Since 1966, the Arno River has flooded again multiple times—however, on a much smaller scale. Some changes have been implemented to lower the flooding risks. Unfortunately, due to space constraints, the Biblioteca Nazionale Centrale de Firenze (BNCF) is once again storing materials in the building's lower levels, which were most damaged in 1966. Looking to the future and Florence's capacity to respond to floods, considerably more work is needed to prevent a repeat of what took place in 1966, as noted by a panel convened in Rome in 2015:

> It is not a question of whether a flood of the magnitude of 1966 or greater
> will occur, but when. In fact, the level of protection that exists in Flor-
> ence at the present time does not yet provide the risk reduction needed

for the city and is not on a level appropriate to the citizens and treasures that rest within the city. If, under current conditions, a 1966-like flood occurred, the consequences to human lives, treasures, other properties and community infrastructure could be much more catastrophic than they were in 1966.[4]

The city of Florence is using the fiftieth anniversary commemoration as a focal point for generating attention and action to improve preparedness and planning.[5] Florence, its cultural heritage institutions, and the Italian government must decide how much protection to provide and the level of risk they can accept. This must be balanced by allocating the funding required for implementation and developing a timetable that takes into account the various risk factors.

Major disasters—encompassing flooding, droughts, tropical cyclones (hurricanes and typhoons), earthquakes, tsunamis, tornadoes, and extreme fires—are products of weather patterns, environmental changes, and, in some cases, human actions. Records of disasters go back millennia and, in a given location, may reoccur on a cyclical basis due to particular risk factors such as communities built on earthquake fault lines or near a river that may overflow with heavy rains. According to the Environmental Defense Fund, "The number of natural disasters has doubled in the past few decades—90 percent of them are weather related."[6] Over the last few years, very significant worldwide natural disasters have taken place in Nepal, Haiti, India, the United States, Chile, Japan, China, and Italy, to name but a few, causing thousands of deaths and major damage to communities, property, and cultural heritage and billions of dollars in losses.

During the last fifty years, emergency management has developed into its own profession with graduate-level education, research, and specializations, including medicine, fire, and security. Experience and knowledge have increased significantly regarding what is needed to prepare for and respond to a cultural heritage disaster.

A historical review provides information on previous disasters and the potential for future ones; however, not all disasters can be anticipated. Assessing risks,[7] followed by planning and preventive actions, is critical in mitigating damage. Risk assessment and preventive strategies that include application of pertinent building codes, materials, and other mitigation strategies are fundamental to preserving cultural heritage over the long term; however, much is still to be done. Such risk assessment and mitigation activities are being undertaken worldwide more than ever before from the collection and building/site levels to the community and regional levels. Mutual concerns by different entities can support efficiency in achieving needed results. Traditional building materials and styles that have stood the test of time are useful to maintain. Modern materials should be selected carefully for appropriateness in the particular setting. Such cultural heritage support can be cost intensive yet invisible until it is put to the test in an emergency. Therefore, it is sometimes considered "unglamorous" for fund-raising purposes. Analysis to determine the costs of cultural heritage disaster losses provides sobering information and cost-benefit support for allocating resources.[8] Numerous sites of global cultural and religious significance were damaged in the 2015 Nepal earthquake. Those sites that had previously been retrofitted for earthquake resilience came through the quake in much better condition than those without the additional structural support.[9]

In growing numbers, heritage preservation professionals have been reaching out to governmental and community emergency networks to connect in advance of disasters in order to understand each other's needs and to develop the best methodologies for working together when required. Examples of these efforts include Alliance for Response[10] networks, of which there are currently twenty-six across the US, as well as the United States Federal National Planning System,[11] which includes five frameworks that address cultural heritage as part of their mandates: protection, prevention, mitigation, response, and recovery. The goals of the US State Heritage Emergency Partnership are to "provide strategies to cultivate close working relationships among state agencies, heighten their commitment to protect cultural and historic resources, and increase the sustainability of statewide initiatives that preserve these resources."[12]

Climate Change: An Inestimable Threat

Climate change poses significant risks to cultural heritage, raising innumerable questions and concerns. There are escalating worries worldwide related to increased sea levels and the growing frequency of extreme weather events that have already been affecting the preservation of cultural heritage—for example, as a result of flooding. Scientific modeling of the rise in sea levels has identified the likely impact on some of the most vulnerable cultural heritage sites.[13] Images of at-risk cultural heritage in Venice, London, India's Elephanta Island, New York City, and Algiers provide vivid visuals of what future to expect.[14] Even if greenhouse gas emissions are reduced significantly over coming decades, extreme weather will continue to increase, as will sea levels, augmenting existing risks and producing new ones, and "the risks of abrupt or irreversible changes increase as the magnitude of the warming increases."[15] It is likely that the Arno River will flood to the 1966 level or higher much sooner than 350 years from now; historically infrequent flooding events are becoming common in many regions around the world as a result of our changing climate.[16]

London's Thames River sea barriers were highly advanced when built in 1984 and have proven very effective. Based on the increasing rate of sea level rise and increasingly frequent and heavy rainfalls, however, the existing sea barriers are expected to reach their limits of effectiveness sooner than anticipated. Efforts are under way to determine the additional protections needed to secure London from future flooding. The risks to English heritage are enormous and are being examined at the highest levels of government in order to avoid or minimize the loss of their highly significant cultural treasures. Coastlines are receding at varying rates with a range of effects on cultural heritage. Peter F. Smith notes, however, that the United Kingdom's largest landowner, the National Trust, "manages some of the most scenic coastal landscape in Britain and has come to the conclusion that some of it will be radically changed or lost . . . because it is no longer possible to hold back the rising seas and coastal erosion."[17]

The international cultural heritage community has been focusing its attention on climate change and its effects on cultural heritage for some time. A joint report from the World Heritage Centre, its advisory bodies, and a broad group of experts to the thirtieth session of the World Heritage Committee, held in Vilnius in 2006, advanced strategies for addressing the most critical issues: "Experience and lessons learned on addressing Climate Change stress the need for using a number of management responses at national and local levels."[18] Looking strategically twenty, twenty-five, or thirty years ahead, working toward five- to ten-year objectives, the World Heritage Centre report identifies a number of key elements to be addressed simultaneously, including the following:

1. "If a Management Plan is specifically designed and formatted to foster its use as a working document which can be updated on a regular basis, then it can become a key tool in the effective stewardship of World Heritage sites under threat from Climate Change and actions in response to Climate Change can be flexibly introduced throughout the document."

2. "No one can work alone in this complex field. Strengthening of existing networks is necessary, along with ensuring that Climate Change issues become a part of the exchange of information within those networks. The environmental effects on cultural heritage such as Climate Change are trans-boundary. At the very least, regional networks need to be strengthened and focused on Climate Change adaptation."

3. "There is a need for more research on the effects of Climate Change on both the physical heritage and the social and cultural processes that they are a part of."

4. "The obligation under the *World Heritage Convention* to develop management systems for World Heritage sites provides an opportunity to integrate Climate Change adaptation measures in the process. Documents such as management plans should include a statement of the objectives necessary for the long-term preservation of the World Heritage sites and its landscape

setting, aiming to balance the interests of conservation, public access, and the interests of those who live and work in the area." Conduct risk and vulnerability assessments.

5. Local, regional, and global public and political support must be developed and expanded well in advance of a crisis.

The following actions are also essential in light of climate change and to prepare for the broad range of emergencies and disasters independent of cause. There is a need to adapt and refine management emergency plans and strategies from the local to regional levels and up. Among the elements needing attention are the following:

i. Enhancement of appropriate education and traditional skills
ii. Rigorous ongoing monitoring and maintenance
iii. Research to support national/regional decision-making
iv. Planning for emergency preparedness
v. Reevaluation of management priorities in response to climate change
vi. Training on the various problems and possible responses to climate change in all aspects of conservation activity—namely, development of traditional skills, monitoring, management, and emergency preparedness

Various efforts to adapt to our changing climate are being implemented effectively locally and globally. Climate change, however, is highly complex and its impacts wide ranging. Fully mitigating its effects is now impossible; even with concerted mitigation efforts worldwide, impacts will be widespread. The impacts of climate change, independent of concerted efforts on the 2015 Paris Agreement, will be felt for the foreseeable future; the immediate goal should be to reduce the effects of this baked-in change and to mitigate greenhouse gas emissions such that future changes are minimized.[19] Cultural heritage institutions have a role in mitigating climate change as outlined in the recommendation of the Intergovernmental Panel on Climate Change 2014 /SPM 4.1: "Adaptation and mitigation responses are underpinned by common enabling factors. These include effective institutions and governance, innovation and investments in environmentally sound technologies and infrastructure, sustainable livelihoods and behavioural and life-style choices."[20]

Human-Caused Disasters

Cultural heritage loss and disasters occur also as a result of actions by people, not just natural causes. Whether inadvertent or intentional, significant damage can occur from neglect or negligence—for example, by not maintaining infrastructure, security, environmental systems, storage, or plumbing. The Convention concerning the Protection of the World's Cultural and Natural Heritage, signed in 1972 and implemented in 1975, initiated the international process of designating World Heritage Sites (cultural and natural) under UNESCO to provide accountability and help guard against loss of the world's most significant sites. World Heritage Sites are identified on the List of World Heritage in Danger with the goal of calling attention to their needs for improvements. Development of the World Heritage Sites list and the Dutch Delta Plan[21] are two significant examples of efforts during the last decades to inventory and assess the needs of cultural heritage on global and national scales, respectively. Such risk assessments are also frequently done at the collection, institutional, or facility level.[22]

Willful destruction of cultural heritage—as a result of arson or vandalism, or for ideological reasons—also takes place. Despite vociferous international pleas to spare them, in March 2001, the supreme Taliban leader in Afghanistan ordered the destruction of the two magnificent and immense Bamiyan Buddhas, which had been carved into the mountain rock 2,700 years ago. The Taliban viewed the destruction as just and important in order to rid Afghanistan of reminders of its idolatrous, non-Islamic past.

Recently in Syria, the Islamic State of Iraq and Syria (ISIS) damaged and looted 70 percent of the remarkable Hellenistic, Parthian, and Roman archaeological site Dura Europos.[23] ISIS has also destroyed ancient statues and devastated other archaeological sites in order to plunder them and sell the artifacts on the black market for their own financial gain. Damage to cultural heritage has long been a casualty of war, whether intentionally or due to a lack of adequate planning, as observed with the looting of thousands of artifacts from the Iraq Museum in Baghdad in 2003. Also, for a variety of reasons, wartime strategic goals have not always taken cultural heritage into consideration. Since the 2003 Iraq War, the US Army has developed a guide for soldiers on the protection of cultural property in a wartime environment to improve protection of cultural heritage.[24]

Following World War II, the International Committee of the Blue Shield was established to reduce loss of cultural heritage during war and at other times. According to its website, "The Blue Shield is the cultural equivalent of the Red Cross. It is the symbol specified in the 1954 Hague Convention for marking cultural sites to give them protection from attack in the event of armed conflict."[25] The International Committee of the Blue Shield "advises and assists in responding to events such as war in former Yugoslavia and hurricane damage in Central America."[26]

Progress in Addressing Cultural Heritage Emergencies

In the fifty years since the Florence Flood, significant communication advances have yielded faster and greater awareness of global events and their impact, as well as sharing of technology and research. Efforts to discuss and address issues of common interest and concern can be beneficial—and also challenging. More than ever, people are increasingly aware and respectful of cultures, perspectives, and values other than their own, despite the contrary examples of the Taliban and others cited above. Global considerations are interwoven with professional, business, cultural, and political activities more today than ever. Conservation strategies have grown more consistent across the globe, due to various factors including the prominent role that international professional organizations play in facilitating communication and collaboration, the accessibility of more professional literature and training, and increased professional travel.

In 2004, the Heritage Health Index determined that "80 percent of US collecting institutions [did] not have a written emergency/disaster plan that include[d] collections and staff trained to carry it out."[27] In the last twenty years, cultural heritage organizations in the US and abroad have dedicated considerable resources to raising awareness about the need to plan for tangible cultural heritage emergencies and have served as catalysts and sources for expertise in improving disaster planning and preparedness. These include the Institute of Museum and Library Services (IMLS); American Library Association (ALA); Society of American Archivists (SAA); the United Nations Educational, Scientific, and Cultural Organization (UNESCO); Heritage Preservation, the Getty Conservation Institute (GCI); the American Institute for Conservation of Historic and Artistic Works (AIC); the five coordinating organizations supporting the International Committee of the Blue Shield—the International Council on Archives (ICA), International Federation of Library Associations (IFLA), International Council of Museums (ICOM), International Council on Monuments and Sites (ICOMOS), and Coordinating Council of Audiovisual Archives Association (CCAAA)—US regional centers; and others. The International Centre for the Study of the Preservation and Restoration of Cultural Property (ICCROM) has been offering train-the-trainer programs for professionals in Africa, Asia, the Middle East, and elsewhere with the goal of significantly expanding available expertise for responding to cultural heritage emergencies, particularly in times of crisis.[28] In the US, May Day has been designated as the day that cultural institutions launch staff and public awareness campaigns related to cultural heritage emergency preparedness on behalf of their collections and to assist the public with their personal collections. Following Hurricane Katrina in 2005, the US Council of State Archivists (COSA) launched a widespread and highly effective initiative to train state and local governments on preparing for emergencies and how to respond in order to ensure the preservation of vital records and other holdings.[29] These are examples of some of the initiatives during the last two decades that have significantly furthered disaster preparedness, response, and recovery readiness in the US and globally.

AIC maintains an emergency response team available twenty-four hours per day that has supported regional emergencies in the United States and Haiti. Large cultural heritage institutions—such as the National Archives and Records Administration, the National Park Service, the Smithsonian Institution, the University of Iowa Libraries, regional conservation centers, and the Library of Congress—have extensive experience in responding to cultural heritage emergencies. Due to a variety of factors, including the age, condition, and location of the facility and the type of emergency affecting it, every cultural heritage emergency presents a unique set of circumstances and requires situation-specific solutions. Each emergency experience, however, builds on those that have come before.

While every disaster is unique, cumulative training and experience continue to improve response and recovery with each event. Today there are far more conservation professionals with the disaster experience and training to take on such challenges than there were in 1966. Over the last fifty years, with the growth of graduate conservation education, the profession has developed significantly. There have been many emergencies that provided opportunities for professionals to get experience in responding to and recovering cultural heritage materials from disasters. Research and experience have also yielded significant advances in disaster response and recovery.

Today's Florence Floods

Disasters will continue, and likely at a higher rate due to increased threats as a result of climate change. We require ongoing risk assessment, vigilance, preparation, and prioritization. Disaster preparedness is an ongoing activity that is never complete. When it is not possible to prevent a disaster through risk mitigation, it is best to have plans in place to manage it and to reduce the disaster's impact, its costs, and its long-term implications.[30] Today, we are better prepared and have better tools to address disasters than fifty years ago due to broader awareness and improved communication, increased numbers of trained preservation professionals, and increased investments in emergency planning.

As a result of international professional efforts, more disaster planning for cultural heritage has taken place than ever before. Increasingly, the cultural heritage field is working together with civic first responders to understand respective priorities and needs in order to be as effective as possible in the event of a disaster. Activities of professional organizations internationally and nationally provide examples of successful coalitions for preserving cultural heritage worldwide, particularly during disasters. Much work is still to be done to have adequate emergency plans, the necessary technology, protective mechanisms, protocols, infrastructure, and strategies to mitigate the greatest risks. Additionally, it is important to think in terms of establishing priorities; otherwise, resource and time limitations often force ad hoc decisions regarding what can or cannot be done. Any discussion of priority setting is fraught with controversy, because explicit statements about what to save are a conscious acceptance of loss.

Significant progress in disaster preparedness, response, and recovery of cultural heritage has been achieved. Nonetheless, substantial disaster preparedness work is still needed to address large-scale and ongoing threats, including the effects of climate change that will affect cultural heritage in the future. Making disaster preparedness a priority, and committing the resources that it requires, has never been more important. More than ever before, stewards of cultural heritage have the knowledge, tools, strategies, and awareness necessary to make a meaningful difference in planning for, preparing for, and responding to disasters in order to preserve cultural heritage for future generations.

Notes

1. The United Nations Educational, Scientific, and Cultural Organization (UNESCO) World Heritage Centre defines intangible cultural heritage as "the practices, expressions, knowledge and skills that communities, groups and sometimes individuals recognise as part of their cultural heritage. Also called living cultural heritage, it is usually expressed in one of the following forms: oral traditions; performing arts; social practices, rituals and festive events; knowledge and practices concerning nature and the universe; and traditional craftsmanship." "Frequently Asked Questions (FAQ): Intangible

Heritage," UNESCO World Heritage Centre, accessed July 20, 2017, http://whc.unesco.org/en/faq/40.

2. Myron P. Gilmore, "Progress of Restoration in Florence," *Renaissance Quarterly* 20 (1967): 100–102; CRIA Committee to Rescue Italian Art, accessed July 16, 2017, http://cria.itatti.harvard.edu/exhibits/show/the-rescue/paper.

3. "Convention for the Safeguarding of the Intangible Cultural Heritage 2003," UNESCO, Paris, October 17, 2003, accessed July 6, 2017, http://portal.unesco.org/en/ev.php-URL_ID=17716&URL_DO=DO_TOPIC&URL_SECTION=201.html.

4. Gunter Bloschl, Gerard Galloway, Marcelo Garcia, Alberto Montanari, Giovanni Seminara, and Luca Solari, *Saving a World Treasure: Protecting Florence from Flooding* (Florence: Firenze University Press, 2017).

5. Firenze 2016's goal was "to perform initiatives on the 50th anniversary of the Florence 1966 flood event to resume memories and to improve prevention in such events to protect better in the future people, cultural heritage, environment and economics." "The Project," Firenze 2016, accessed July 16, 2017, http://toscana.firenze2016.it/en/the-project/.

6. "Why You Need to Care about Climate Change—Now," Environmental Defense Fund, accessed July 25, 2017, https://www.edf.org/climate/why-you-need-care-about-climate-change-now.

7. "Risk is often represented as the probability of occurrence of hazardous events or trends multiplied by the magnitude of the consequences if these events occur. Therefore, high risk can result not only from high probability outcomes but also from low probability outcomes with very severe consequences. This makes it important to assess the full range of possible outcomes, from low probability tail outcomes to very likely outcomes." Core Writing Team, R. K. Pachauri, and L. A. Meyer (eds.), *Climate Change 2014: Synthesis Report* (Geneva: IPCC, 2014), 36, accessed July 25, 2017, http://ar5-syr.ipcc.ch/ipcc/ipcc/resources/pdf/IPCC_SynthesisReport.pdf.

8. Dilani Dassanayake, Andreas Burzel, and Hocine Oumeraci, "Evaluation of Cultural Losses," December 10, 2012, accessed July 20, 2017, https://www.tu-braunschweig.de/Medien-DB/hykuxr/43_dassanayake_et_al_xtremrisk_evaluation_of_cultural_losses.pdf.

9. Gunda Achterhold, "About 700 Projects in Asia Alone," How Germany Ticks Deutschland, April 18, 2016, accessed July 19, 2017, https://www.deutschland.de/en/topic/politics/development-dialogue/about-700-projects-in-asia-alone; Randolph Langenbach, "Understanding What Works: Lessons from Earthquake Resistant Traditional Construction," in *Heritage at Risk, Special Edition: Cultural Heritage and Natural Disasters/Risk Preparedness and the Limits of Prevention*, ed. Hans-Rudolf Meier, Michael Petzet, and Thomas Will (Munich: ICOMOS, 2007), 87–98, accessed March 18, 2018, https://www.icomos.org/images/Cultural_Heritage_and_Natural_Disasters.pdf.

10. "Alliance for Response," Foundation for the American Institute for Conservation of Historic and Artistic Works, accessed July 19, 2017, http://www
.heritageemergency.org/initiatives/alliance-for-response/afr-home/.

11. "National Planning Frameworks," Federal Emergency Management Agency, accessed July 19, 2017, https://www.fema.gov/national-planning-frameworks.

12. "State Heritage Emergency Partnership," Foundation for the American Institute for Conservation of Historic and Artistic Works, accessed July 19, 2017, http://www.heritageemergency.org/initiatives/state-heritage
-emergency-partnerships/shep-home/.

13. Ben Marzeion and Anders Levermann, "Loss of Cultural World Heritage and Currently Inhabited Places to Sea-Level Rise," *IOPScience Environmental Research Letters* 9 (2014), accessed July 5, 2017, http://iopscience.iop
.org/article/10.1088/1748-9326/9/3/034001/pdf.

14. Sara Kramer, "Five Priceless Locations That Are Slowly Drowning under Water," *Business Insider*, May 25, 2016, accessed July 5, 2017, http://
www.businessinsider.com/rising-oceans-locations-under-water-2016-5/#1
-venice-1.

15. *Climate Change 2014*, 16.

16. European Parliament, "Policy Department Economic and Scientific Policy: Climate Change and Natural Disasters: Scientific Evidence of a Possible Relation between Recent Natural Disasters and Climate Change: (IP/A/ENVI/FWC/2005–35)," accessed July 25, 2017, http://ecologic.eu/sites/
files/project/2013/Brief_CC_and_natural_disasters_scientific_evidence_of
_relation_Jan_2006_EP_version.pdf.

17. Peter F. Smith, *Climate Change and Cultural Heritage: A Race against Time*, chapter 5, "Predictions for the UK" (New York: Routledge, 2014).

18. May Cassar, Christopher Young, Tony Weighell, David Sheppard, Bastian Bomhard, and Pedro Rosabal, in collaboration with the World Heritage Centre and its Advisory Bodies, *Predicting and Managing the Effects of Climate Change on World Heritage*, updated to account for the suggestions of the group of experts during the Meeting on Climate Change and World Heritage, held at UNESCO headquarters on the March 16 and 17, 2006 (Vilnius, Lithuania: UNESCO, 2006), accessed July 6, 2017, http://whc
.unesco.org/document/6670.

19. "The Paris Agreement," United Nations Framework Convention on Climate Change, accessed July 24, 2017, http://unfccc.int/paris_agreement/
items/9485.php.

20. "SPM 4.1," *IPCC, 2014: Climate Change 2014*, 26, accessed July 25, 2017, http://ar5-syr.ipcc.ch/ipcc/ipcc/resources/pdf/IPCC_SynthesisReport.pdf.

21. Gerrit De Bruin, "An Assessment of Deltaplan: The Dutch National Preservation Strategy," *Liber Quarterly* 14:356–67.

22. Robert Waller, "Risk Management Applied to Preventive Conservation," in Society for the Preservation of Natural History Collections, *A Preventive*

Conservation Approach, ed. C. L Rose, C. A. Hawks, and H. H. Genoways (Iowa City: Storage of Natural History Collections, 1995), 21–28, accessed July 24, 2017, http://www.museum-sos.org/docs/WallerSPNHC1995.pdf.

23. Deborah Amos and Alison Meuse, "Via Satellite, Tracking the Plunder of Middle East Cultural History," radio program, *All Things Considered: National Public Radio*, March 10, 2015, accessed July 16, 2017, http://www .npr.org/sections/parallels/2015/03/10/392077801/via-satellite-tracking -the-plunder-of-middle-east-cultural-history.

24. Headquarters, Department of the Army, "GTA 41-01-002," *Civil Affairs Arts, Monuments, and Archives*, August 2009, accessed July 21, 2017, http:// www.au.af.mil/au/awc/awcgate/army/gta41-01-002_arts_monuments_and _archives.pdf.

25. "ICOM and the International Committee of the Blue Shield," International Council of Museums (ICOM), accessed July 16, 2017, http://archives.icom .museum/emergency.html.

26. The International Committee of the Blue Shield (ICBS) addresses the needs of museums, archives, libraries, monuments, and sites. It draws on the expertise, capabilities, and international networks of the five organiza- tions sponsoring cultural heritage organizations. "ICOM and the Interna- tional Committee of the Blue Shield: The International Committee of the Blue Shield (ICBS): Working for the Protection of the World's Cultural Heritage," accessed July 16, 2017, http://archives.icom.museum/emergency .html. Also see Blue Shield International, http://www.ancbs.org/cms/en/ home2.

27. Heritage Health Index, *A Public Trust at Risk: The Heritage Health Index Report on the State of America's Collections* (Washington, DC: Heritage Pres- ervation and Institute of Museum and Library Services, 2005), 62–63, American Institute for Conservation of Historic and Artistic Works, accessed July 19, 2017, http://www.conservation-us.org/docs/default-source/hhi/ hhifull.pdf.

28. See course: "First Aid to Cultural Heritage in Times of Crisis (FAC)," ICCROM, accessed March 18, 2018, https://www.iccrom.org/news/first -aid-cultural-heritage-times-crisis.

29. "Emergency Preparedness," Council of State Archivists, accessed July 14, 2017, https://www.statearchivists.org/programs/emergency-preparedness/.

30. Rohit Jigyasu, "Building Resilience by Reducing Disaster Risks to Cul- tural Heritage," Prevention Web, accessed July 20, 2017, http://www .preventionweb.net/experts/guest/collection/44401.

DISASTER PREPAREDNESS
GOES DIGITAL

Shannon Zachary

Since the early 1980s, I have watched the business of library preservation mature into its own profession and then watched first the beginnings and then the explosion of digital information in our libraries. I am not a digital preservation specialist. My own training and roots are firmly in the preservation and treatment of paper and books. But from managing a traditional preservation program in a library at the cutting edge of the digital revolution, I have had a ringside seat watching the translation of preservation principles from books to bytes. The technological transitions, and even more so the cultural clashes, have been fascinating to witness.

By the 1990s, disaster planning was firmly entrenched as a Good Thing that every library, and particularly every preservation officer, should do. If ever the impetus provided by the Florence Flood waned from memory, it seems there was always another high-profile disaster to jolt libraries into action: the Los Angeles Public Library fire of 1986, the fire at the Library of the Russian Academy of Sciences in 1988, Hurricane Katrina in 2005, the collapse of the Historical Archive of

Cologne in 2009, and floods in Prague and central Europe in 2013 and again in 2015, just to name a few that have caught the wider attention of the Western world. Others at this symposium describe many of these tough situations and tragic losses from both natural and human causes. Disaster planning has been part of the core curriculum for library school preservation classes since such classes came to be, and textbooks, workshops, and how-to guides abound.

The Getty *Art and Archeology Technical Abstracts* (AATA) includes listings of resources related to disaster mitigation.[1] A close look at index listings by decade for the subject designations of "disaster planning" or "disaster recovery" demonstrates a marked and dramatic increase in published attention to these two topics. Prior to the Flood in Florence, the AATA logs fewer than 40 publications on disaster-related topics. In the five decades since, AATA indexes 49 publications for the decade of the 1970s, 120 for the 1980s, 340 for the 1990s, and a peak of 400 publications for the 2000s. The current decade has seen a decline in this rate of growth but is still on track for several hundred publication references to disaster planning or disaster recovery. While there are quirks and artifacts in this visualization that derive from the history and development of AATA, it provides a quick profile of the rise of disaster preparedness as a topic for the care and management of physical collections in cultural heritage institutions—both museums and libraries.

Despite the abundance of literature, the 2004 Heritage Health Index survey found that only 30 percent of archives in the US and 22 percent of libraries and museums had disaster plans that included collections.[2] The Heritage Health Index was a broad survey of cultural institutions of every type and size. The situation was rather better among academic and research libraries. In the 2013 American Library Association (ALA) Preservation Statistics, a survey of forty mostly academic libraries, 70 percent of libraries reported having disaster plans; another 15 percent said there was a plan, but it was not up-to-date; and 7.5 percent had no plan but asserted a plan was being developed.[3] *Knowing the Need*, a 2011 survey of eighty-six libraries and archives in the UK and Ireland, found 62 percent of items surveyed—the survey only looked at physical books and documents—were covered by an up-to-date written emergency control plan.[4]

Yes, some libraries still do not have a disaster plan yet, or the plan is slipping out of date; but today's preservation officers know enough to feel guilty about that. The reminders are frequent: in addition to the headliner events, 72 percent of libraries in the 2013 ALA survey report experiencing "some type of disaster in fiscal year 2013."[5]

But what about the digital collections?

While the roots of digital information go back much earlier, the real game changer began to hit research libraries in the 1990s. Those early project names roll off the tongue: Project Gutenberg, Making of America, Project Open Book, Advanced Papyrological Information System, American Memory Project. Research libraries began creating digital libraries. I remember Carla Montori, the preservation officer at the University of Michigan Library at the time, making the pitch to administration in the late 1990s that this new format of digital information needed a new sort of preservation expert—a digital conservator, as it were—to grow up with the new technology. That pitch did not succeed—or at least not then at the University of Michigan. It does, however, highlight the way we were thinking.

More precisely, perhaps, I should say that those of us who managed preservation in traditional libraries and archives thought in analogies to the more familiar world of books. A separate stream of digital managers was also coming into being: information technology experts who were educated in computer science and worked in a world completely separated from the world of cultural heritage preservation. I have participated in cross-professional conversations around this question: Is a grounding in book and paper preservation necessary to better success in the preservation of digital libraries? The response of course was split: those of us familiar with traditional library and archive preservation felt that knowledge greatly informed our high-level understanding of the management of digital collections; those who had never worked in traditional preservation equally asserted they never missed it.

It may, in fact, be those coming from the analogy of book and paper preservation who have most strongly insisted on the word *preservation* in the digital context. I have listened to impassioned arguments that the words *curatorship* or *stewardship* more accurately reflect the full life cycle involvement required for sustained access to digital materials.[6] *Preservation*, goes the argument, means intervention that begins only late in the cycle, while digital stuff needs management from the point of creation. Personally, I've always felt that preservation involved action at any stage of the life cycle of books and documents, but I respect the nuanced distinction.

So the question also arises about digital disaster planning: Is a "disaster plan," as conceived analogously to traditional library plans, even relevant to digital collections?

A number of the early guides to disaster planning for digital collections focused on the recovery of drives and portable media—floppy disks, CDs—from water, fire, and other natural events, much in the way such guides described the recovery of books or photographs. The 1994 handbook *Disaster Response and Prevention for Computers and Data* by Miriam Kahn provided welcome practical information at a time when it was hard to come by. Kahn went on to produce several useful guides on the general management of digital collections.[7]

What is different about disaster planning for digital collections is the ability to leverage their capacity for identical copying: the ability to make backups. Mother Nature can do her worst on the primary copy, but with a good backup copy, stored in a remote location, there is no need even to try to salvage the original. But is the creation and deployment of backups disaster planning or just good management?

More and more urgently through the 1990s was the call for standards for the good management of digital collections. The Commission on Preservation and Access's 1996 report on *Preserving Digital Information*—the authors of which included several leaders in traditional library preservation—called for the creation of a community-agreed definition of a trustworthy digital repository.[8] From that report came, in 2002, *Trusted Digital Repositories: Attributes and Responsibilities*

(TDR), published jointly by the Research Libraries Group and OCLC.[9] Out of TDR grew, in 2007, *Trustworthy Repositories: Audit & Certification* (TRAC),[10] which more recently has become a standard under the International Standards Organization.[11] The entire genealogy of standards—stemming from the Commission on Preservation and Access report through TDR, TRAC, and ultimately to the Open Archival Information System (ISO 16363) reference model[12]—firmly asserts that disaster plans, in those precise words, are a necessary component to what makes a digital repository worthy of trust.

The existence of these standards, however, has not meant implementation has been automatic or easy. University of Michigan School of Information doctoral student Rebecca Frank and professor Elizabeth Yakel conducted a study in 2012 investigating motivators and barriers to the creation of a disaster plan for a digital repository. The key incentive they found was clear and nearly universal: repositories seeking TRAC certification were motivated to create a disaster plan. But they also found a disconnect: the IT-trained managers seemed to have difficulty imagining or comprehending a disaster plan, while converts from traditional preservation took that need for granted.[13]

I've watched the scenario they describe play out here at the University of Michigan Library: while the need for and role of a disaster plan seems obvious and instinctive to those with a background in traditional preservation, the demand to write a disaster plan often puzzled those from other backgrounds. This is not to say that digital repositories neglected emergency planning altogether. Our colleagues simply observed that best practices for stewardship already specifies backups, actions against security breaches, hardware failure, software failure, obsolescence, and so on. What more do we need?

What is a digital disaster? Certainly it is true that all digital information has a physical reality somewhere on spinning disks or computer drives or portable media. All of these can be damaged by flood, fire, or building collapse. But digital files are also vulnerable to so much more: hardware failure, network configuration errors, malicious attacks, format obsolescence, software failure, operator error, security breach, and media degradation. Is the preparation for these risks disaster planning or, again, just good management?

And what should a digital disaster plan look like? It is notable in the current literature on digital preservation that even now guides and descriptions are few and models are still hard to find. If libraries struggle to create a disaster plan for their book collections, even more do managers struggle to create disaster plans for their digital repositories. A search of Charles Bailey's ninety-page *Digital Curation Bibliography* from 2012 finds no titles with any variation of the words *disaster planning* or *disaster recovery*.[14] More recent versions of the bibliography show little progress in publication on these topics.

I have observed that while the digital preservation world has struggled at times with the concept of disaster planning, it is comfortable with and has embraced the broader and overlapping concept of risk management. Disaster planning looks at emergencies and response; risk management looks at all causes of loss, whether sudden emergencies or slow deterioration, and encourages the development of strategies to reduce loss. In a risk management framework, the possibility of an earthquake can be lined up alongside the likelihood of bit rot and prioritized for mitigating action.

Bailey's bibliography of digital curation cites six titles on risk management/assessment. Tellingly, European models for digital repositories, except where they are strongly influenced by the American thread, have tended to go with the risk management model. The Digital Repository Audit Method Based on Risk Assessment (DRAMBORA) is all about risk management, as expressed in its name.[15] In the literature, studies exhorting a risk management approach to the preservation of digital collections—or the selection of file formats or long-term access to online journals—abound.[16]

In fact, the concept of risk management has reflected back into the physical world with growing popularity. As mentioned earlier in this presentation, the Getty *Art and Archaeology Technical Abstracts* showed a marked burst in attention to *disaster preparedness* and *disaster recovery* following the Florence Flood. The same AATA source demonstrates the emergent dominance of concepts of *risk assessment* and *risk management*. With almost no uses of the terms prior to 1990, AATA logs early interest in the 1990s with just over fifty citations. The decade of the 2000s, however, has over 450 publications on risk listed in the index, with the first six years of the 2010s already listed with 450 publications. In the meantime and most recently, disaster preparedness topics have waned.[17]

In the concept of risk management, the digital and the physical can come together in parity. For the past decade, I have taught basic preservation to School of Information master's students, students who are increasingly aware of and keen to learn about the management of digital information. While the students and I have struggled to make the traditional preservation management tools (needs assessments and disaster plans) bridge across formats, the risk assessment approach works equally well in both realms.

I should add, however, that while risk assessment is good for developing management strategies, it is not itself a disaster plan. I do still argue that *disaster plan* has some meaning for digital collections. Details of what to do in an emergency do need to be thought through in advance, written down, and drilled.

Finally, I have wondered, has there yet been a digital Florence Flood, one that might still motivate international action on digital risk? Maybe not. Most of the digital disasters we know about involve the accumulation of small losses, more analogous, say, to those perennial water leaks in our library storage facilities that impact ten, fifty, or a few hundred books at a time.

What would a digital Florence Flood look like, anyway? By that, I mean a cultural catastrophe so large that it catches worldwide media attention and attracts people from many countries to volunteer to join the recovery effort. Big digital disasters that hit the news tend to be security breaches into large corporations, or banks, or governments, or political parties. Yes, these breaches make the news, and some of them spur hackathons and other pro bono communal efforts to find solutions. Yes, these breaches are serious and have the potential for significant economic, social, and political influence on our lives collectively and as individuals. But do we perceive them as threatening our communal heritage? Have they resulted in loss? Do they capture our imagination in the way the Florence Flood of 1966 did?

Digital disasters tend to happen not with a bang but with a silent "poof!" They don't make for vivid images on television or social media. They are discovered after the fact, sometimes long after. Maybe we will witness a digital Florence Flood. I hope not. But meanwhile, it is our collective mandate to imagine what it might be and to mitigate the loss.

Notes

1. Art and Archeology Technical Abstracts (AATA). October 2016. http://aata .getty.edu/.
2. Heritage Preservation and the Institute of Museum and Library Services. 2005. *A Public Trust at Risk: The Heritage Health Index Report on the State of America's Collections.* Washington, DC: Heritage Preservation. http:// resources.conservation-us.org/hhi/home/full-report-by-section/. See also Langa, Lesley A., Annie Peterson, and Holly Robertson. 2015. *Preservation Metrics Today: Heritage Health Information and Preservation Statistics* [recorded webinar]. Washington, DC: American Institute for Conservation of Historic and Artistic Works, Connecting to Collections Care, June 11, 2015. Archived at http://www.connectingtocollections.org/preservation -metrics-today-heritage-health-information-and-preservation-statistics/.
3. Peterson, Annie, Holly Robertson, and Nick Szydlowski. 2014. *Preservation Statistics: A Survey for U.S. Libraries, FY2013 Report.* Chicago: American Library Association/ALCTS/PARS. http://www.ala.org/alcts/resources/ preservation/presstats.
4. Peach, Caroline, and Julia Foster. 2013. *Knowing the Need: Optimizing Preservation for Library and Archive Collections.* London: Preservation Advisory Centre. http://www.bl.uk/aboutus/stratpolprog/collectioncare/ publications/reports/reports.html.
5. Peterson et al. 2014, 16.
6. Lazorchack, Butch. 2011. "Digital Preservation, Digital Curation, Digital Stewardship: What's in (Some) Names?" *The Signal* [blog]. Washington, DC: Library of Congress, August 23, 2011. http://blogs.loc.gov/thesignal/ 2011/08/digital-preservation-digital-curation-digital-stewardship-what's-in -some-names/.
7. Kahn, Miriam B. 1994. *Disaster Response and Prevention for Computers and Data.* Columbus, OH: MBK Consulting; Kahn, Miriam B. 2004. *Protecting Your Library's Digital Sources: The Essential Guide to Planning and Preservation.* Chicago: ALA Editions.

8. Garrett, John, and Donald. J. Waters. 1996. *Preserving Digital Information: Report of the Task Force on Archiving of Digital Information.* Washington, DC: The Commission on Preservation and Access & Research Libraries Group. See also Hedstrom, M. 1997. "Digital Preservation: A Time Bomb for Digital Libraries." *Computers and the Humanities* 31:189. doi:10.1023/A:1000676723815.

9. *Trusted Digital Repositories: Attributes and Responsibilities.* 2002. An RLG-OCLC Report. Mountain View, CA: Research Libraries Group. http://www.oclc.org/content/dam/research/activities/trustedrep/repositories.pdf.

10. Research Libraries Group and National Archives and Records Administration. February 2007. *Trustworthy Repositories Audit & Certification: Criteria and Checklist* (TRAC). http://www.crl.edu/archiving-preservation/digital-archives/metrics-assessing-and-certifying.

11. International Organization for Standardization (ISO). 2012. *ISO 16363:2012: Space Data and Information Transfer Systems—Audit and Certification of Trustworthy Digital Repositories.* http://www.iso.org/standard/56510.html.

12. Lavoie, Brian. 2004. *Open Archival Information System: Introductory Guide.* Technology Watch Report 04–01. Digital Preservation Coalition. http://www.dpconline.org/advice/technology-watch-reports; Lavoie, Brian. 2014. *Open Archival Information System: Introductory Guide.* 2nd ed. Technology Watch Report 14–02. Digital Preservation Coalition. http://www.dpconline.org/advice/technology-watch-reports.

13. Frank, Rebecca D., and Elizabeth Yakel. 2013. *Disaster Planning for Digital Repositories.* Montreal: ASIST 2013, November 1–6, 2013. http://www.asis.org/asist2013/proceedings/submissions/papers/59paper.pdf.

14. Bailey, Charles W., Jr. 2012. *Digital Curation Bibliography: Preservation and Stewardship of Scholarly Works.* Houston, TX: Digital Scholarship. http://digital-scholarship.org/dcbw/dcb.htm.

15. DRAMBORA Digital Repository Audit Method Based on Risk Assessment. Digital Curation Centre and DigitalPreservationEurope. http://www.repositoryaudit.eu/; see also Data Seal of Approval (DSA), https://www.datasealofapproval.org/en/.

16. See, for example, Cervone, H. F. 2006. "Disaster Recovery and Continuity Planning for Digital Library Systems." *OCLC Systems & Services* 22 (3): 173–78; Kenney, Anne R., et al. 2003–14. *Digital Preservation Management: Implementing Short-Term Strategies to Long-Term Problems* [online tutorial]. Cambridge, MA: Massachusetts Institute of Technology and Cornell University. http://www.dpworkshop.org/dpm-eng/eng_index.html; McGovern, N. M., and L. Stuchell. 2009. *Disaster Planning.* Ann Arbor, MI: Inter-university Consortium for Political and Social Research (ICPSR). http://www.icpsr.umich.edu/icpsrweb/content/datamanagement/disaster/; New York State Archives. 2012. *Records Advisory: Electronic Records Disaster*

Preparedness and Recovery. October 2012. http://www.archives.nysed.gov/records/mr_disaster_assistance_erecords.shtml; Swanson, M., P. Bowen, A. W. Phillips, D. Gallup, and D. Lynes. 2010. *Contingency Planning Guide for Federal Information Systems.* NIST Special Publication 800–834 Rev. 1. Washington, DC: National Institute of Standards and Technology. http://nvlpubs.nist.gov/nistpubs/Legacy/SP/nistspecialpublication800-34r1.pdf.

17. These are the Art and Archeology Technical Abstracts article counts by decade with index terms *disaster planning* or *disaster recovery* and article counts with index terms *risk assessment* or *risk management.* Data source: Art and Archeology Technical Abstracts (AATA), October 2016. http://aata.getty.edu/.

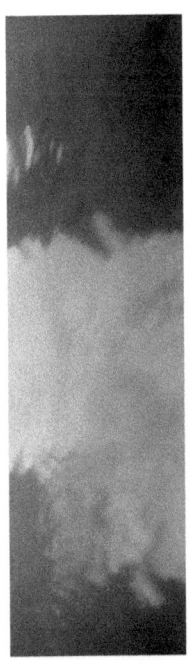

THE FLORENCE FLOOD ON FILM

FLORENCE: DAYS OF DESTRUCTION: A FILM BY FRANCO ZEFFIRELLI

Bryan Draper and Carla Q. Montori

I WAS THERE.

—Franco Zeffirelli

Tuscany is the land where I was born and spent my formative years. . . . When the flood of 1966 devastated Florence, I grabbed two movie cameras and rushed out to film the disaster so that the world could see it. I like to think that those images, broadcast all over the world, were the spur which prompted the Mud Angels to come to the city's rescue and encouraged the Florentines themselves not to lose heart, to roll up their sleeves in the name of a shared culture and civilization to be protected and preserved.

—Erasmo D'Angelis[1]

Introduction

The University of Maryland Libraries thanks the University of Michigan's Florence Flood symposium planning committee for the opportunity to share its rare copy of Zeffirelli's film, *Florence: Days of Destruction* during the fifty-year retrospective symposium. Maryland's copy of *Florence* was the first of two films to be screened the evening of November 3, 2016, in the Helmut Stern Auditorium of the University of Michigan's Museum of Art. Zeffirelli's *Florence* film is a dramatic and emotional record of the 1966 flood and the devastation it caused. The second film shown, Roger Hill's *The Restoration of Books, Florence, 1968*, illustrates the rational and creative response developed at Florence's Biblioteca Nazionale Centrale di Firenze (BNCF) to reclaim the printed and written heritage that had been damaged in the flood.[2] Screened together for the first time, the films illustrate events that had profound effects on the development of the conservation of cultural heritage generally and specifically in the field of book, library, and archives conservation.

History of the University of Maryland Libraries' Copy

The University of Maryland, College Park, is the largest university library system in the Washington, DC, area; its nine libraries support the education, research, and scholarship of the university's students, faculty, and staff and of the citizens of the state of Maryland. This copy,[3] on 16 mm film, of Franco Zeffirelli's *Florence: Days of Destruction*—or its Italian title, *Per Firenze*—is held in the Libraries' Media Services (LMS).[4]

The media format of choice in educational settings in the 1950s, '60s, and '70s was 16 mm film. With the advent of video and the ease of video playback—as opposed to setting up a film projector and threading a fragile film through a lot of wheels and sprockets—institutions began disposing of their films, sometimes even just throwing them away. We believe that in the mid-1980s, the university's School of Architecture, Planning, and Preservation was disposing of its outdated films and gave its copy of *Florence: Days of Destruction* to the Libraries' Media Services department. The Libraries own a second copy of the second reel of the film, held in the Historic Preservation Collection; the core of this collection is the library donated to the university in the 1980s by the National Trust for Historic Preservation.[5]

Linda Sarigöl, the now retired manager of the Libraries' film collection, was aware of the copy held in LMS in the early 1990s. In 2008,

LMS film technician and Zeffirelli enthusiast Juana Godinez and Sarigöl viewed the film and were moved by the images of destruction of the beautiful city. At the same time, they were confused by the fact that some scenes are in color, some in a reddish black and white. Recognizing that this film "deserved higher visibility in our collection," Godinez undertook the first digital transfers of the LMS copy to DVD and experimented with color correction as her skills and equipment allowed. These DVD transfers became our first access copies.

In the fall of 2009, Sarigöl told the relatively new members of the preservation department staff, Carla Montori and Bryan Draper, of the existence of this rare film in our collection. We immediately scheduled a viewing and were completely astounded by this visual record of this natural disaster and Zeffirelli's dramatic portrayal of the devastation it caused to the people, the built environment, and the precious cultural heritage of the city of Florence.

As we researched the film and our copy of it, its rarity became quickly evident. In 2010, we were able to confirm the existence of just four full copies of the film:

- a streaming Italian version at Radiotelevisione Italiana (RAI), Italy's national public broadcasting company
- a nonstreaming English-language version at RAI
- a nonstreaming English-language copy at the British Film Institute
- the University of Maryland Libraries copy

In 2015, a record was added to OCLC, reflecting two unviewed copies of the film at Harvard University.

Showing the Film

We agreed with our media services colleagues that this film deserved greater visibility and made the decision to preserve and promote the Libraries' copy of *Florence*. Our first public screening in early 2010 was to a small group of the Potomac chapter of the Guild of Book Workers. We

were delighted by the enthusiasm of our audience and further aston-
ished by the response our announcement[6] of the screening would have:
inquiries came from Australia, Magdalene College, Oxford, and many
libraries and museums in the US about obtaining a copy or requesting
a loan.

With the approach of the forty-fifth anniversary of the 1966 flood,
we were invited by the National Gallery of Art (NGA) in Washington, DC, to have a public screening on Saturday, November 5, 2011,
as part of their film series. This venue offered a large auditorium with
exceptional cinematographic capacities. In preparation for this occasion, we engaged ColorLab of Rockville, Maryland, to produce a new
digital transfer, which they delivered on a digi-beta tape with deriva-
tive access copies on DVD. The film was screened from the digi-beta
tape by the NGA and was the highest quality any of us had yet seen.
We followed the screening with a short program of presentations by
Sheila Waters and Norvell Jones, who spoke about their roles and
experiences participating in the salvage efforts at the BNCF. Finally,
there was a very enthusiastic question and answer session.[7] The audience was estimated to be about four hundred, and our desire to bring
our Libraries' film to greater visibility was clearly achieved. Since 2010,
we have made our copy of the film available for presentations at conferences and professional meetings or via interlibrary loan to groups and
individual researchers.

As the fiftieth anniversary of the 1966 flood approached, many invi-
tations to show and requests to borrow *Florence* came in. In Washington, DC, the Italian Cultural Institute (IIC), an overseas office of Italy's
Ministry of Foreign Affairs and International Cooperation, partnered
with the Italian Embassy and the University of Maryland Libraries to
show the film at the National Gallery of Art. IIC arranged to have RAI's
English-language version of the film copied to DVD. It was this, now
the fifth known copy of the film, that was shown at the Gallery on
November 4 and November 6; introductory remarks were made by staff
of both the IIC and the University Libraries.

Due to the high demand to show the film and the importance of
the fiftieth anniversary, the Libraries decided that a new digitization

to current preservation standards was in order. In addition, there was the issue of the Historic Preservation Collection's copy of the second reel: no one had viewed it, but we believed that it contained additional footage showing Senator Edward M. Kennedy's visit to Florence on November 7, 1966. He had attended a conference in Geneva and went to Florence to see the flood damage himself. He visited the Uffizi Gallery and the Biblioteca Nazionale and spoke with many of the volunteers who had come to Florence to help in the rescue effort.[8] Kennedy later wrote of the volunteers, "It was if they knew that this flooding of the library was putting their soul at risk."[9]

The Libraries' second copy of the film (in the Historic Preservation Collection) does include the added Kennedy footage. We have since learned that both RAI's streaming Italian and its nonstreaming English versions of the film include the Kennedy footage. Of the four copies of the reel that we have seen, only the copy held in our Library Media Services department shows the film as originally produced: without the Kennedy footage.

In his appearance in the film, Kennedy promoted the work of the Committee to Rescue Italian Art (CRIA), an American fund-raising effort. Established within days of the flood, and with Jacqueline Kennedy as its honorary president, CRIA set its goal as raising $2,500,000—worth nearly $19,000,000 in 2017—for the repair and restoration of works of art damaged by the flooding. Within a month, there were fifty branches of CRIA across the United States; its first grants were made in early December, a tribute to the generosity of those moved by the plight of the city of Florence. Zeffirelli's film was produced, distributed, and shown at CRIA fund-raising events in the United States and Europe.

Robert Clark's book *Dark Water: Flood and Redemption in the City of Masterpieces* was published in 2008, after he had attended the forty-year commemoration of the flood in 2006. Clark provides information about the genesis of Zeffirelli's film. In November of 1966, Franco Zeffirelli—a native Florentine—was in Rome doing postproduction for his film *The Taming of the Shrew*, starring Richard Burton and Elizabeth Taylor. Around dawn, Zeffirelli's phone rang: it was his sister who lived east of the Duomo in the historic center of Florence, telling him about the flooded streets below her window. He immediately contacted the state-owned public service broadcaster, RAI, borrowed a helicopter, and quickly assembled a film crew. He was filming in Florence before any other news agency, including RAI's.[10]

Zeffirelli himself conducted the interviews in his footage, and you can see him make a fleeting appearance about forty-two minutes into the film. The finished version combines Zeffirelli's footage with that of RAI television crews. The film was produced in a week's time.[11]

Katherine Taylor, an American writer living in Florence during the flood, recorded in her diary that while spending Thanksgiving with friends in France three weeks after the flood, "one evening, the Richard Burton film appeared on television and gave our friends their first look at the tragedy they had only heard about".[12]

The film premiered in London on November 20[13] and was shown on television in the United States on December 22.[14]

Though Zeffirelli shot in black and white, he added stock color footage of preflood Florence at the beginning of reel one and toward the end of reel two. Prints for distribution were made on color film stock that redshifted over time. The version of the film shown in Ann Arbor in 2016 during the fiftieth anniversary of the 1966 flood is the result of the second digital transfer performed by ColorLab. Although we did not request ColorLab to undertake a full digital restoration, the color correction and higher quality is a vast improvement over previous digital transfers. In addition, we are able to show the film with the additional Kennedy footage for the first time.

In recent years, many individuals have endeavored to preserve, promote, and make this film accessible to a wider audience. However, that effort was only possible due to the many anonymous people through whose hands these reels of 16 mm film passed over the last fifty years and who did not discard or trash them. Due to their intentional stewardship or benign neglect, the University of Maryland Libraries can share this important perspective on an event that has so profoundly influenced the field of conservation.

Notes

1. D'Angelis, Erasmo. 2016. *The Mud Angels: The "Best of Youth" in Florence at the Time of the Flood, Fifty Years Later.* 1st ed. Firenze: Giunti, p. 112.

2. Hill, Roger, Peter Waters, Christopher Clarkson, Royal College of Art (Great Britain), and Italian Art and Archives Rescue Fund (Great Britain), dirs. 2006. *The Restoration of Books, Florence, 1968: A Film Based on the Work in the National Library of Florence Resulting from the Floods on 4 November 1966.* University of Utah Library. http://stream.lib.utah.edu/index.php?c= details&id=284.

3. Burton, Richard, Furio Colombo, Franco Zeffirelli, Roman Vlad, Radio audizioni Italia, and Committee to Rescue Italian Art. 1966. *Florence: Days of Destruction.* Committee to Restore Italian Art. https://umaryland.on .worldcat.org/oclc/959295493.

4. University of Maryland Libraries Media Services. Accessed on March 19, 2018. https://www.lib.umd.edu/lms.

5. University of Maryland Libraries. Special Collections. "Historic Preserva-tion." Accessed on March 19, 2018. https://www.lib.umd.edu/special/ guides/preservation.

6. Announcements were shared on the Conservation DistList and the Book_ Arts Listserv.

7. National Gallery of Art. Audio and Video. *Florence: Days of Destruction.* Accessed March 18, 2018. https://www.nga.gov/audio-video/audio/florence -flood-film.html.

8. Clark, Robert. 2008. *Dark Water: Flood and Redemption in the City of Masterpieces.* 1st ed. New York: Doubleday, pp. 177–79 and 333.

9. Spande, Helen, and New York University. 2009. Institute of Fine Arts. Con-servation Center. *Conservation Legacies of the Florence Flood of 1966: Pro-ceedings of the Symposium Commemorating the 40th Anniversary.* London: Archetype, p. xviii.

10. Clark (2008), p. 136.

11. Clark (2008), p. 197.

12. Taylor, Kathrine Kressmann. 1967. *Diary of Florence in Flood.* New York: Simon and Schuster, p. 137.

13. Clark (2008), p. 222.

14. *New York Times*, December 9, 1966, p. 95 (announcement to air film on Channel 13 at 9:00 p.m.) and December 22, 1966, p. 50 (film appears in the evening television lineup).

THE RESTORATION OF BOOKS, FLORENCE, 1968: A FILM BY ROGER HILL

Cathleen A. Baker

In 1968, Roger Hill was lecturer in filmmaking at London's Royal College of Art, where Peter Waters was lecturer in bookbinding. With financing from the Italian Art and Archives Rescue Fund, they traveled together to Florence to make this film. Hill was on a very tight budget, and the film was made in a minimal amount of time so that Peter could take it on his February 1969 lecture tour across the United States as a fund-raiser for the Biblioteca Nazionale Centrale di Firenze, a tour about which Sheila Waters spoke in her lecture. I learned in late October 2016 that the original of *The Restoration of Books, Florence, 1968*, was in the British Film Institute; the whereabouts of the original Hill film had been unknown up until then. Randy Silverman, who first approached me (The Legacy Press) to publish Sheila Waters's book *Waters Rising: Letters from Florence* (Ann Arbor, Mich., 2016), also arranged for Mikio Moriyasu at the University of Utah to perform a fantastic remastering of the digital version for a DVD that is included with every copy of Sheila's book. Among other conservation techniques performed in this film, Christopher Clarkson (1938–2017) covers a book in a limp vellum binding, while Peter Waters (1930–2003) demonstrates a binding in full leather.

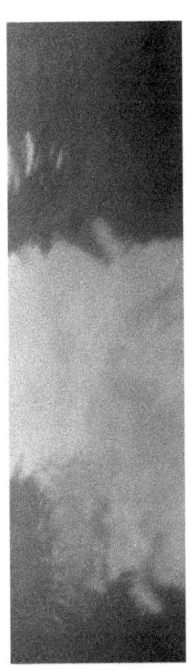

THEME PANEL: CONSERVATION EDUCATION AND TRAINING

WHENCE AND WHERETO LIBRARY AND ARCHIVES CONSERVATION EDUCATION?

Ellen Cunningham-Kruppa

Today we will take an abbreviated journey down the Daedalean path the field of library and archives conservation has traveled in higher education over the past thirty-five years. The story begins in 1981 with the opening of the new Conservation Education Programs—known as the CEP—in Columbia University's School of Library Service (SLS). Ten years later, as the school closed its doors in the early 1990s, the CEP relocated in 1992 to the Graduate School of Library and Information Science at the University of Texas at Austin. Between 1981 and 2011, the two schools graduated just over one hundred conservators and an equal number of preservation administrators. These professionals have led and defined the field's practice and research. Curiously, however, despite the successes of the graduates, the conservation and preservation administration specializations never found long-term stability in either school. Given the field's troubled history in defining and stabilizing itself in a disciplinary home, it is critical that we understand what has and has not moored it in library and information science (LIS).

The question of the disciplinary "fit" of library and archive conservation education is under question at this very moment. The Andrew W. Mellon Foundation is weighing whether to support (at least for the next five-plus years) an educational program within the art conservation domain or in that of information studies—or perhaps both.[1] We might ask, Why do we care in which intellectual domain library and archives conservators are educated? If Mellon is generous enough to fund an educational program, does it matter? I will suggest today that there are clear reasons it does matter. Today and in this room filled with many of the brightest minds in our field, this conference provides us a fortuitous moment to interrogate the disciplinary nature of our field, to give it the critical consideration it demands and deserves.

The Road to Higher Education

Paul Noble Banks was a primary architect of library and archives conservation education in the United States. His work toward the professionalization of the field, beginning as early as 1960, was determined and arduous. Banks was one of two named conservators in 1964 hired into professional positions to oversee conservation operations within libraries in the US.[2] In his position at the Newberry Library, he worked as both an administrator and a conservator and began to think about the need for "conservation administrators" to oversee operations, write policy, and the like. Two years later, he became involved with the Florence rescue for seven years, from 1966 to 1973, through his work as chair of the Committee on the Rescue of Italian Art's Study Committee on Book Conservation to consider book conservation problems, and especially the proposal for a book conservation center in Florence. The historical record documents his longtime quest for resources, long before the National Endowment for the Humanities or any other federal agency was funding such endeavors. They reveal his struggles to, first, define a new area of study and, second, gain attention from those who could fund it. By the late 1960s and into the very early 1970s, he and the director of the Newberry Library, Bill Towner, began working with Verner Clapp, the founding director of the Council on Library Resources, to fund a professional educational program at the Newberry. When that failed, they turned to the Independent Research Libraries Association, in which Bill Towner was a leader.

In 1974, the possibility that New York City might be a home for a program was beginning to be considered by Columbia University's School of Library Service. The record is clear, however, that until 1979, library and archives conservation could have moved either into LIS or into art conservation education—specifically into the program at New York University's conservation center in the Institute of Fine Arts. As late as 1979, Banks remained equivocal—at least in published writings. We know, however, that he had become increasingly adamant that conservators needed a graduate degree to be on equal institutional footing with curators, bibliographers, and the range of librarians who purchased, cataloged, and provided public services for research collections. The conservator's role was far-reaching; to engage at the professional level in library institutions and to influence library policy meant that the job needed to be at the professional level, which at the time meant that the conservator required a master's of library science, the currency of the realm.[3] Furthermore, Banks was interested in specifying the education of the preservation administrator (PA), to whom the conservator would report. The IFACC would have been hard-pressed to establish the kind of program for PAs that was envisioned for the SLS.[4]

Columbia's SLS, a well-established library school boasting an Ivy League parent institution and with a humanities-oriented curriculum, promised to be an ideal home for the new programs. Within the SLS itself, the possibility of working with Terry Belanger and his newly established and thriving rare books specialization promised a collegial intellectual collaboration and prime courses for the preservation administration and conservation specializations. Beyond the SLS, Columbia had a history of supporting cultural preservation programs, having founded the first historic preservation program in 1964. Clearly, New York City was the very heartland of libraries, museums, and archives. Finally, with the prestige of significant funding from the

National Endowment for the Humanities (NEH), the Andrew W. Mellon Foundation, and the Carnegie Corporation of New York, among others, the programs commenced with a seemingly promising future.

Though few on the outside would have known it (or on the inside acknowledged it), by the time the program opened its doors in the SLS, it was already on unstable ground. The CEP existed on soft funding, faculty without the credentials of the academy (who did not obtain tenure), and the collaborative goodwill of NYU's graduate art conservation program that provided three courses on the science and conservation of paper. Significantly, the CEP was situated within a school and discipline undergoing substantive philosophical disruption. In the case of the SLS and more than a dozen other like schools in the 1980s and '90s, they faced institutional displacement. Columbia itself was having significant financial difficulties; the upper administration was hot on the tail of the SLS, a school that brought in little in the way of endowments and whose enrollment had been declining precipitously.

With substantial support from NEH, as Columbia's SLS was closing its doors in the early 1990s, the CEP moved to the University of Texas at Austin in 1992. In 2003, the Graduate School Library and Information Science (GSLIS), under the leadership of a new dean, changed its name to the School of Information. Like other schools in the iSchool movement that made this name change—with Apple product naming as its seeming basis—the school branded itself the iSchool. Six years later, in 2009, the school's faculty voted to discontinue the certificate of advanced study for conservators.[5] It was not a particularly propitious financial moment in the US for another LIS school to establish an expensive conservation program.[6] On the other hand, given that 70 percent of the nation's cultural record resides in libraries and archives,[7] it seemed incomprehensible that the LIS domain would abdicate its responsibility to educate conservators.

In response to the closing of the UT program, the Mellon Foundation stepped in to provide competitive funding to the nation's three art conservation programs to build pilot library and archives curricula. Effectively overnight, the specialization moved from one intellectual domain (LIS) to another (art conservation). While each art conservation program had graduated some number of students over the decades specializing in rare book conservation, the Mellon Foundation encouraged the programs to propose "imaginative ideas for the pilot training programs."[8] In response, each program incorporated in their proposals foundational elements from the LIS discipline.[9] Though clearly invested in the success of the pilot projects, the Mellon Foundation expressed concerns about the integration of library and archives conservation into the art curriculum: "Although we hope to be able to give each pilot program a full run, we are very concerned both about the mission appropriateness and the sustainability of the programs at each institution. As we move forward, we want to be certain that these new program areas are not putting new strains on each of your institutions and diverting attention away from core strengths."[10] Would library and archives conservation "fit" in art conservation?

What does the recent move of the library and archives conservation specialization from the LIS domain to that of art conservation mean? Do university restructurings and disciplinary consolidations really matter to a field's study and praxis? Disciplines evolve, shift, merge, and even disappear in institutions.[11] What does it mean that the LIS/iSchool domain chose (at least for the past six years) to not educate library and archives conservators? Are there principles and practices that ally disciplinarily the education of all conservators who work in and with collections found in cultural institutions such as libraries, archives, museums, heritage societies, and the like? Why do we even care about disciplines?

Well that's a lot to chew on! For a productive approach to untangling these threads of inquiry, let's try launching from a single question. What might the evolution of the LIS discipline over the past thirty years tell us about the fit of conservation education in that intellectual domain?

Dean Richard Darling brought the CEP and the rare books program into the school intentionally as unique, distinguishing programs to attract more students and to build the SLS's financial resources and standing in the university. In his 1990 report of a university review of the SLS, Provost Jonathan R. Cole—who played a critical role in the eventual close of the school—singled out the CEP and the rare books program in particular, noting especially that the former had the support of large monies from the NEH and the Mellon. Indeed, the CEP was seeking renewal of both grants in 1991. Yet he and the 1990 committee report, the latter of which singled out rare books and the CEP as having "large international reputations and . . . significant sources of distinction for the University," also voiced that the CEP presented long-term financial concerns given the soft nature of its funding.[12]

Indeed, as the 1980s came to a close, the cooperative educational agreement with the NYU Institute of Fine Arts' conservation center ended. The SLS had to teach the three courses previously offered by NYU. Additionally, had the programs remained at Columbia, the university would have had to "secure additional laboratory space at Columbia or another institution for these activities," amounting to a possible five hundred thousand outlay.[13]

Despite prospective financial obligations, educating "scientific" conservators and preservation "administrators" appeared to fall in line with Columbia's drive for what it promoted as "selective excellence."[14] As Cole reflected on the CEP, "Within the School of Library Service the programs in preservation-conservation and rare books make a significant contribution to Columbia's academic vitality and distinction." However, Cole equally pointed out that the CEP had two nontenured faculty and a full-time research appointment (Banks) and that the program enrolled "fewer than 10 students annually." He noted similar faculty issues with the rare books program. With these considerations in mind, Cole asks, "Is the quality of these . . . excellent but small programs enough to justify the continuation of programs whose contribution to the most promising fields of inquiry within the profession and related disciplines in the University is marginal? Is it possible to close SLS degree programs and preserve programs in preservation-conservation and rare books?"[15] In other words, while the rare books program and the CEP were not without costs, in the minds of the SLS's reviewers at least, these programs represented an "other" with merits. The programs were considered among but also distinguishable from the SLS's concerns. At least in Cole's mind, the programs could be considered distinct from the SLS and, congruently, the intellectual domain of LIS.

The CEP was bold and newfangled for a school of library service. What, however, does the "unlikeness" or "uniqueness" of the programs mean given their integration into the SLS?

By interrogating the ontology of the conservation education program in particular—apart from the program's financing, faculty status, and intellectual networks—we begin to understand that library and archives conservation education acted more as an appendage rather than an integral intellectual component in the SLS and, arguably, in LIS. While conservation resonated intellectually most especially with the SLS's library science focus (including rare books/special collections) and, at UT Austin, the archives specialization, the study and practice of conservation differed somewhat dramatically from other areas of study within the LIS domain. The genesis of the iSchool at UT Austin in 2002 promised further intellectual distancing.

The formal application process and entrance requirements to the conservation course of study distinguished the specialization from the SLS master's program. While students applying to other SLS specializations did not need to meet requirements other than those of all master's program applicants, conservation applicants had to meet a number of additional requirements, ones that were modeled on those for admission to the art conservation education programs. Applicants presented portfolios of "craft or artistic work that demonstrate[d] manual ability and creative problem solving." Additionally, the applicant interviewed with CEP faculty on campus, during which he or she took "a bookcraft aptitude test" that was scored to suggest the applicant's degree of manual dexterity. Finally, applicants had to have completed one year of college-level chemistry, including a semester of organic chemistry, in advance of applying.[16]

Likewise, the conservator student's coursework differed substantially from that of other SLS master's students. To begin with, unlike other foci of study defined as specializations within the SLS, the CEP tracks were called "advanced programs."[17] In keeping with the "advanced" status of the programs, in addition to a specially reduced nine-credit-hour "core" requirement for the MLS (referred to as a "basic education in librarianship"), conservator students took sixty-three more hours, composed of many courses new to the SLS, such as Introductory Technology and Structure of Records Materials, Fundamentals of Conservation Treatment (the first of a number of book and paper conservation treatment laboratory courses), Protection and Care of Records Materials, and Administration of Preservation Programs plus select courses required for the rare book specialization.[18] Unlike any other specialization in the SLS, the conservator's course of study included a required third-year internship in an established conservation laboratory, in keeping with the curricular requirements of art conservation education programs.[19]

The preponderance of courses in the conservator curriculum required that the students inhabit spaces apart from the traditional classroom in which all other SLS students matriculated. In addition to the school's classrooms, conservator students matriculated in laboratories outfitted to serve a primary element of their intellectual domain: the "modern" science and "historical" craft duality. The labs, located across campus from the SLS in Schermerhorn Hall, which originally housed the sciences, announced an "other" intellectual domain.

The lab itself functioned as something other than a passive classroom lecture environment. Students gathered around an instructor, who demonstrated binding and treatment techniques, which they each physically repeated. Students sat on high stools/chairs at large "benches" and wore the same white lab coats sported by doctors. "Treatment" of book and paper objects required a range of tools not found in any other LIS classroom, including industrial-era bookbinding equipment, archival papers and boards, special mending papers, sewing threads, and hand tools galore. The scientific component of treatment called for a large stainless steel washing sink with a filtrated water supply, a chemical fume hood, personal respirators, beakers, gram scales, microscopes, and chemicals. In this lab space, conservator students spent the preponderance of their time—including after class hours and weekends. Punctuating the differences between their work and that of other SLS students, only conservator and preservation administration students were permitted to take lab courses.[20]

The CEP's curricular affiliation with NYU's Institute for Fine Arts Conservation Center embodied a distinct disciplinary as well as physical disjunction from the SLS and spoke to the ambiguous disciplinary nature of library and archives conservation education at the time. Located on the city's East Side—in a building across from the Metropolitan Museum—library and archives students took three courses (Chemical Problems in Library and Archives Conservation I and II and Treatment of Manuscript Materials [laboratory]) off campus from Morningside Heights in an art conservation program.[21] Rounded instruction required that students learn principles and techniques founded in the art conservation domain. The SLS could not fulfill the academic needs of the library and archives conservation specialization. The conservation science component required faculty specialists in the physical sciences, which was and remains a foreign concept to a humanities/social sciences discipline, and used expensive, analytical laboratory technologies.[22] Ironically, while the scientific elements of conservation fostered an otherness in the LIS domain, the field's theoretical and practical grounding in science (a recognized intellectual concern) smoothed the path for the admittance of library and archives (and art) conservation to the academy. As early as 1968, Banks commented that the possibility of a "rational discipline of book conservation" was made possible due to the "advent of the scientist" who studies book materials.[23] Modern science permitted conservation to move away from an apprentice model.

The iSchool Movement

As the story of the SLS's closure highlights, increasingly in the 1980s, the role of "information" in LIS intensified as an intellectual focus. Examining the rise of information as a prominent domain within LIS provides another lens through which we can examine the theoretical fit of the conservation of library and archives specialization within the discipline. As a 1983 SLS faculty-generated review reports, at that time approximately two-thirds of the ALA-accredited "library schools" in the US and Canada had changed their names to include *information*—"Information Studies, Information Management, or Information Science."[24] While the 1983 report noted that the addition of the *I* proved to be more cosmetic than substantive in a number of instances, this naming nonetheless reflected a shift in the field that began as early as the 1950s.[25]

Within this model, however, LIS increasingly emphasized the commonalities of information practice, transferrable to a range of institutional and noninstitutional settings in the information environment.[26] Schools may have viewed information science as an add-on, but the fact that *information* became incorporated in the names of schools signified a critical shift.

By the late 1980s, the duality of library science and information science gradually manifested in a rift in the LIS discipline. A new "iSchool" movement began to coalesce. This movement is important to our analysis of the increasing difficulty of framing library and archives conservation in the LIS discipline and, particularly, within an iSchool. Referring to themselves as the "Gang of Three," in 1988, the School of Library and Information Sciences (now the School of Information Sciences) at the University of Pittsburgh, Syracuse University's School of Information Studies, and Drexel University's College of Information Science and Technology began to meet at annual Association of Library and Information Science Educators (ALISE) meetings. Their objective was "to share information and to foster development of a community of colleagues addressing such questions as 'How do you explain information science (IS) to your provost?'" In 1996, the University of Michigan became the first graduate program to rename its school simply as the "School of Information." Other schools followed suit over the next decade. By 2003, the "Gang" had grown to ten, at which point "the group's agenda became more focused on building a sense of identity and community among the 'information schools,' or 'iSchools.'"[27] The group was formally named "The iSchools Caucus" in 2005, substantiating the collective "production and diffusion of ideas and knowledge" central to the emergence of intellectual movements.[28]

The iSchool movement, incorporated as iSchools Inc. in 2015, states that it emerged and evolved as schools realized in 2003 that there was an explosive growth in digital information. While some in the new "iField" have suggested broad theoretical conceptions of "information," the dominant discourse focuses on *computed* information, not historical technologies such as books, paper, analog audiovisual recordings, and the like.

Increasingly, the requirement of "hand skills" separated the education of conservators within an information science–oriented domain. While the theoretical and philosophical underpinnings of conservation resonated with new preservation issues associated with digital information, hand skills were linked (albeit via a questionable intellectual dichotomy) to "old," "fragile," "rare," and "special" items in disrepair and situated in a traditional, nonprogressive, trade or artisanal past rather than engaged with a modern-day Information Society.[29] Moreover, the faculty who taught conservation did not have PhDs, further relegating them as "other" and relatively impotent in the academy.[30] Hence as LIS began to separate "traditional" library work from that involving the new information environment, information scientists found little intellectual alliance with analog "book" and "paper" conservation.

Now let's return to the move of the CEP from Columbia to its new home in the summer of 1992 in GSLIS at UT Austin. Once again, the program's new labs and classrooms were housed on the periphery of campus (a ten-minute walk uphill from the GSLIS proper) in a decidedly unattractive off-site storage library. After seventeen years in the GSLIS/iSchool at UT Austin, the faculty voted to discontinue its advanced study certificate in conservation education in 2009, after "significant examination of the goals and objectives" of the school's programs, in light of its "move to new facilities, significant new faculty hires and the shifting funding model for higher education."[31]

While the financing of the program was a legitimate concern, the closure of the program and its subsequent move into art conservation suggests that the LIS/iSchool domain could not—or chose not to—support it. Designed as an expensive program graduating few students per year, it would have been counterintuitive for an LIS/iSchool in 2009 to attempt to reconstruct it without significant external support.[32] Moreover, as a specialized area of study, the increasingly tenuous intellectual and cultural fit of library and archives conservation in the LIS/iSchool domain was inherently problematic.

Art Conservation

In 2010, as the art conservation programs commenced with their Mellon-supported pilot projects, the field of library and archives conservation entered an experimental phase, albeit at an advanced stage of its history and development. As the Mellon Foundation and the faculty of the art conservation programs predicted, the transitional period has resulted in changes and adjustments, most particularly with regard to the intellectual framing of the library and archives specialty.

In my roles as library and archives program liaison between the three art conservation programs, adjunct assistant professor in the Winterthur/University of Delaware Program in Art Conservation, and former chair of the visiting committee that advised the initial phases of the new library and archives specialization within the programs, I have had the opportunity to engage with the programs' administrations, the faculties, and the students. Library and archives conservation has the opportunity for both stability and growth within the art conservation domain. The pilot period's "success" can be measured by one significant metric: the almost twenty library and archives students who have graduated from the programs since 2012 hold conservator positions in Association of Research Libraries institutions, in the National Archives and Records Administration, in regional conservation facilities, in the National Park Services, in independent research libraries, and in a museum holding extensive archival collections. Institutions have not required the MLIS. In effect, by hiring these graduates, the primary institutional stakeholders in library and archives conservation have invested their dollars and professional trust in the ability of the art conservation programs to produce the professionals they seek to fulfill their missions.

We understand today that library and archives conservation became part of the LIS domain for particular reasons. At the risk of oversimplifying the intellectual grounding of the field, the disciplinary basis for library and archives conservation rested to some degree in the ideas that books and records are not art and libraries are not museums. Today, those reasons have less resonance, particularly given the significant intellectual and cultural changes that the LIS/iSchool domain has undergone in recent decades. I suggest that presently, within art conservation, discernible factors speak to the potential that library and archives conservation has a solid disciplinary home for its continued development.

First, the intellectual-cultural dynamics within art conservation promise to be conducive to the systematic intellectual growth of the library and archives specialty. To a great extent, library and archives conservation education modeled itself academically and culturally on the older, more developed field of art conservation. As we have seen today, a substantial drawback for library and archives conservation within the LIS domain rested on an observable degree of intellectual and cultural misalignment. To an extent, this misfit restricted library and archives conservation intellectually through a choice not to support the full intellectual, cultural, or financial development of the field. For example, from the beginning, art conservation programs normalized the role of physical scientists on faculty to conduct research and to guide students in scientific, instrumented studies of cultural records. The curricula are designed to produce scientifically literate graduates capable of the essential understanding of the fundamental chemical and physical properties of cultural materials and the technology of their manufacture, through and with a focus on instrumental analysis techniques and the proposal, interpretation, and writing of experimental research. In LIS, little funding was directed to in-depth scientific and instrumental analysis of cultural records.[33] To date, library and archives conservation in praxis has been predominantly production (treatments, etc.) oriented, with little opportunity for institutionalized scientific and technical research.[34] Students emerging from the art conservation programs will affect the work of these institutional operations. They will bring the culture (and skills) of rigorous scientific research; in time, they may evolve how conservation departments in libraries see and perform their work. Congruently, the library and archives institutional

environment and its evolving mission will influence the research conservation professionals find important. As a result, we may witness
increased interdisciplinary collaboration among library and archives
conservators, scientists, curators, scholars, and communities to document and call attention to the role of the cultural record in its range of
meanings for the scholarly community and the public at large.[35]

Second, the collectivist cultural orientation and sense of mission
that a broad field such as art conservation encompasses suggests not
only collegiality and "likeness" of mind-set but also the singular focus
of financial and intellectual resources on conservation education.[36] All
three programs have stated that library and archives conservation is
now part of their domain and that they are committed to sustaining
and developing the specialty.[37] Outside funding support is oftentimes
critical to the sustenance of an academic program. The art conservation
programs have proven to be highly adept at creating and responding to
educational needs by augmenting their budgets with private and federal short-term funding. However, at least at present, the art conservation programs rest on relatively stable financial bedrock; in addition
to short-term funds, they have garnered long-term support from the
private and federal sectors toward building large endowments. Moreover, they have merited the continued support of their parent institutions. The longevity of these programs, the strength of their leadership,
and the visibility they have created through research, national and
international community-based projects involving the conservation of
material culture, and substantial fund-raising has reflected positively
on parent institutions. Finally, three programs are better than one.

Concluding Thoughts

Significant challenges remain during this transitional period from one
intellectual domain to another. Beyond producing practicing library
and archives conservators, the field must continue to progress in its
scholarship, undertaking the advanced and interdisciplinary scientific, technical, and historical-cultural research required to support
new thinking and praxis toward the continued survival of the cultural

record. To this end—and toward the long-term stability of cultural conservation writ large in the academy—the field must increasingly produce teaching and research faculty who hold the PhD, the currency of the research university.[38] In the near future, I suggest, the master's will no longer suffice as the end degree for those who direct programs and teach conservation in the academy. Not a few of the issues that library and archives conservation faced in the LIS domain evinced from the program's instructors being denied entrée into the ranks of tenured faculty. Without tenured faculty holding the highest degree of academic currency, the field risks a diminished voice and status within the academy and a limited opportunity to create potentially powerful coalitions across academic disciplines.

Finally, I suggest that it is time for the art conservation programs to consider a renaming to represent the spectrum of the cultural record. *Cultural record conservation* may serve as a term acceptable to any number of audiences. The word *record* speaks to the full spectrum of human existence, creativity, and experience in all their nuances. Naming the field as such speaks directly to its intellectual, disciplinary, and sociocultural domain. By clearly identifying and communicating the nature and significance of the field's work, the cultural record has a better chance of serving its many purposes and constituencies through preventive and remedial conservation measures, interdisciplinary research, and community-based engagement.

Notes

1. In September 2017, the Andrew W. Mellon Foundation awarded a grant of $2,100,000 to the State University of New York College at Buffalo to support for approximately eight years an advanced degree program of study in the conservation of library and archival collections. A cooperative educational undertaking, the funding will be shared among three graduate art conservation education programs: Patricia H. and Richard E. Garman Art Conservation Department, State University of New York College at Buffalo; Conservation Center, Institute of Fine Arts, New York University; and Department of Art Conservation, University of Delaware. Earl Lewis to Katherine S. Conway-Turner, September 27, 2017. In the author's possession.

2. The Boston Athenaeum hired George M. Cunha as its conservator in spring 1964.

3. Paul N. Banks, "Education for Conservators: A Proposal for Training Conservators of Library and Archival Materials," *Library Journal* 104 (May 1, 1979): 1016. Banks stated that the training program "must be affiliated with or be within a university." It is clear, however, that he favored being "within" the university. He continued, "We are really talking not only about training conservators, but, of necessity, about developing the whole field of library conservation. This also suggests that the university environment, which is traditionally hospitable to such activities as research, writing, and editing publications, professional societies, and so on, is the appropriate place for a conservation training program." Banks never stated directly that library and archives conservation education should be within LIS; however, he did articulate the subject matter that a program should contain: history of the book, descriptive bibliography, rare book librarianship, and "perhaps a survey or core course in libraries and librarianship, which are offered at most library schools" (1016). In a 1978 article Banks wrote for the *Encyclopedia of Library and Information Science*, he suggested that education for "conservation administration could presumably be effectively carried out as a specialty in a library school which has a strong commitment to the physical book." Banks, "Preservation of Library Materials," *Encyclopedia of Library and Information Science* (New York: Marcel Dekker, 1978), 214.

4. Suggesting in a talk he gave at the IFA-CC that museum conservation might be interested in the ideal of specialized training for PAs, by 1983, Banks was clearly sold on the role of the PA in research libraries. Banks, "A Library Is Not a Museum," in *Training in Conservation: A Symposium on the Occasion of the Dedication of the Stephen Chan House* (New York: Institute of Fine Arts, New York University, 1989), 65.

5. The UT Austin iSchool continues to offer a certificate of advanced study in "preservation studies"; the curriculum is less prescribed in its current iteration, requiring only twelve credit hours of specialized coursework. The former certificate was named "Administration of Preservation Programs in Library and Archives."

6. In 2009, there were fifty-nine American Library Association–accredited LIS programs in the US, Canada, and Puerto Rico.

7. Heritage Preservation, Inc., and Institute of Museum and Library Services, *A Public Trust at Risk: The Heritage Health Index Report on the State of America's Collections* (Washington, DC: Heritage Preservation, 2005), 28.

8. Donald Waters, email to Debra H. Norris (with copy to author), "Proposal from UD/Winterthur," September 20, 2010.

9. For example, in the first round of grants, Buffalo hired a specialist in preservation administration as an adjunct faculty member to teach short courses on management topics, and NYU partnered with the Palmer School of Library

and Information Science, Long Island University; the Morgan Library and Museum; and the Columbia University Libraries to incorporate the following courses: Introduction to Descriptive Bibliography: Understanding the Material Book, History of Book Structures Practicum and the Treatment of Bound Materials in the Research of Library and Archive, and Introduction to the History of Bookbinding (Columbia University Libraries); History of the Book, Collections Librarianship, and Introduction to Preservation (The Palmer School); Special Topics in the Conservation and Exhibition of Rare Books and Manuscripts (The Morgan Library and Museum). Delaware partnered with Simmons College Graduate School of Library and Information Science to incorporate the following courses: Preservation Management in Libraries and Archives, History of the Book, Introduction to Archives, Digital Stewardship, and a six-week internship. The Library of Congress provided a ten-month internship, and North Bennet Street School created a five-week lab course called Historical Bookbinding Structures.

10. Waters, email to Norris.

11. See Andrew Abbott, *The Chaos of Disciplines* (Chicago: University of Chicago Press, 2001). Abbott argues that the intellectual world today reaches across disciplines in ways hitherto unimagined, while the disciplinary system—the departmental structure in the US—has remained largely unchanged since its instantiation between 1890 and 1910. He further posits that the system of disciplines could (and does) survive the destruction of some of its elements (e.g., departments); the other disciplines fill in the intellectual space it used to occupy.

12. Ibid., 20.

13. Ibid., 21, 33.

14. Ibid., 27.

15. Ibid., 31.

16. Columbia University School of Library Service, *Conservation and Preservation Education Programs*, December 1982, 4, box 2, folder 68, Conservator's Administrative Files, 1964–89, Conservation Department, Office of the Preservation Librarian, Newberry Library Archives.

17. Jonathan R. Cole, *Report of the Provost on the School of Library Service at Columbia*, appendix 3, "Report of the Review Committee for the School of Library Service" (New York: Columbia University, January 25, 1990), 4. The committee reported that in fall 1989, the SLS had defined a number of fields of "advanced work" as it revised its curriculum from thirty-six to forty-eight credit hours. After a "common core," students had to select a field of major emphasis from the following: Academic and Research Librarianship, Archives Management and Organization, Bibliographic Control, Information Science and Systems, Information Services, Management and Administration, Public Librarianship, Rare Books and Special Collections, and Special Libraries.

18. Allert Brown-Gort, *Final Performance Report to the National Endowment for the Humanities on the Conservation Education Programs at the School of Library Service, Columbia University* (New York: Columbia School of Library Service, 1990).

19. Ibid., 5–6.

20. PAs took one lab course designed specifically for their needs.

21. Columbia University School of Library Service, *Conservation and Preservation*, 5–6.

22. For example, art conservation master's programs now typically have a wide range of analytical equipment, including scientific instrumentation for organic and inorganic analysis that allow the identification of paint media, pigments, alloy assay, fibers, and photographic processes. Labs contain equipment for forensic imaging of artwork by X-ray, ultraviolet, and infrared techniques.

23. Paul N. Banks, "The Scientist, the Scholar and the Book Conservator: Some Thoughts on Book Conservation as a Profession," in *Atti Della XLIX Riunione Della Societa Italiana per Il Progresso Delle Scienze* (Rome: Societa Italiana per il Progresso delle Scienze, 1968), 1215.

24. Faculty of the School of Library Service, *Columbia University School of Library Service: New Directions* (New York: Columbia University, 1983), 33.

25. Tefko Saracevic, "Information Science," *Journal of the American Society for Information Science* 50, no. 12 (October 1999): 1061. Jesse H. Shera, long-time dean from the 1950s to 1970s at Western Reserve University (now Case Western Reserve) and regarded as one of the early principles of information science in the US, founded there the Center for Documentation and Communication Research in 1955. Soon, the library school at Western Reserve began to incorporate "information"-oriented courses, which acted as electives appended to the library school curriculum. Rather than modify the library science curriculum, information science (or a variation) became a specialty of library science. Schools in the US and in other countries copied Shera's model, which, as of 1999, remained prevalent.

26. June Lester, "Education for Librarianship: A Report Card," *American Libraries* 21, no. 6 (June 1, 1990): 580.

27. The iSchools Organization, "Origins," http://ischools.org/about/history/origins/. Accessed online March 18, 2018.

28. Scott Frickel and Neil Gross, "A General Theory of Scientific/Intellectual Movements," *American Sociological Review* 70, no. 2 (April 2005): 206.

29. As Glenn Adamson argues in *The Invention of Craft*, the "bifurcation" between craft and other more objective ways of making and knowing that occurred during the Industrial Revolution continues to linger in our cultural narratives. He demonstrates that what had once been an undifferentiated complex of human production evolved into a set of constructed binaries: "craft/industry, freedom/alienation, tacit/explicit, hand/machine, traditional/progressive." The professional field of library and archives

conservation emerged from deep historical roots in a Western European apprenticeship model or a trade school education in "trade" and craft binding. Other fields have emerged similarly (including LIS) in the twentieth century and have wrangled with like questions. Like Adamson in *Shop Class as Soulcraft* (2009), Matthew B. Crawford attempts to place these kinds of questions in a broader context. He scrutinizes what he calls the recent educational imperative to turn students into "knowledge workers," which he says is based on a misguided separation of the work of the hand from that of the mind. Crawford traces the partition between hand and mind to the invention of the assembly line, arguing that attempting to segregate handwork from "thinking" work is a false concept. In its enactment in the workforce, he argues that separating handwork and abstract thinking promotes denigration of work on either side of the divide. Glenn Adamson and Victoria and Albert Museum, *The Invention of Craft* (London: Bloomsbury Academic, 2013); Matthew B. Crawford, *Shop Class as Soulcraft: An Inquiry into the Value of Work* (New York: Penguin, 2009).

30. For example, conservation instructors could not sit on the faculty executive committee in the iSchool. While the instructors and director of the program participated in graduate studies committee meetings, as non–tenure track faculty, their vote on school concerns (including curriculum and the direction of the school) did not count officially at the university level.

31. Mary Lynn Rice-Lively, "Curriculum Changes at University of Texas School of Information," *Conservation DistList*, January 13, 2010. The posting does not mention that in 2009, as part of the school's move to new facilities, the university funded and built two expensive, custom book and paper laboratories to support the certificate of advanced study offerings in conservation and preservation administration.

32. Beginning with its founding at Columbia in 1981, the National Endowment for the Humanities (NEH) supported the conservation and preservation administration specializations with significant funding. August 31, 2010, marked the end of NEH funding for the program at the UT Austin iSchool. NEH senior program officer Nadina Y. Gardner commented that outside reviewers of that final proposal to the NEH from the iSchool were concerned about the financial commitment of UT Austin to the specializations: "They . . . expressed concern that the conservation aspect of the curriculum was on the softest ground in terms of funding and that the university was not providing enough support for a program with high, national ranking in the field. In spite of their concerns about the lack of a substantial institutional commitment to the program, the panelists acknowledged that it is the premier program of its kind in the nation and merited the highest priority for support." Nadina Y. Gardner, email to author, January 28, 2008.

33. For example, at UT Austin, chemistry coursework depended on the program contracting a lecturer to teach the two core chemistry classes. With no

science lab and little available instrumentation, faculty and students were hampered in their ability to undertake rigorous scientific analysis. This said, students performed a level of scientific research and a range of other kinds of research (historical and social science based) that advanced knowledge in the field. For example, at the annual conference of the Association of North American Graduate Programs in Conservation between 2005 and 2008, two conservator and two doctoral students from the UT iSchool presented papers on the following topics: "Revealing Networks: A Case Study of Disaster Response and Recuperation" (Maria Gonzalez, doctoral student); "The Nature of Forgeries: Iron Gall Ink and Paper Aging in Relation to Forged Historical Documents—an Independent Study" (Tish Brewer, conservator student); "Revisiting the (Recent) History of Publishers' Bindings as Artifacts" (Fletcher Durant, conservator student); and "See No Evil, Hear No Evil: Audiovisual Evidence, Forensics, and Preservation in Law Enforcement" (Snowden Becker, doctoral student).

34. Office of Survey Research, Annette Strauss Institute for Civic Participation, *Program Evaluation: Conservator Graduate Questionnaire*, Executive Summary (Austin: University of Texas at Austin, June 2009). This study of the UT Austin iSchool's conservation certificate program was funded by the Mellon Foundation. This particular component of the evaluation surveyed UT conservator graduates to better understand how well the iSchool and the conservator curriculum in particular prepared them for the workplace. The survey instrument was prepared by the iSchool's Kilgarlin Center for Preservation of the Cultural Record; the author directed the center at the time this survey was undertaken. Of the findings, only 13 percent of the alums felt prepared to examine cultural objects using lab equipment. Fewer than one in ten (9 percent) felt "very prepared" to design a scientific experiment.

35. One example illustrating this kind of collaboration is the Archimedes Palimpsest Project. See http://archimedespalimpsest.org.

36. Frickel and Gross, "A General Theory of Scientific/Intellectual Movements," 218–19. The authors suggest, "It may be easier for SIMs to win followers and become institutionalized in fields or at moments in a field's history when its repertoire tends toward collectivism, because a collectivist cultural orientation conduces toward collective action. Each of the mobilizing structures on which SIMs must rely—departments, communication networks, and scholarly organizations—become more efficient tools for it to the extent that the individual actors who compose them have a collectivist orientation."

37. Ellen Cunningham-Kruppa, personal meeting notes from the Mellon Visiting Committee on Library and Archives Conservation Education, August 7–8, 2014, Buffalo State Art Conservation Department. In the author's possession.

38. Other than the scientists on faculty in the three programs, few permanent and adjunct faculty hold the PhD. The end degree in art conservation has, to this point, been the master's.

EDUCATING LIBRARY AND ARCHIVES CONSERVATORS IN ART CONSERVATION GRADUATE PROGRAMS

Morgan Adams

I would like to begin by sharing my path to a career in library conservation. I am a 2013 graduate of New York University's Institute of Fine Arts Conservation Center. I first learned about conservation as an undergraduate intern in the Harry Ransom Humanities Research Center at the University of Texas at Austin, working with book conservators Olivia Primanis and Mary Baughman. After graduating, I moved to Ann Arbor, Michigan, and Olivia introduced me to Shannon Zachary and Julia Miller, who in turn introduced me to Cathleen Baker and all the wonderful book and library people in Ann Arbor. Over the next four years, I prepared to apply to conservation graduate programs, taking chemistry and art history classes at night and bookbinding workshops on the weekends, all while working in the University of Michigan Special Collections Library and then the conservation lab. I enrolled in the NYU program in 2009, pursuing a major in book conservation with the ambition of working in a university research library. The Conservation Center did not offer a concentration in book conservation when I started; however, I knew that previous students had focused on books in the past, and I intended to supplement the paper conservation curriculum with book-specific internships and independent studies with book conservators in New York City. My timing was fortunate, as the Conservation Center faculty started planning programming for a libraries and archives specialty during my second year. I was lucky to be an unofficial guinea pig for new courses and workshops. This is the perspective I can share with you today, that of a recent graduate of an art conservation program who now works in a research library. I will briefly review how the art conservation graduate programs adapted to train library and archive conservators and then consider the benefits and challenges of this educational model.

As Ellen Cunningham-Kruppa outlined for us in her theme paper, in 2011, three of the four American conservation programs—Buffalo, Delaware, and NYU—each added a specialization in libraries and archives conservation, with funding from the Andrew W. Mellon Foundation. A specialty in book conservation needs to include the following:

- bookbinding training, including working with leather, parchment, wood, cloth, and preparing and maintaining tools and knives

  Learning historical techniques with a conservator's eye is essential to appreciating how a binding's features impact its function and deterioration. The value of historic reconstructions to technical studies of art has been recognized since at least the work of Edward Forbes at the Fogg Museum.[1]
- connoisseurship of the history of bookbinding and related crafts, such as printing and the production of manuscripts, paper, and parchment
- book conservation treatment experience with book conservators
- experience with circulating collection care and book repair
- introduction to library preservation and special collections librarianship, as well as descriptive bibliography and book and manuscript studies

To meet these overall expected requirements, the graduate programs collaborated with many book conservators, book historians, libraries, and institutions, as well as library and information schools, to provide instruction in book conservation treatment, book history and descriptive bibliography, and library-related courses.[2] For example, NYU partnered with Columbia University Libraries for a winter intersession course on the history of bookbinding (four days of lectures, with time for the students to examine hundreds of books and practice writing binding descriptions), plus introductions to paleography (one day) and descriptive bibliography (two days). Any of these subjects could fill a semester or more, but there is not time in the already full curriculum. Instead, the short courses function as introductions to the topics, with the expectation that the students will seek further education as their careers progress.

The first and primary benefit of educating library conservators in tandem with art conservators is that shared coursework provides exposure to and interaction with the wider world of conservation. Students learn about the technology and structure of textiles, photographs, paper, leather and parchment, wood, paintings, metals, stone, ivory, bone, horn, glass, plastics, and time-based media. This equips students with a broad knowledge base to inform their own practice.

At NYU, I tailored my coursework to my specialization in books, working in the NYU Libraries' conservation lab during the semesters, interning in libraries every summer, and selecting relevant art history seminars along the way. At the same time, I had two experiences that, at first glance, had nothing to do with books: first, I worked as a conservator on an archaeological dig, and second, I took an objects conservation course in which I treated a folding paper lantern. These experiences provided general training, valuable to every conservator, such as improving my hand skills, treatment planning, and documentation skills. They honed specific techniques useful in a library setting, such as efficiently creating custom housings for three-dimensional objects. This kind of cross-specialty sharing is valuable, particularly early in one's career, because it encourages innovation and can lead to creative problem solving.

A second benefit of cotraining book, paper, and art conservators, as Ellen highlighted, is that art conservation graduate programs have a particular advantage in providing a more well-developed curriculum in conservation science. In addition to studying material science, students learn to apply and interpret analytical techniques. This is essential to the goal of creating scientifically literate conservators who are capable of planning and carrying out technical analysis themselves or in partnership with scientists. Technical studies are an area of increasing interest to the fields of book and art history, and conservators should be centrally engaged in these discussions.

Third, shared graduate education results in increased integration of library conservators with the art conservation world. Classmates become objects conservators, paintings conservators, and textile conservators and form an important professional network for a library conservator to draw on for expertise throughout his or her career. This is valuable, as libraries contain more than just books and documents. As a particularly extreme example, my colleague and classmate Jessica Pace, preventive conservator in the Barbara Goldsmith Preservation and Conservation Department for NYU Libraries, recently built custom housing for a stuffed alligator in the David Wojnarowicz Papers.[3] Furthermore, rare book libraries are increasingly engaged in exhibitions and loans with museums, and it benefits library conservators to be more connected to their museum colleagues.

For me, the most valuable part of my graduate school experience was learning how to think about my own work and where it fits into the broader field, its history, and its theories. The scope of activities and diversity of approaches included within "conservation" is much more wide-ranging than I had realized. I learned that the goals and activities of a conservator are specific to each collection and context. And I realized that the history of conservation is more vital to our work today than I had previously appreciated. Perhaps most important, I came to understand that the theories of conservation are not static. They have evolved in response to events such as the Florence Flood and to changes in technology, material science, and the arts themselves.[4] As professional conservators, it is essential that we continue this conversation about what our work means with each other and the wider library and museum communities.

There are some important challenges in a model of integrated conservation training. Art conservation students in an integrated program are not necessarily exposed to the broader library and archives community; they may not attend professional association meetings, such as the biannual American Library Association conferences, and do not learn to "talk the talk" with librarians. Whereas book and paper conservation students in the NYU program take classes with art history graduate students, who will become their colleagues in the museum world, library conservation students have to educate themselves about the work of rare books librarians and build an equivalent network. Courses at Rare Book School are an opportunity for building this type of professional network.

In preparing for this symposium and considering conservation education from the perspective of educational institutions and instructors, rather than that of the student, I was continually awestruck that the training of conservators, whatever the educational model, relies entirely on a tremendous amount of work put in by some extremely dedicated and determined teachers and the institutions who support their educational work. Clearly, no student becomes a conservator in just three or four years of graduate school. Rather, the graduate programs provide a framework: the student learns what it means to be a conservator and gains the tools to seek the additional education and experience that he or she needs to work responsibly in our field. It is through many years of work, continuing education and training, relationships with mentors, curiosity, and drive that we become conservators. It has been more than three years since I graduated, and I am still building my treatment experience. My "bench training" is ongoing.

Book conservation is the *intersection* of multiple disciplines. This alluring combination of art and science applied to historical artifacts makes it interesting and rewarding to practitioners and fascinating to outsiders. It is also what makes educating conservators awkward and challenging: the needs are many and diverse; the equipment is expensive, highly specialized, and often situated all over campus; and the job market for new conservators is never as large as the need for conservation.

In considering the future of library and archives conservation education, let's look at the unique contributions book conservators make to libraries. Beyond treatment, which is itself an essential contribution, conservators understand the technical and historical aspects of the collections in ways that are frequently unique within an institution. It is precisely our training across disciplines combined with our hands-on work that puts us in a position to interpret and contextualize data prepared by scientists or to assist curators and researchers in recognizing material evidence to understand the creation and history of an object. In addition to serving others, we conduct our own research contributing to the wider scholarship in history and material culture. I suggest that the question motivating us when we consider the future of conservation education and the field should be this: How do we communicate our unique value to libraries and prepare future conservators to best contribute?

Notes

1. Norbert Baer, Michele Marincola, and Margaret Holben Ellis, email messages to author, May 25–26, 2017; Francesca G. Bewer, *A Laboratory for Art: Harvard's Fogg Museum and the Emergence of Conservation in America, 1900–1950* (Cambridge, MA: Harvard Art Museum, 2010), 42, 56–57. Edward Forbes directed the Fogg Museum at Harvard University from 1909 to 1944 and founded the (Straus) Center for Conservation and Technical Studies. In his own training, Forbes practiced historical painting techniques to better understand the materials and aging properties. He required students to copy paintings as a part of his early courses in art history and technical studies at Harvard in the 1920s. The NYU Conservation Center graduate program modeled its early curriculum on Forbes's courses, and students were painting frescoes and panel paintings as early as 1960. Over the past fifty-seven years, Conservation Center students have also practiced papermaking, spinning and dying wool, weaving, printing, photography, stone carving, ceramics, and mosaic work. Reconstructions remain an important part of the Conservation Center curriculum today.
2. Collaborating institutions included the Palmer School of Library and Information Science, Long Island University; the Simmons College Graduate

School of Library and Information Science; the Rare Book School; the North Bennett Street School; the Library of Congress; Columbia University Libraries; and the Morgan Library & Museum.

3. "Stuffed Reptile" (catalog #092.2.0541), David Wojnarowicz Papers, Fales Library and Special Collections, New York University.

4. For example, installation art and time-based media have pushed conservators to new definitions of what constitutes a treatment.

THE FUTURE OF LIBRARY AND ARCHIVES CONSERVATION EDUCATION

Cathleen A. Baker

In my brief remarks, I will sketch the trajectory that has brought the conservation field to its present state of educational offerings. I will then speculate about promising future developments, contextualizing my remarks with two suggestions for making conservation education more diverse and more effective.

The list below is the timeline of the degree-granting North American programs that have offered majors in art on paper and/or library and archives conservation over the past fifty-six years.

DEGREE-GRANTING NORTH AMERICAN PROGRAMS
WITH MAJORS IN ART ON PAPER AND/OR LIBRARY
AND ARCHIVES CONSERVATION (LAC)

1960–present	New York University / Institute of Fine Arts / Conservation Center
1968–78	Oberlin College / Intermuseum Conservation Association
1970–present	SUNY–Oneonta State College, Cooperstown, NY, and SUNY–Buffalo State College

1974–present	University of Delaware / Winterthur Museum
1974–present	Queen's University, Kingston, Ontario, Canada
1981–2011	Columbia University and University of Texas at Austin
2011–present	Mellon Library and Archives Conservation Fellowships at Buffalo, Delaware, and NYU

The book and archives conservation program at the University of Texas at Austin stopped admitting students in Fall 2009, and in 2011, the Andrew W. Mellon Foundation began to support the discipline of book and archives conservation within the three fine art programs through its Library and Archives Conservation Fellowship.

In 1969, three years after the Florence Flood of 1966, a team consisting of James Lewis and Peter Waters of the Conservation of Library Materials Research Group, Imperial College of Science and Technology, along with Emanuele Casamasima of the National Library in Florence, issued a pamphlet titled "Proposed International Centre for the Preservation of Books and Manuscripts."[1] Too long to quote in full here, the "subjects for study" to be covered were the following:

1. Historical development of book technology, experimental construction of nondestructive bindings, composition and testing of book materials, practical studies of the reversible restoration of artifacts, assessment of mass deacidification
2. Principle causes of deterioration, day-to-day care, techniques in surveying collections to establish conservation priorities
3. Emergency measures, after treatment and storage of disaster-damaged artifacts
4. Study of the book in relation to conservation practice as it affects the scholar, scientist, and restorer
5. Administration of preservation programs in libraries

It is not surprising that these subjects were also central to the Columbia/Texas programs, and they are at the core of a new book and archives program under consideration now. In early 2016, an advisory committee was formed with funding from the Mellon Foundation to look into the advisability and practicality of a graduate program that would focus on the education of library and archives conservators at the University of California, Los Angeles. This committee consisted of members from a variety of institutions and geographic locations, including myself. Other committee members included the following:

- Elmer Eusman, Library of Congress
- Lisa Forman, Getty Research Institute
- Doris Hamburg, National Archives and Records Administration, retired
- Penley Knipe, Harvard Art Museums
- Chela Metzger, UCLA Library
- Holly Moore, Huntington Library
- Janet Ruggles, Balboa Art Conservation Center
- Jennifer Hain Teper, University of Illinois–Urbana Champaign
- Nancy Turner, J. Paul Getty Museum

The committee was headed by Ellen Pearlstein, who is director of the UCLA/Getty Program in the Conservation of Archaeological and Ethnographic Materials. Significantly, she is a full professor on the faculty of the Department of Information Studies, within the UCLA Graduate School of Education and Information Studies. Among other things, the UCLA advisory committee was charged with defining admission prerequisites, the type of degree to be awarded, the length of the program, and the curriculum within the Department of Information Studies, as well as staffing and the design and equipping of appropriate teaching spaces. If the committee's recommendation to establish such as program is accepted by the school, this conservation program could become a reality within a few years.

Here I offer my thoughts on two topics: admission prerequisites and the length of conservation programs. I want to make it clear that what follows are my personal opinions and should not be interpreted as representing those of the committee or any of the other members.

In other talks at this symposium, mention was made that the three art conservation programs have different academic requirements for admission and that these prerequisites differed from those required by the Columbia/Texas program. While a few students apply to any program with all the prerequisites in hand, most have to go back to college to pick up required courses. I would argue that the required general and organic chemistry courses (four semesters for art conservation and two semesters for the Texas program) present the greatest obstacle for the nonscience students, psychologically and financially. Over the years, I have advised many studio art and art history students who want to become conservators, but for many prospective students, the idea of taking four semesters of chemistry is out of the question. We can discuss the validity of their reasons for making this decision, but the fact remains that many highly qualified, potentially fantastic people have excluded themselves from the pursuit of this profession most often because of the science courses prerequisite. And the message that this prerequisite could send to our larger audience is that conservators graduating from a program are actually scientists. If you ask program graduates, I do not think any of them would describe themselves as such, including the Winterthur/Delaware graduates who receive a master of science degree. But I suspect that nonprofessionals would agree with that description, for after all, don't conservators work in labs and wear lab coats?

I think it would be far better for our profession if we recognize and celebrate the fact that practicing conservators are first and foremost not scientists—that, in fact, they have other, equally valid, skills and knowledge that enable them to solve real preservation, conservation, and treatment problems and that the acquisition of these skills and knowledge is just as rigorous as attaining an MS (one could argue more rigorous). If the preservation of collections, whether in museums, libraries, or archives, is to be accomplished in reasonable, practical, and cost-effective ways, science must be able to explain the observations of the knowledgeable conservator, not the other way around. Conservators need to have much more confidence in their abilities to act as advocates for their collections, to critically analyze how artifacts function in terms of their use and how they have aged based on their environments, and then to make sound recommendations based on those observations and conclusions, backed up by the methods of scientific investigation.

My radical suggestion is that the science courses prerequisite be dropped by all the existing conservation programs, including the proposed UCLA program. Instead, I recommend that the programs as a group provide one intensive, preprogram, science-based summer course for all newly admitted students, taught by program scientists. This would bring into the applicant pool a much more diverse group of potential conservators. Admittedly, the number of applications each year would rise above the present one hundred plus for the ten or fewer places in each program, but it would be worth solving that administrative headache in favor of a wider variety of individuals from which to choose. On the other side of the coin, applicants with science backgrounds find having to take the required courses in art history, studio art, and/or information studies equally daunting. A solution to this problem might be to establish a science major within the conservation programs, enabling those students to graduate as conservation scientists, a designation that is now given to scientists who work with conservators.

Second, I would like to address the length of an academic program. Not including the essential internship located away from school, I believe that two years in any academic program, focusing on conservation, is not long enough to educate students to the level that they need to attain by the time they leave for their internships. Instead, I would recommend three years in the classroom. When interviewing internship supervisors and employers of new program graduates, the common complaint is that the students/graduates simply do not know enough and/or do not have the requisite hand skills in order to fully benefit from the internship supervisor's instruction or to be a productive employee within a conservation department or business.

Before leaving for their internships, students should (1) gain extensive knowledge about the scientific, historical, and technological aspects of a variety of artifacts; (2) learn to think critically about what they read or hear and relate that to what they observe to be true; (3) acquire extensive hand skills (and, additionally for book conservators, bookbinding skills); and (4) perform numerous routine and advanced treatments under the guidance of the instructor in their major. The success of attaining these four goals in the classroom can only occur in conjunction with the accumulation of a deep and wide understanding of artifacts gained only by handling and examining many artifacts—certainly hundreds, and perhaps thousands. Condition surveys of collections undertaken as summer projects would be ideal opportunities for students to garner this information and turn it into knowledge.

As has been pointed out during this panel's presentations, the exposure to the materiality of and conservation problems associated with art and museum artifacts that LAC students now receive in the art conservation programs is essential if we are to graduate well-informed library and archives conservators, because such collections are seldom composed of just books and documents. I would suggest that the UCLA program include one course that would bring in lecturers for a few weeks to cover paintings, objects, art on paper, and photographs. Thus the library and archives conservation students will be better prepared to understand artifacts materially, historically, and culturally, and then decide on the most appropriate policy for their preservation.

If these extra courses and summer projects are to occur without overloading students or teachers, I think that three years in the classroom are warranted, followed by the crucial internship. Funding to support these courses, projects, and the third year would have to be found, but I truly think that more knowledgeable graduates possessing better hand skills would result in a richer profession as well as better served and preserved collections.

Each of the present North American programs has been in existence for many decades now, and since their beginnings, they have essentially operated within the same program structures and over time have required even more academic prerequisites. Especially in the light of achieving diversity in the conservation profession, if they haven't done so already, it is time for the programs to take a critical look at themselves to determine how they can be less exclusive and more inclusive without compromising each program's unique characteristics.

Serving on the UCLA committee and being a panelist at this symposium have given me opportunities to articulate my ideas about these issues, albeit here briefly. Certainly I do not expect all of you to agree with what I have said, and that is fine, because what I am hoping for is that these proceedings will open up meaningful dialogs across the conservation field.

Note

1. Lewis, James, and Waters, Peter, "Requirements for an International Center for Preservation of Books and Manuscripts," *Bollettino dell'Istituto di Patologia del Libro* 1970 (1–4): 60–84.

PRESERVATION EDUCATION THROUGH IN-SERVICE TRAINING: AN INTERNATIONAL PERSPECTIVE

John F. Dean

The Florence Flood of 1966 provided a focus for preservation training in the United States and directly influenced many conservators and volunteers with hands-on experience in the emergency handling and remedial treatment of water-damaged library and archives materials. The news about the flood and resultant publicity encouraged many in the United States in particular to consider book and paper conservation to be a worthy profession.

It did not, however, lead directly to the establishment of preservation programs around the world, nor did it result in the formation of international standards of practice. These events have still yet to come to pass, but there had been considerable discussion long before 1966. This is not to suppose that the field was moribund. The body of preservation knowledge and practice on which Western systems are built is the result of a long evolution from the wholly craft-trade-based bookbinding tradition to the present level of quite sophisticated and technical practice.

In the United States, the Florence Flood events lead to the appointment of Peter Waters as head of preservation at the Library of Congress, and his far-reaching influence changed the general approach to conservation at the Library of Congress and throughout the United States. Peter was ably assisted in his endeavors by Don Etherington and Christopher Clarkson (regrettably now deceased). However, the development of preservation programs in the United States has actually been rather spotty and has waxed and waned along with the ability of institutions to pay for them. The lifeblood of funding in the United States, from private and public foundations, has altered direction along with changes in new technologies. In the seventies and eighties, the strong lobbying efforts of the Research Libraries Group (RLG) and the Council on Library Resources (which became the Commission on Preservation and Access, which became the Council on Library and Information Resources) claimed most of the national preservation funding for microfilming projects, and the few voices on the RLG Preservation Committee calling for the consideration of some allocations for conservation funding were in vain and often ridiculed.

Meanwhile, there still remained gaps in education and training. Some of the main issues were articulated by Warren Haas in his report to the Association of Research Libraries in 1972.[1] Haas noted in his *Specifications for a Nationwide Preservation Program* that what was needed was the setting up of a graduate program to educate preservation administrators and a national apprenticeship program to train conservators and technicians, similar to the ones in Europe. The Haas report led indirectly to the creation of the Columbia University graduate program, which was later moved to the University of Texas and is now sadly defunct.

The idea of a nationwide preservation apprenticeship program has still not occurred in the United States, although a five-year program was established at the Johns Hopkins University in 1975 (until budgetary constraints abolished it some years later), and a number of pioneering efforts were launched to attempt to fill the gaps. Although there were few effective institutional preservation programs in place at that time, it was seen that they would have to take the lead in helping jump-start new efforts to develop and strengthen conservation skills where they existed. For example, an Andrew W. Mellon Foundation–funded project was established at the Johns Hopkins University in 1979, which provided for a series of three-month internships, workshops, and consultancies. This proved to be so successful that three more three-year projects were funded by the Mellon Foundation to be held at the Johns Hopkins University. In 1985, similar programs were established at Cornell University.

In 1997, a three-year project was developed at Cornell to train the staffs of libraries and archives in eleven Southeast Asian countries, each internship consisting of six months of exposure to work in the university's conservation facilities. This program was supported by a variety of funding sources, including the Christopher Reynolds Foundation, the Toyota Foundation, the Harvard-Yenching Institute, the Soros Foundation Burma Project, the Henry Luce Foundation, and various Cornell faculty and alumni. The twelve interns subsequently developed preservation programs in their respective libraries and archives on their return to their own countries, and their programs have continued to be a success. For example, one intern from Cambodia is now director of the National Archives and one is director of the Sino-Nom Institute in Hanoi, Việt Nam. An intern from the University of Malaya converted a British-trained production bindery into a more conservation-oriented operation, and a former director of the General Sciences Library in Ho Chi Minh City is now a preservation consultant funded by a Dutch foundation. The project at Cornell University was followed by a similar project to train librarians from four institutions in Beijing in a series of three-month internships funded by the Henry Luce Foundation. Cornell also developed a project to provide conservation training to Native Americans to care for tribal libraries and archives, also a three-year project.

The idea of a full graduate program as recommended by Haas is certainly an excellent one, preparing students to develop and administer preservation programs. The Columbia and later University of Texas programs have provided some talented graduates, but the type of education and its acceptance by the library and archives profession has not proved sustainable. The high cost of tuition at both the Columbia and the Texas programs has tended to reduce the number of graduates, and the general lack of enthusiasm for preservation at many institutions has kept salaries for preservation administrators low, with no adequate reward for the high tuition. Grant funding to support graduate programs seems very scarce, and when available, foundations are reluctant to provide open-ended support. Meanwhile, library and archives materials continue to deteriorate for lack of preventive and remedial treatment. It seems that a partial answer to the lack of the formal apprenticeship programs envisioned by Haas is to rely on the strengths of existing operational programs through a series of internships, workshops, seminars, and consultancies.

Perhaps the most important factors pertaining to internships are the abilities and credentials of the institutions or individuals conducting the programs and the length and overall effectiveness of the internship training sessions. The selected intern will be a person with some knowledge and basic experience of preservation and will have the support of his or her employing institution. Typically, the internship would consist of a controlled rotation through the various work stations of the host institution, with some particular aspects tailored to the employing institution's needs.

Workshops and seminars can be useful ways to help raise awareness of the main challenges in preservation and identify some general areas where attention should be concentrated. These affairs are usually of a few days' duration and are very helpful in demonstrating special techniques or in introducing new approaches to old methods. They can be valuable to preservation administrators, especially if used to augment existing skills.

Apprenticeship programs are based on the incremental acquisition of skills and knowledge by serving a formal hands-on schedule of training and working in a facility where a high standard of work is performed. For conservators and technicians, this is probably the most effective way to develop high levels of skill and knowledge and to start addressing the most immediate preservation problems.

My own training in preservation was through formal apprenticeship and required supplemental craft and technical courses at the University of Manchester College of Science and Technology (UK) for the City and Guilds of London Institute certification, beginning in 1951. As a continuation of Cornell University's training and needs assessment programs since 1987, I have worked every year for more than twenty-five years in Southeast Asia and in nations in other regions, making training and consultancy visits, and worked at many libraries and archives, all with funding from various outside sources. A few examples of these have included efforts to reclaim and restore manuscripts and printed books in 1987, 1989, and 1991 to address extensive damage by the Khmer Rouge in Cambodia; establishing conservation facilities and staff training at the National Archives in Afghanistan after the ravages of the Taliban; and a continuing seven-year project to restore early printed books and manuscripts at the National Library in Việt Nam. In every case, this required developing conservation facilities from scratch and training local staff. In the latter case, the results have been outstanding, with staff now performing quite advanced work.

Sometimes disasters can occur over a period of time and collections can be deteriorated and neglected over a period of time rather than being the result of some cataclysmic event such as the great Florence Flood. Often major disasters occur more insidiously through years of neglect and lack of resources. In some countries, and especially in Southeast Asia (the region with which I am most familiar), library and archives materials are especially susceptible because of unfriendly climates and national economies that are unable to support the care of collections.

There are many examples of seriously damaging events in countries outside the United States. In Burma, the premier library was destroyed by bombing during the Second World War, along with two of the college libraries, resulting in the loss of a great deal of research materials and valuable scholarly notes.[2] Despite early training of the staff by the India Office Library and Records training program (unfortunately now long defunct), the conservation training given to the staff was more than fifty years out of date, there being no opportunity for current staff to avail themselves of further overseas training due to a repressive regime.

During the Vietnam War, more than two million tons of bombs were dropped on Laos and in Viêt Nam; Hanoi was on the receiving end of more explosive power than was unleashed by all belligerents during the Second World War. This war officially ended in 1973, but it wasn't until 1992 that the first steps toward the normalization of relations with the United States and other Western nations were taken, seriously delaying recovery that is still incomplete in both countries. In more recent times, the conflicts in Bosnia have seen the destruction and damage of many famous collections, the great library of Mosul has been devastated by the so-called Islamic States, and the manuscripts of Mali have been deliberately destroyed by Boko Haram. Strong efforts have been made to bring these damaged collections back to a semblance of usability, but the necessary resources are lacking. In 1991, Irene Nordlung and Jonas Palm of the Nordic Institute of Asian Studies reported that the wholesale evacuation of books and manuscripts from Hanoi to places of relative safety during the war years resulted in the gradual recovery of some important collections.[3] There can be no doubt that some of the lessons learned in Florence on recovery techniques continue to aid some of these salvaging efforts.

As Bernard Middleton has pointed out to me, given the ongoing narrative of the destruction of books and manuscripts throughout history, it is amazing that so much is left for us today. The international cooperative efforts to save the vast collections in Florence in 1966 is a signal and inspiring event in this otherwise doleful tale. The training and education of conservators to restore these culturally important research materials continue apace in developing countries, and I am grateful for their growing knowledge and level of sophistication. For example, the conservation staff of the National Library of Viêt Nam now work in a well-equipped facility. They are intelligent, skillful, and enthusiastic and have made remarkable progress since my first staff training session there in 1990.[4] I hope that someday there will be much greater integration among conservators throughout the world, to combat what Decherd Turner has called the "wave of deterioration" sweeping through our collections, so that we may be prepared to address the next catastrophe.

Notes

1. Warren J. Haas, "Preparation of Detailed Specifications for a National System for the Preservation of Library Materials," Association of Research Libraries Report, Washington, 1972.
2. T. Birkelund, "Burma Libraries," UNESCO Report, April 1969.
3. Irene Nordlung, Rasmussen, and Jonas Palm, "Report of a Survey of Libraries in Laos and Viêt Nam," Nordic Institute for Asian Studies, Copenhagen, 1991.
4. See also John F. Dean, "Burma, Cambodia, Laos and Viêt Nam: The Road towards Recovery for Library and Archival Collections after War and Civil Unrest," in *Disaster and After: The Practicalities of Information Service in Times of War and Other Catastrophes*, ed. Paul Sturges and Diana Rosenburg, London: Taylor Graham, 1999; and John F. Dean, "Preservation in Tropical Climates: An Overview," *International Preservation News* no. 54 (August 2011).

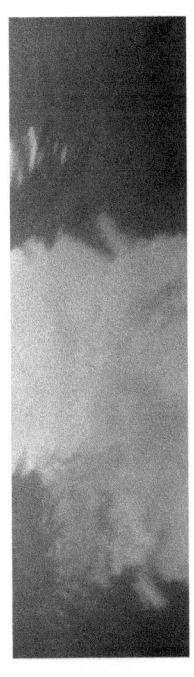

CLOSING
KEYNOTE

MATERIALITY AND MEANING
IN A DIGITAL WORLD

Michael F. Suarez, SJ

I think that we would all agree that the sensibility at this conference over this past day and a half has been remarkable. I think that this group has had a profound sense of privilege to be gathered here. Certainly, I have felt that, even though I come to you this morning very much as an auslander. I'm neither a conservator nor a librarian. I am—and I like putting this on my passport application—a bibliographer. I'm an academic who happens to run a school for the study of rare books and manuscripts and digital materials, and I am honored to be among such accomplished and committed individuals who are doing so much to secure the future of the textual record for the generations to come.

Accordingly, I'd like to reflect today on what I think it is you do and why I believe it is culturally important—supremely so. Then I'd like to spend a little time thinking about what the landscape looks like for the decades ahead. Let me begin by telling you about my ancestors: They were idiots. I come by my surname from Asturias in the north of Spain; my grandfather was a peasant farmer there, and so my great-great-great-great-great-great-great-ancestors were perhaps numbered among the conquistadores.

We know that when the conquistadores arrived in Central and South America, they came into contact with rich civilizations, where they encountered much of great cultural and practical value that they failed to recognize. The indigenous peoples practiced terrace farming, and a staple food in that agricultural regime was the potato. Not one kind of potato, but more than one hundred kinds. In any given season, perhaps forty or fifty types were grown simultaneously. One was unaffected by problems associated with too much rain, while another one did well when there was a drought. Some were resistant to blight; others tasted sweet or stored well through the winter, while still others could be most easily pounded into flour.

This was not a civilization of monoculture. Yet in the midst all this ingenious agricultural variety—a genetic and phenotypical diversity cultivated for long-term flourishing—in the midst of this brilliant commitment to agricultural sustainability, the foolish and short-sighted conquistadores brought back one potato, the one that they thought tasted best. They were good soldiers, perhaps, but they were terribly narrow-minded. The result of their bringing back a single type of potato was, in time, of tremendous consequence: the Irish potato famine, the "Great Hunger" in which between 1 million and 1.5 million people starved to death. Another million people immigrated, with the cumulative result that the economy of Ireland was devastated and did not recover for more than one hundred years. Ladies and gentlemen, this is the price of monoculture. When you cannot predict the changing environment and you opt for homogeneity rather than diversity, you die.

You die because eventually conditions arise that you are completely unprepared to handle. Although there were other factors at work, certainly, the Irish potato famine was largely caused by a colossal lack of human vision, nothing less.[1]

Now, you may have never heard of one of the greatest collectors in the history of humankind, because Nikolai Vavilov (1887–1943) was not a book collector nor a manuscript collector nor even a collector of great works of art. No, he collected seeds. Vavilov was in charge of the biological and genetic program for plants in the Soviet Union.[2] He learned fifteen different languages in addition to his native Russian.

He made some 115 collecting trips to sixty-four different countries on five continents. He met with indigenous peoples, with farmers, with fellow scientists, and with government officials. Over the years, with great labor, Vavilov and his team collected 270,000 different species of seeds in order to establish an unprecedented potential for future hybridity—the future hybridity Vavilov believed could at some future time feed a hungry world.

His strategy was the opposite of those myopic conquistadores. In addition to collecting and preserving the seeds of 270,000 different species, he traded with other collectors around the globe, amassing an additional 100,000 species. Thus he established what would eventually become the Vavilov Scientific Institute in Leningrad (now St Petersburg), with 370,000 different species cataloged and preserved so that the world might be fed from such diversity, no matter what conditions would arise in the future.

The Millennium Seed Bank in Sussex, England, is probably the most advanced expression of Vavilov's idea today. (If anybody asks you where the most biodiverse place in the world is, the answer might not be the Amazonian rainforest but Sussex, England.) The ultimate goal of the Millennium Seed Bank is to collect 50 percent of the surviving plants in all the world. Some of you may have heard of the pink yunnan banana (*Musa itinerans*) because the Millennium Seed Bank publicized it as the acquisition that enabled the MSB to cross the threshold of the holding 10 percent of all the world's species, much like a library does when it acquires its millionth book. They focused on this plant because many scientists believe that it has the potential to feed a starving world. The Millennium Seed Bank is now up to about 15 percent of all plant species. They're trying to create a store of hybridity for future conditions that cannot be predicted today.

The most culturally diverse place on earth is the Library of Congress; depending on how you count, it has 164 million items. There is a bit of a counting competition with the British Library, which also has a legitimate claim be the most culturally diverse bank of information and knowledge, and of language and thinking in the world. (It is interesting to remember that both of these institutions are the legacy libraries of global empires. We'll prescind from that today, but it's important to the ways we consider what our cultural heritage is and how it came to us.) We might usefully think of these national libraries, and indeed of the dispersed university library system and other such cultural institutions, as a kind of strategic reserve not unlike the strategic grain reserve or the strategic oil reserve.

Why do we hold our textual heritage in trust for future generations? For many of the same reasons that Vavilov collected his seeds: to have future hybridity (of thought), to avoid the perils of (intellectual) monoculture, to understand the record of humanity (especially human love and loss). We protect and communicate the richness of that heritage to remember and so to revivify the lives of those who have come before us so that in an increasingly fast-paced and complex world, we ourselves might understand a little bit better what it means to be human at all. The work that the conservation community does is essential to the preservation of our humanity. It's essential to our future survival as a people, nothing less.

It was Ludwig Wittgenstein who said, "To imagine a language is to imagine a form of life."[3] It seems to me that our libraries and archives and other cultural heritage institutions preserve forms of life—forms of life and human thinking and creativity that we can go back to if we're wise enough, if we prepare the coming generations well enough to help humanity not merely survive but thrive. Many of you will know the famous stained-glass window in Canterbury Cathedral called *Adam Delving*. I call that twelfth-century masterwork to mind because it leads us to consider the word *cultivate*, meaning to grow a garden, to dig the soil, to help things grow.

I want to remember also that we ourselves seek to be cultivated individuals. To do that, we do the labor not merely of digging into the earth but of delving into our historical past, to know the riches of Emily Dickinson and Montaigne, to read Cicero and Confucius, to understand the cave paintings at Altamira, to know what it is to be a human being, and to equip ourselves for citizenship in a complex and fast-paced world. This is work we need to do, and this capacity for delving, for becoming cultivated citizens of our time, is a vital capability that we need to pass on.

Unfortunately, the image of the Temple of Baal in Palmyra, Syria, is now hauntingly familiar to us, as is the scene of its destruction. Even those of us who have no special interest in Middle Eastern archeology or in this great crossroads of the spice trade now know about this site because of the most regrettable and abhorrent actions of ISIS to destroy our cultural patrimony as a way of attacking the roots of our culture. As reprehensible as we find this, it's extremely cunning, for to destroy the monuments of our past is to vitiate our ability to learn from that past and so provide for the future. Yet even in Palmyra, all is not lost.

Consider, if you will, that in the West, the Temple of Baal and all of the city of Palmyra came into human consciousness through a book in a library, a book that still endures: *The Ruins of Palmyra, Otherwise Tedmor, in the Desert.*[4] It was this beautifully illustrated volume that changed the shape of Western archeology, which had hitherto been overwhelmingly Greco-Roman. Many antiquaries were wrongly attributing some of the Greek artifacts they found to the Etruscans, and they didn't really understand the difference, but archeology was predominantly Greco-Roman. Then *The Ruins of Palmyra* fired the imaginations of a generation of young men. They went out to the Middle East, and they began to study. The book was a transformative agent, and it exists still to this day. Although Palmyra is in many ways lost to us, it has fired the human imagination for centuries, in no small measure because of its transmission in a book. Jorge Luis Borges was a secular man, but Borges was firm in his belief that "A book, any book, is for us a sacred object"[5] ("Un libro, cualquier libro, es para nosotros un objeto sagrado"). That's a powerful thing for him to say, and *The Ruins of Palmyra* is a good case in point.

We come together in these days to remember the Florence Flood and all that we have learned from the great rescue operation that followed; yet, at the same time, we come to look forward in this, our digital age. The digital is here, and it has many marvelous affordances. But it is also true that the digital domain is one of loss and gain. I need not spend a great deal of time celebrating the gains, but let me gesture toward one of those now. Some of you will know that I am an employee of the University of Virginia. That means I work for the Commonwealth and am therefore obliged by contract, and blood pact as well, to mention Thomas Jefferson in every lecture I give for the rest of my life, so here is the T. J. moment.

Looking at Jefferson's draft of the Declaration of Independence, one can see that there is an anomaly in the manuscript, a word that is smudged in a way that nothing else in the manuscript is. Fenella France, who is chief of the preservation research and testing division at the Library of Congress, was able through some multispectral imaging to show what happened, that Jefferson had originally written "subjects." As soon as he wrote it, however, he knew it was wrong, and he smeared it out, and wrote over in bold ink "citizens." I like to tell my students, though admittedly it's a bit reductive, that at this moment at Jefferson's drafting table, the United States of America was born: we are not subjects but citizens.

Yet in the midst of such wonderful work that the digital has made possible, we ought also to remember that, from a conservation and preservation perspective, the digital is fragile and vulnerable. We talked a little bit yesterday about the perniciousness of a cyberattack. We need to keep our heritage collections secure and integral, no question about it. It's also true that there are other threats that need to be considered, threats such as our very own sun. A solar flare, or coronal mass ejection, is a massive outrushing of electromagnetic energy, and it's entirely possible that some time in the not too distant future, a solar flare could send so much electromagnetic energy to the earth that most of our digital records would be destroyed (to say nothing of the power grid and satellite system).

In September 1859, just such a solar flare occurred. Often known as the Carrington Event, after the astronomer who first saw it happen, this sudden bombardment of electromagnetic energy effectively brought down the telegraph system in Europe and North America.[6] A 2013 Lloyd's of London study estimated that a Carrington-like coronal mass ejection would cause damage costing between $600 billion and

$2.6 trillion in the US alone.[7] So when we think about the Aurora Borealis and its incomparable beauty, we ought perhaps also to remember that the electromagnetic energy that rushes toward the earth in this entirely benign way could also change the course of human civilization if the scale were changed. Scientists tell us it could be. How should we react to this possibility?

For some people, the solution seems to lie in the dark archive, which of course takes multiple forms. One particularly unusual permutation on this strategy is the Memory of Mankind project.[8] What ought we do if we might lose a substantial portion of the historical record? Well, if you're inspired by cuneiform tablets that were baked in fire and have lasted for five thousand years or more, you make the equivalent by inscribing key texts on ceramic tiles with lasers. Then you find a salt mine in Austria, of course, and deposit the texts far from the maelstrom of history. How will people know five thousand years from now where your hidden salt mine in Austria happens to be? Well, you drop baked ceramic tokens all over the earth, so that somebody will find them and say, "Hmm, MoM, that must be memory of mankind." They'll find their way. It's like a bad episode of *Star Trek*. Oh, by the way, the public largely funds the project. You too can have your story in the Memory of Mankind archive for a fee, so that the undertaking becomes a kind of vanity press directed at readers five thousand years from now. That's akin, in my view, to naming a star after your grandfather.

Yet Brewster Kahle, who gave us the Internet Archive, is not crazy. Brewster Kahle is a proven visionary. Given the vulnerability of the digital record and the importance of books to the history of humankind, he variously says he wants to collect and preserve ten million books or, even more ambitiously, one copy of every book ever published. In 2011, he spent some three million dollars to buy and operate a storage facility in Richmond, California, where he's archiving as many books as possible in specially outfitted temperature- and humidity-controlled containers.[9] That's one way of thinking about the problem of long-term survival. Much as I admire what he has accomplished, however, I hope it's not our way of thinking about this problem. Hide the stuff away in an ark. Don't let anybody touch it for a very long time. Given what is at stake, we need a variety of strategies to address a situation with far-reaching consequences.

As this group well knows, print is perishable, but the World Wide Web is far more transitory. What's the average life of a webpage in the United States of America? Not in Bosnia nor in Syria, but in the United States of America? One hundred days. The web is profoundly ephemeral. Since the internet is now a primary vehicle for the transmission of human knowledge, what redress can we find for that? Well, some very smart people—at Los Alamos, no less—have developed the Memento Project, which I highly recommend to you.[10] It's a wonderful tool for looking at old web pages, with the caveat that "obviously, you will only get to see old versions of a resource if some exist, for example, in a web archive or a content versioning system." *Nemo dat quod non habet*—"No one can give what he does not have."

The Memento Project, or even the Wayback Machine of the Internet Archive, can't give you what doesn't exist anymore. That seems pretty insidious, but perhaps even more insidious is this: the web we know is deep, deep, deep, deep. There are millions and millions of web pages out there. And what do we do? We Google, using a keyword search, but almost unavoidably we have what I call our "Google Goggles" on, because our search results are optimized to confirm our own preferences and biases, and none of us have access to the algorithm. It's proprietary. For most of us, then, far from being unfathomable, the web is a thousand miles wide and a millimeter deep.

A similar problem occurs when, say, the British Library microforms the copy of the book that it has from the seventeenth century, with the result that the particular copy becomes the copy of record—all the more so when the microfilm is digitized. Then other institutions imagine that they don't need to digitize their copies because there's already a good copy from a reputable institution on the web, and digitization costs money. But if everybody acts according to that logic, then the variations in that handpress book as it exists in multiple repositories around the globe are essentially erased, because researchers are all looking at the same copy. As a student of book history and bibliography, as a scholarly editor, I believe that variation among copies is centrally important. Yet such cases are legion and prompt these questions: How should we deal with the flattening effects of the internet? How is the problem of "the one and the many" impoverishing our scholarship?

It's also true that we often celebrate the access afforded us by the web, and so we should, but all too often we neglect to ask the question, "Access to what?" How would you know from your laptop (or phone or tablet) say, what Picasso's great history painting *Guernica* (1937) actually looks like unless you already knew? I remember as a little boy of nine years old or so being taken into the Museum of Modern Art (MoMA) in New York by my mother and being terrified at what I stood before. The painting was so large and powerful and violent and unlike anything I had ever experienced that I had nightmares for a couple of weeks. Although I cannot have even remotely comprehended the meaning of that mural-sized oil painting, the moral enormity of the work had its effect on me in no small measure because of its scale.

Today, looking at hundreds of versions on the internet, I am compelled to ask, "Which is the real *Guernica*, and how would you know unless you knew?" This is what conservators, many of you, in part devote your lives to. We have to have recourse to the original object. As it's transformed in the digital world, we must have recourse to the original object over and again, so that it becomes the referent for everything else that we know and do. In the world of libraries and archives, for you to preserve such a cultural loadstone, the priceless referent from which everything else comes, is a grand vocation for a lifetime.

And which is the best representation? One needs to ask, Which is the most accurate representation? And how would you know unless you knew? How would you know unless you had studied it? That's very different than merely being contented with the velocity of access that the internet gives us; we must continually ask, "Access to what?" It's also true that the efflorescence of the digital is changing the way that we see the printed book. The efflorescence of the digital is changing the ways that we consume printed matter, both in its remediations and in our own paper-based reading habits too.

Jason McElligott, a quondam professor of history at Trinity College Dublin, and now the Keeper (or head librarian) of Marsh's Library

in Dublin, has observed, "Most of our students here [at Trinity] pre-
fer using EEBO (Early English Books Online), even with the great
[printed] resources we have, but even the best of them have great difficulty relating what they see on their screens to anything like the historical, physical object."[11] McElligott's students had access to the Long
Room, an exceptionally fine library, but they would much rather look
online at the sources that they need to study than to go into the library
and handle the material artifacts because it is more convenient to so.
But here's the problem: they've handled so few textual artifacts that
they don't understand the correspondences between artifact and simulacrum. If digitizing the printed world is something of loss and something of gain, how would you know what was lost and how would you
know what was gained unless you were fluent in bibliography (which
after all is a form of literacy, the ability to read the object in history)?

The British Library in its drive for popular appeal has gone to great
lengths to make pictures of manuscripts and books seem to behave in
the ways that actual books might in theory behave (but don't) via its
Turning the Pages software. I'm delighted to have excerpts from the
Lindisfarne Gospels online. I can't take my students to London to see
that manuscript, so it's great to have. Nonetheless, to pretend that what
we see on screen is a book, and to pretend that one can use a mouse
or track pad to manipulate that "book" is intellectually dishonest. It's a
palliative, a skeuomorph.

Even in the area of medical imaging and informatics, the distance
between image and presence has proven to be problematic. Medical
schools and hospitals have found that while med students and young
physicians are adept at reading diagnostic images, many are ill-equipped
to interrogate the bodies of their patients. The *New York Times* reported
that a leading US neuropathologist discovered that his specialist residents knew surprisingly little about the actual physical anatomy of the
human brain. His solution was to invite them to a weekly brain dissec-
tion, an old-fashioned gross anatomy clinic. Amazed at how much he
had learned from studying the object rather than the image, one of the
residents observed, "It is like the difference between looking at a map of
a place and driving around it."[12] I recommend this kind of learning to all

here present. It is what we do at Rare Book School at the University of Virginia. Although there are certainly things that images can reveal to us about objects that would be otherwise unintelligible to us ("citizens," not "subjects"), I recommend hands-on learning to you because, in the world of textual artifacts, it is the artifact's materiality that instantiates culturally imbedded meanings. To claim to know and interpret those meanings and yet be largely ignorant of their material forms is folly.

I don't know how many of you have read *Cutting for Stone* by Abraham Verghese (2009), a splendid novel. I recommend it most warmly to you. Verghese was a physician in the so-called third world before coming to the US. Eventually, the Stanford University School of Medicine hired him to develop the Stanford Medicine 25, a set of protocols for physical exams, because students didn't know how to read human bodies as well as they should. For the Stanford Medicine 25, Verghese and his colleagues taught students and residents how to execute diagnostic techniques at the patient's bedside and how to see and understand the embodied, physical evidence before their very eyes.[13] In a sense, this is akin to bibliography for the human body; in both cases one has to learn how to read materiality. What literacies are at risk of being lost, not merely in the medical world but concomitantly in the library world, in the archive world, in the cultural heritage world more broadly?

It's also true that the affordances of the digital are teaching us that collections we were on the brink of throwing out as redundant, as unnecessary, as outdated, or illegible now have new power. Archives, museums, and libraries holding photographic plates that captured images from telescopes as far back as the 1860s are a good case in point. Those glass plates are cumbersome, smelly, and expensive to store. Besides, why would we be interested in those outdated images? We have Hubble, the best technology for optical astronomy the world has ever known. Why would we want old images from instruments that don't have anything like the resolution of the Hubble telescope or any of the other scopes that scientists are getting research time on today?

Well, there's a new discipline called "archival astronomy." Digitizing the images on these old plates, astronomers can now compare images of a particular sector of the sky at a documented date and time with contemporary images in order to learn more about how the universe is evolving. Repurposing the once "obsolete" data, scientists are now making new advances in cosmology. The plates were once thought to be useless, and now they turn out to be priceless.[14] I owe my knowledge of archival astronomy to Abby Smith Rumsey's marvelous book *When We Are No More: How Digital Memory Is Shaping Our Future.*[15]

Another case in point is an ambitious genome-sequencing program for the avian world, the Avian Phylogenomics Project.[16] Where did they find the DNA to map some of the extinct and endangered species representing particular phyla? From taxidermic specimens languishing in basements, forgotten in metal cabinets, at the Smithsonian Institution, at the Museum of Natural History, and so on. They're from a bygone era. Nobody wants to see them. If we were efficient, we might have thrown them out fifty years ago. Now they're providing scientific data of enormous consequence for the comprehensiveness of the project. And this audience will know all about the marvelous work that Brent Seals and his team is doing to read the scrolls from Herculaneum with a powerful amalgam of advanced X-ray tomography, supercomputing, and multispectral imaging.[17] What was once known to be irretrievably lost is now digitally restored.

These projects are magnificent achievements. Yet we should also remember that just as the digital can help us see what would be otherwise impossible to perceive, so too does digitization sometimes obscure what we could easily apprehend from the textual artifact itself. Over the course of several years, I've been visiting special collections libraries to look at a book that has been digitized by institutions as diverse as the Bibliothèque Nationale de France and the Ernst Mayr Library of the Museum of Comparative Zoology at Harvard University. Louis Renard's *Poissons, ecrevisses et crabes, de diverses couleurs et figures extraordinaires,* first published in 1718, exists in three editions, but their title pages are not reliable in telling us which sheets were actually used in any given copy (i.e., a copy of the second edition may be made wholly or in part from sheets of the first edition). Accordingly, I needed to examine as many physical copies as possible, scrutinizing and documenting the watermarks on every page of every surviving copy I could see, because you don't get the watermarks from digitized images—not yet anyway. In fact, for this bibliographical problem, all that the digitized copy really told me was that a copy of the book, purportedly of a particular edition, was held at a particular library. It was thus no better than a catalog record.

In an altogether different vein, I wonder if any of you have ever read John Cleland's *Fanny Hill*, or *Memoirs of a Woman of Pleasure* (1749), which seems to be the best-selling pornographic novel of eighteenth-century England. People bought it because it was lascivious. So I ask you, What keyword would you enter to search a digital copy of *Fanny Hill* in order to retrieve its prurient content? In this instance, the problem is compounded by the fact that, hoping to escape any future prosecution for obscenity, Cleland used only euphemisms and circumlocutions; there is not a "dirty" word in the whole book. In fact, *engine* is probably the best word for your salacious search, but how could you know that, unless you had read the novel?

The keyword search is a blunt instrument. Consider, if you will, Henry Fielding's comic masterpiece *Tom Jones* (1749). What keywords would you enter to discover the funny parts? Or, thinking a bit more academically, we know that the humor in *Tom Jones* owes much to the Greek satirist Lucian of Samasota. What words would you put in a search box to retrieve the Lucianic content in Fielding's novel? It's a big book. It came out in four volumes. You don't want to read the whole thing. Certainly not. You've got to go fast. But how would you know unless you had read the book slowly and carefully? The keyword search is good—and it's garbage. We use it all the time, and we forget its profound limitations. How will such a basic dimension of the digital change the ways that my students and their children think about the world, think about literature, and think about the cultural record as informing the richness of our humanity?

We also have a problem that I adverted to earlier: if you digitize one copy and that becomes the copy of record to the effective exclusion of other copies, then researchers don't really see the pluriformity of the multiple copies. I spent a long time studying John Pine's edition of the works of the Roman poet Horace (*Quinti Horatii Flacci Opera*,

2 vols. [London: 1733, 1737]), which is engraved throughout. I wanted to examine as many copies as I could find, but people said, "You're crazy. It's fully engraved. There is one variant, and only one, and it is well documented." Well, why would anyone look at more than a hundred sets? I'll tell you why: because Howard Nixon believed that one set of Pine, in the Bodleian Library, had the greatest Irish binding of the eighteenth century. Because I found the book in an astonishing variety of contemporary bindings. Because a few sets were annotated. Others had particularly significant provenance information. And on the ninety-forth set I examined, I found both volumes in their original workaday boards—they were hiding in a pair of red Morocco slip cases made in the nineteenth century. For the bibliographer and book historian, nothing obviates the need to examine multiple physical copies.

What you do as conservators matters, in part, because having one copy of record is frequently misleading. What you do matters both locally and more broadly because discovery and, where possible, careful comparison are central to the study of textual artifacts. To be studied, it has to be found, and to be found, it has to be saved. Lionel Walter Rothschild (1868–1937), who amassed the greatest private natural history collection ever put together by a single person, when asked why he had some two million butterflies in his collection (and that was just the butterflies), is reputed to have replied, "I have no duplicates in my collection." For those of you charged with the stewardship of handpress books, Lord Rothschild's answer is worth remembering.

What is the digital world for? Obviously, in many respects, it's for velocity of access. But here is my problem with that; here is what I do not understand. I was taught a very long time ago that if I gave my life with great generosity and discipline to studying the historical past, sedulously dedicating myself to what was good and true and beautiful, then perhaps over time, if I was very fortunate, and I taught my students wisely and generously, then perhaps my life and the lives of my students might become a little more good, and a little more true, and a little more beautiful. I do not understand what that could possibly have to do with mere velocity of access. "Where is the knowledge we have lost in information?" asked T. S. Eliot more than eighty years ago.[18]

Those of us who are bibliographically knowledgeable need to have a place at the table in conversations about the futures of human knowledge, the future structures of the academy, and the future of our cultural heritage institutions. In the end, a simulacrum is a representation of what is absent. How, we need to ask, are we creating an environment that promotes sustained engagement? Could it not be that the wonder occasioned by the textual artifact, the wonder and the passion for the past that conduce from close contact with embodied knowledge, could lead students and scholars alike to sustained engagement?

If we don't preserve our textual heritage in all its many forms wisely and well, we will be utterly lost. For the most part, the library and archive of the twentieth century did not include digital materials, although now both the born-digital and the digitally remediated are essential parts of the twenty-first-century historical record. That is a good thing, and there would be no running away from it even if it weren't, but the central importance of the digital has to change the ways we think about digital curation and digital preservation. We need to not put digital objects in a lockbox and hide them away but use and to repurpose again and again over time that which is digital, so it will remain accessible and of use.

Of course, this means that a very intensive selection process has to happen as we decide what to preserve. Then automation is required to do this to scale. We are far, far away from where we need to be, and digital curation is the sixty-four-trillion-dollar question.[19] In the time it has taken me to give this lecture, human agents have created more terabytes of information than the equivalent of the entire holdings of the Library of Congress. A lot of it is junk, but some of it is not; most has no metadata, and so whether it's junk or priceless, it will have no future.

This learned audience will likely remember that to celebrate the nine hundredth anniversary of the making of the Doomsday Book—a magnificent medieval manuscript codex that recorded a comprehensive inventory of all the lands, riches, and people of England and parts of Wales—the BBC decided, "Let's make a new Doomsday Book. We'll get the school children of Britain involved. We'll spend £2.5 million doing so and put it on what we know is an imperishable medium, a laserdisc

(LV-ROM)." Twelve years later, it was unreadable by any machine in the world, and the University of Leeds and the University of Michigan spent some $150,000 on a digital emulation project to make it legible once again. Yet if you know a little Latin and your paleography is up to speed—that is to say, if you have the literacies you need to read the object in human history—then the original Doomsday Book in the National Archives at Kew is legible to you still.

I wonder whether any members of this distinguished group of librarians and conservators have attempted to visit the International Center for the Preservation of Books and Manuscripts in Florence, Italy. For in truth, such a center does not exist. One of the reasons this is so is because we have failed as heritage professionals to make our case. Across the board, universities, museums, and libraries have been derelict in their duty of advocacy. Do a gut check and ask yourself a question, "How much of my time as a fully employed person is spent on advocacy for the public, and with the public?" *Advocare*, "to speak toward"; *curation*, "to care for," because one cares so much about. Do we have the conversations with those publics who will determine future spending on our cultural heritage, to preserve, and protect, and defend it? It is an old scholastic adage that one cannot love what one does not know. Accordingly, we need to help others know.

How can we most effectively advocate and educate? How can we put out a clarion call to the public at large in order let them know that the future of human civilization may be at stake—nothing less—and that the literacies that are being lost are impoverishing our human societies? If we lapse into a kind of monoculture, that will perforce over the long run lead to famine. Preserving cultural heritage, communicating cultural memory, is not about the moldy past; it's ineluctably about the human future. We shouldn't commit ourselves to this enterprise because we care about books. We should do this because we care about humanity.

Recall that Nikolai Vavilov collected those 370,000 different species of seeds and stored them in Leningrad. He himself fell afoul of Joseph Stalin, languished in a jail, and perished. In 1942, during the siege of Leningrad in which seven hundred thousand human souls perished, Vavilov's twelve principal assistants locked themselves into the laboratory and lived there to protect the seeds they believed were the inheritance that would feed a world sometimes weakened by famine, sometimes broken by war. Rather than consume the seeds in their care, one by one, every man and woman in that lab died. Ladies and gentlemen, much is at stake: more than we like to countenance in our day-to-day lives. May I submit to you that it is incumbent upon us to preserve, protect, and defend our textual heritage. It is we who must cultivate the garden entrusted to our care.

Notes

1. John Reader, *Potato: A History of the Propitious Esculent* [New Haven: Yale University Press, 2009].
2. Gary Paul Nabhan, *Where Our Food Comes From: Retracing Nikolay Vavilov's Quest to End Famine* [Washington, DC: Island Press, 2009].
3. Ludwig Wittgenstein, *Philosophical Investigations* [New York: Macmillan, 1953], section 19.
4. Paul Fourdrinier, Giovanni Battista Borra, and Robert Wood, *The Ruins of Palmyra, Otherwise Tedmor, In the Desart* [London: n.p., 1753.]
5. Jorge Luis Borges, "Del culto de los libros [On the Cult of Books]," in *Borges, Selected Non-Fictions*, trans. Eliot Weinberger [New York: Penguin, 1999], 358.
6. Stuart Clark, *The Sun Kings: The Unexpected Tragedy of Richard Carrington and the Tale of How Modern Astronomy Began* [Princeton: Princeton University Press, 2009].
7. The American Association for the Advancement of Science, "How to Predict and Prepare for Space Weather," *Economist*, February 25, 2017, accessed online October 27, 2017, https://www.economist.com/news/science-and -technology/21717348-tales-wonder-how-predict-and-prepare-space -weather.
8. Memory of Mankind, https://www.memory-of-mankind.com/.
9. David Streitfeld, "In a Flood of Digital Data, an Ark Full of Books," *New York Times*, March 3, 2012, accessed online October 27, 2017, http://www .nytimes.com/2012/03/04/technology/internet-archives-repository-collects -thousands-of-books.html.
10. Memento Project, mementoweb.org.
11. Quoted from remarks delivered at the Perils of Print Culture conference, Trinity College Dublin, September 2010. Jason McElligott (ed.), *The Perils of Print Culture: Book, Print and Publishing History in Theory and Practice* [London: Palgrave Macmillan, 2014].

12. Elissa Ely, "In an Age of Images, Teaching Pathology by Hand," *New York Times*, September 11, 2007, accessed online October 22, 2017, http://www.nytimes.com/2007/09/11/health/11prof.html.

13. See the Stanford Medicine 25 website, accessed online March 17, 2018, https://stanfordmedicine25.stanford.edu/.

14. "Stars in Dusty Filing Cabinets," *Science* 324 (April 24, 2009), accessed online November 23, 2017: sciencemagazine.org.

15. Abby Smith Rumsey, *When We Are No More: How Digital Memory Is Shaping Our Future* [New York: Bloomsbury Press, 2016]; see also Dava Sobel, *The Glass Universe* [New York: Viking, 2016].

16. Avian Phylogenomics Project, http://avian.genomics.cn/en/.

17. See, for instance, John Seabrook, "The Invisible Library," *New Yorker*, November 16, 2015, accessed online March 17, 2018, https://www.newyorker.com/magazine/2015/11/16/the-invisible-library.

18. T. S. Eliot, *The Rock: A Pagaent Play* [1934]; [New York: Houghton Mifflin Harcourt, 2014], 7.

19. The LOCKSS Program (Lots of Copies Keep Stuff Safe) based at Stanford University is among the most advanced digital preservation protocols extant today; see https://library.stanford.edu/projects/lockss.

Contributors

Morgan Adams is conservator for special collections for the Columbia University Libraries. She has a BA from the University of Texas at Austin and an MA in art history and an advanced certificate in conservation from the Conservation Center, Institute of Fine Arts, New York University (2013). In 2011, she was awarded the James H. Frantz prize for student research. Prior to her current position, she worked in the conservation departments at the Morgan Library and Museum; the New York Academy of Medicine; Bobst Library, New York University; and the University of Michigan.

Cathleen A. Baker, a paper and book conservator and educator for more than forty-five years in England and the United States, is author of numerous articles and books including the award-winning *From the Hand to the Machine: Nineteenth-Century American Paper and Mediums: Technologies, Materials, and Conservation* (2010). She holds an MA in art history from Syracuse University, and an MFA in book arts and a PhD in communication studies from the University of Alabama. Cathy taught paper conservation for fifteen years in the SUNY graduate program at Cooperstown and in Buffalo, New York. For the 2015 fall semester, she was the Judith Praska Distinguished Visiting Professor in Conservation at the Conservation Center, Institute of Fine

Arts, New York University. Cathy is conservation librarian emerita at the University of Michigan Library and currently serves on an advisory committee to develop a book and paper conservation graduate specialization within UCLA's Department of Information Studies. Cathy is also proprietor of The Legacy Press, established in 1997, which specializes in publishing books about the printing, paper, and bookbinding arts.

John Comazzi is associate professor of architecture in the College of Design at the University of Minnesota and was the director of the undergraduate BS degree program (major in architecture) from 2012 to 2015. His areas of research and scholarship focus on architecture photography, mid-century Modern architecture and design, design theory and criticism, design-build, and active learning environments for PK–12 education. He is the author of *Balthazar Korab: Architect of Photography* (Princeton: 2012), which is the first monograph on one of the most prolific and celebrated architecture photographers of the Modern era. He holds a master of architecture and MS in architectural history and theory from the University of Michigan. He taught at the University of Michigan as a lecturer in architecture (1999–2006) before joining the faculty at the University of Minnesota in Fall 2006.

Martha O'Hara Conway is director of the Special Collections Research Center at the University of Michigan Library. In this position, which she has held since July 2011, she provides vision, leadership, strategic direction, and administrative oversight for the operations, services, programs, and resources of the Special Collections Research Center. She worked previously for the Newberry Library and at the Yale University Library and the Library of Congress. She has a BA from Mount Holyoke College, where she studied French and Russian, and a MILS from the University of Michigan, and is an active member of the Rare Books and Manuscripts Section (RBMS) of the Association of College and Research Libraries (ACRL).

Paul Conway has been associate professor at the University of Michigan School of Information since 2006. His research and teaching focus on archival science and the digitization and preservation of cultural heritage resources. His research projects at Michigan have included developing a model of expert user interaction with large collections of digitized photographs, modeling and measuring the quality of large-scale digitization as represented in the HathiTrust Digital Library, and exploring the conceptual roots of e-books in nineteenth-century photographically illustrated books. His prior career includes serving as archivist at the National Archives and Records Administration and as a senior administrator for the libraries at Yale and Duke universities. The American Library Association awarded him the Paul Banks and Carolyn Harris Preservation Award for his contributions to the preservation field. He is a fellow of the Society of American Archivists and holds a PhD from the University of Michigan.

Ellen Cunningham-Kruppa is associate director and head of preservation and conservation at the Harry Ransom Humanities Research Center, University of Texas at Austin. She received an endorsement of specialization in administration of preservation programs for libraries and archives from Columbia University's School of Library Service and has a PhD in American studies and an MLIS from UT–Austin. From 1985 to 1987, she was project archivist at the Johns Hopkins University Peabody Institute. In 1988, she became the first preservation officer for the UT–Austin General Libraries and, in 1996, the first Digital Programs Librarian for the Libraries. Ellen was the founding director of the William and Margaret Kilgarlin Center for Preservation of the Cultural Record, a position she held from 2005 to 2009, in the UT–Austin School of Information. From 2005 to 2009, she was president of the Association of North American Graduate Programs in Conservation, she is an affiliated assistant professor with the University of Delaware/Winterthur Program in Art Conservation, and she consults with the art conservation education programs on the library and archives specialization. In 2016, Ellen was awarded the American Library Association's Paul Banks and Carolyn Harris Preservation Award.

John F. Dean became Cornell University Library's first conservation and preservation librarian with the establishment of the program in 1985 and served as director for nearly twenty years before retiring in 2003. John's background includes a six-year apprenticeship in bookbinding in his native England and a few years as a journeyman bookbinder. He was leader of preservation programs at the Newberry Library and Johns Hopkins University, and has two graduate degrees in library science and in liberal arts with a concentration in the history of science. In 2003, John was the recipient of the American Library Association's Paul Banks and Carolyn Harris Preservation Award for his contributions to the field. John remains passionate about preservation and conservation and has endeavored to help institutions around the world through education, training, and consultancies in developing countries, including Laos, Indonesia, Thailand, Viêt Nam, Myanmar, Java, and Cambodia. He created seminal online tutorials for library conservation and preservation in Southeast Asia, Iraq, and the Middle East to give librarians and archivists a set of basic guidelines to inform their preservation efforts. In retirement, John continues to assist local institutions in caring for their book collections.

Beth Doyle is the Leona B. Carpenter senior conservator and head of the conservation services department for the Duke University Libraries. Following an undergraduate arts degree in photography from the University of Dayton, she earned her master's in library and information science and certificate in library and archives conservation at the University of Texas at Austin. She worked as a book conservator for Harvard University before joining the Duke University Library in 2002. An active blogger on all things library conservation, she has written on topics from edible books to disaster planning to ergonomics for conservation labs.

Bryan Draper is the special collections conservator for the University of Maryland Libraries. His interest in conservation was sparked by the

Terry Sanders 1987 film *Slow Fires: On the Preservation of the Human Record.* His first job in preservation was at the University of Delaware Library as conservation technician. After coordinating aspects of the conservation program at the Library of Virginia, Richmond, he pursued an apprenticeship at the Etherington Conservation Center, North Carolina. In 2007, he assumed the conservator position at Maryland. He has graduate training from Winterthur and a certificate from the Rare Book School.

Jeanne Drewes has been the chief of binding and collections care at the Library of Congress since 2006. After earning a BA in English from the University of Missouri–Kansas City and her MLS from the University of Missouri–Columbia, she spent a year as a Mellon preservation intern at the University of Michigan—and found her career. She has held positions as preservation services manager at Pittsburgh Regional Library Center, head of preservation at Johns Hopkins University's Milton S. Eisenhower Library, and assistant director for access and preservation at Michigan State University. A person of tireless energy, she has been an active leader, presenter, and writer in the context of many professional organizations, including the American Institute for Conservation of Historic and Artistic Works, the American Library Association, and the International Federation of Library Associations. She has fostered the translation of preservation literature into Spanish and worked to extend training opportunities to the people of Cuba. In 2015, she received the American Library Association's Paul Banks and Carolyn Harris Preservation Award.

Don Etherington has been engaged in bookbinding and conservation professionally for more than sixty years. After extensive training in England, including a year working with conservators Roger Powell and Peter Waters, he established a four-year program in bookbinding and design at Southampton College of Art in 1960. From 1967 to 1969, he was a training consultant to the Biblioteca Nazionale Centrale in Florence, Italy, and trained regional volunteers in book conservation after the 1966 flood. In the 1970s, he served as training officer to the conservation staff of the Library of Congress and, in the 1980s, as the assistant director and chief conservation officer at the Harry Ransom Humanities Research Center, University of Texas at Austin. He established and served as the first president of the Etherington Conservation Services, a division of ICI, from 1987 until his retirement in 2001. Since then, in addition to his work as director of the book conservation program at the American Academy of Bookbinding, he engages in an intensive teaching schedule and continues work in private practice. His fine bindings are held in major libraries internationally.

Doris A. Hamburg has been director of preservation programs at the National Archives and Records Administration (NARA) since 2001, where she oversees preservation of collections across twenty-four facilities nationwide. Following a bachelor's degree in medieval studies from Mount Holyoke College, a master's in art history from Columbia University, and an MS and certificate in conservation from the Winterthur/University of Delaware program, she joined the Library of Congress as a paper conservator. She rose through several positions of increasing responsibility at the Library of Congress, including eight years as the head of the preventive conservation unit, before moving to her current position at NARA. She has presented and published broadly on topics of conservation and preservation management. In 2003, she was called to aid what became a significant project to salvage records documenting Iraq's Jewish community, which were found by US troops in the flooded ruins of a basement under Saddam Hussein's intelligence agency in Baghdad.

Megan Holmes is a professor of Italian Renaissance art history at the University of Michigan in Ann Arbor. She received an MPhil from the Courtauld Institute of Art and her PhD from Harvard University. Her scholarship has been supported by fellowships from the Harvard University Center for Italian Renaissance Studies at the Villa I Tatti, the Getty Research Institute, and the National Endowment for the Humanities. Her scholarly interests include Italian Renaissance social and cultural history, miraculous images and image cults, popular religion, monasticism and the arts, early modern print culture, and iconoclasm. She has published two books, *Fra Filippo Lippi the Carmelite Painter* (New Haven: Yale University Press, 1999) and *The Miraculous Image in Renaissance Florence* (New Haven: Yale University Press, 2013), the latter receiving the College Art Association's Charles Rufus Morey Award and the Ace/Mercer Award. She is currently working on a short book on the scratching and marking of Italian panel paintings circa 1250–1550.

Nancy E. Kraft joined the University of Iowa Libraries as the preservation librarian and head of the preservation and conservation department in 2001. Circumstances—including the 2008 flooding of the Iowa River and the Cedar River—rapidly developed her expertise in disaster recovery for cultural heritage. She received the Midwest Archives Conference Presidents' award the following year for her assistance to local institutions, including the Johnson County Historical Society, the National Czech & Slovak Museum & Library, and the African American Museum of Iowa, as well as the UI libraries. In addition to teaching in the University of Iowa Center for the Book, she has taught workshops and courses on disaster planning widely across the US and in Europe. She is a member of the American Institute for Conservation Collections Emergency Responders Team. She holds an MLS degree from the University of Iowa.

Julia Miller, educated as a historian, trained in book conservation with Jean Gunner in Pittsburgh. She left her position as a conservator at the University of Michigan Library in 1993 and has since engaged in researching the history of bookbinding. Her widely acclaimed *Books Will Speak Plain: A Handbook for the Identification and Description of Historical Bindings* was published in 2010 by The Legacy Press. Julia has taught and lectured widely on historical book structure both in the US and in Europe. At the University of Michigan, she has curated five exhibits related to the history of the book. More recently she has served as series editor for *Suave Mechanicals: Essays on the History of Bookbinding*, also published by The Legacy Press, of which volume 3 was released in late September 2016. At present, she is writing a second book with the working title *Looking Again at Selected Historical Bindings*. She received the Laura Young Award for service from the Guild of Book Workers in 2014.

Carla Q. Montori is the head of the preservation department at the University of Maryland Libraries. In this position, she has managed the transition from a comprehensive preservation program to one focused on the assessment, care, and conservation of special collections and archives held by the Libraries. Her prior positions include preservation projects manager and head of the preservation division at the University of Michigan Library, head of the preservation department at Indiana University Library, Mellon Intern for Preservation Administration, and conservator for general collections at the Yale University Library. She has written about the preservation of library and archival materials and has spoken and led workshops and seminars worldwide.

Sherelyn Ogden recently retired as head of conservation at the Minnesota Historical Society and currently continues her work as a conservator in private practice. Previously director of field services at the Midwest Art Conservation Center (NEDCC) and the director of book conservation at the Northeast Document Conservation Center, she has taught, published, and consulted widely on conservation. Her books *Preservation of Library and Archival Materials: A Manual* (NEDCC, 1992) and *Preservation Planning: Guidelines for Writing a Long-Range Plan* (American Association of Museums, 1997), and her numerous advisory leaflets have provided go-to resources for heritage organizations for more than forty years. She originally trained in conservation at the Newberry Library in Chicago. She holds a BA from Bucknell University, an MLS degree from the University of Chicago, and is a fellow of the American Institute for Conservation of Historic and Artistic Works.

Michael F. Suarez, SJ, has served as director of Rare Book School, professor of English, university professor, and honorary curator of special collections at the University of Virginia since 2009. He formerly held a joint appointment as J. A. Kavanaugh Professor of English at Fordham University and as fellow and tutor in English at Campion Hall, Oxford University. He received a DPhil, MSt, and MA/BA from Oxford University, an MTh and MDiv from the Weston Jesuit School of Theology, and a BA from Bucknell University. He has written widely on various aspects of eighteenth-century English literature, bibliography, and book history and has held research fellowships from the Radcliffe Institute for Advanced Study at Harvard University, the National Endowment for the Humanities, the American Council of Learned Societies, and the Folger Shakespeare Library.

Sheila Waters is a renowned calligraphic artist and instructor whose career has been devoted to calligraphic commissions for royalty, museums, libraries, corporations, maps for publishers, and art works for collectors for nearly seventy years. Born in England in 1929, she gained her master's at the Royal College Art and Fellowship of the Society of Scribes and Illuminators, London, in 1951. She married fellow RCA student, designer-bookbinder Peter Waters, in 1953. They immigrated to the USA in 1971 with their three sons when Peter became chief of conservation at the Library of Congress, a direct result of his work at the National Library of Florence after the flood of 1966. Sheila has taught across North America and abroad, and continues to lecture and teach workshops and master classes. Her best-known works include the *Roundel of the Seasons* wall panel and the illuminated manuscript of Dylan Thomas's play *Under Milk Wood*. Her classic textbook, *Foundations of Calligraphy*, was published in 2006, and her book *Waters Rising: Letters from Florence* was published by The Legacy Press in 2016.

Shannon Zachary has been a conservator and library preservation specialist for the University of Michigan Library's collections since 1994 and has been head of the library's Department of Preservation and Conservation since 2005. She began studying bookbinding and conservation with Anne and Theodore Kahle at the Capricornus School of Bookbinding in Berkeley, California, in 1977 while a graduate student of classics and comparative literature at the University of California. Subsequently she earned a City and Guilds of London Institute Certificate in Bookbinding at Brunel Technical College in Bristol, England, and a Higher National Diploma in paper conservation at the Camberwell College of Art in London. She was book conservator for rare and special collections at the Cornell University Library from 1987 to 1992 before moving to Ann Arbor to earn a master's degree in library studies at the University of Michigan. She teaches library and archives preservation as an adjunct lecturer at the U–M School of Information.